THE UMPIRE IS *OUT*

THE
UMPIRE
IS *OUT*

CALLING THE GAME AND
LIVING MY TRUE SELF

DALE SCOTT with ROB NEYER

Foreword by BILLY BEAN

UNIVERSITY OF NEBRASKA PRESS

Lincoln

Library of Congress Control Number: 2021039681

Set in Lyon Text by Laura Buis.
Designed by N. Putens.

CONTENTS

ILLUSTRATIONS

FOREWORD

BILLY BEAN

On April 24, 1995, I was driving home from Jack Murphy Stadium after a night game. I was playing for the San Diego Padres, and we were near the end of a very bizarre spring training. The well-documented lockout of 1994, which saw the cancelation of the World Series the previous October, was catastrophic for players like me. Baseball was trying desperately to erase one of the darkest moments in its history. Because of the work stoppage, we started spring training later than usual, and it was shortened with the aim of getting players back on the field as quickly as possible.

Like every spring, my mind was focused on making the ball club, but when I arrived home, I could immediately tell that something was wrong. The front door was open, and I could not find my partner, Sam. As a Major League player deeply submerged in the closet, an open front door was never okay. I found Sam upstairs in our bedroom, unconscious on the floor.

Because of his recent HIV-positive diagnosis, I fully understood the severity of the situation. I rushed Sam to the hospital as fast as I could and held on to his hands all night long; he died at around seven that next morning. As I left the hospital, in complete shock, it dawned on me that I had to be in Anaheim, to play against the Los Angeles Angels, in less than three hours. I walked through the parking lot with Sam's clothes in a clear plastic bag that the hospital had given to me. As I sat in my car, the sad, lonely isolation of the closet tore through me. I was afraid to cry, because I knew I might not be able to stop. None of my teammates had ever met Sam or knew he existed. It was a secret life, one I devoted way too much attention to keeping that way.

It's all I ever thought about. Now I began to realize he was gone forever, as if he had never existed.

I played in the Major Leagues from 1987 through 1995. For the first few years of my career, I didn't once think there might be another gay player or umpire. Then in 1990 I heard a couple of players make comments about a recently fired umpire named Dave Pallone, who came out, and I would come to learn about Glenn Burke and his heartbreaking story toward the end of my career. Glenn and I remain the only two Major League players in the 152-year history of MLB to publicly disclose our sexual orientation as gay. The awful stereotypes I learned growing up made it seem to me that no Major League player or umpire could possibly be gay. When I began to realize my own sexual orientation, so began the never-ending internal voice telling myself I didn't deserve to play in the Majors. By the end of that 1995 season, grieving the loss of Sam, still hiding my secret from my family, friends, and teammates, I walked away from baseball and the life I had dreamed of living since I was a little kid.

My story didn't surface publicly until over four years after my last game. I was completely unprepared for the attention that it brought. At that time, aside from a few former players in the NFL, there had been no representative of male athletes in the four major team sports to ever publicly come out as gay. In December 1999 it was much easier to hide and keep to yourself than it is now. However, I still received more letters, messages, and calls than I could count. My life changed overnight, solely because I had played baseball in the Major Leagues.

During my career, Dale Scott and I exchanged pleasantries on the field during games, but I can't remember anything beyond that. Players and umpires in my era did not engage the way they do now. Dale saw my story on TV and learned that I was living in Miami Beach. About a year later, I received a message from him, for which I am forever grateful. On the phone, he shared the dates his crew would be coming to Miami for a homestand with the Marlins, and we committed to lunch prior to one of his games. We met at a restaurant close to the stadium, and when I sat down in the booth, my heart was pounding. Thoughts of Sam rushed through my mind, and before we even started talking, I felt like I was looking at a long-lost brother. All I could think was: Why couldn't we have had this moment before I walked away from the game?

Anyone who has ever met Dale will tell you that he may be the most easygoing, self-effacing, generous, funniest, and nicest guy they've ever met. On the field, he could give it to you good or give it right back with the best of them, but away from the field, he simply makes everyone feel better when they are in his company. We became brothers during that lunch, and we've remained family ever since. I held on to his and Michael's secret until 2014, when he came out publicly.

Dale's thirty-year MLB career makes him a Hall of Famer in every sense of the term. I've often told him that he will never know how many lives he has impacted by representing the LGBTQ community and MLB in such a profound way. Lucky for us, his work is just beginning, and this book will allow many new fans to get to know him and learn why his story is so important. Dale and I are forever linked, and I would walk to the moon and back for him. I can't wait to see where life takes him next, but his MLB legacy will last forever. And I'm so grateful to call him my friend. Settle in . . . because Dale's story is literally one of a kind.

THE UMPIRE IS *OUT*

1

Nutcutters, Polebenders, and Shithouses

Like just about every profession, I guess, umpiring has its own language.

Take *nutcutter*, for example.

Now, this one's tricky, because it's got two completely different meanings.

Yes, a nutcutter is a foul ball to . . . well, to the nuts. But it's also a really close play.

Wait. It's actually got three meanings. You can also have a nutcutter game, which is a close, intense game with maybe a few lead changes, and it feels like the whole world might depend on every play, every pitch.

Once, in Minnesota, I took a (nearly literal) nutcutter when Steve Balboni was hitting for the Royals. After two strikes, the next pitch came in and sent a line drive right into my cup. I can hear it even now—sounded like a tee shot with a golf ball. *Thwwockk*.

Next thing I remember, I'm looking straight up at the roof of the Metrodome. The trainer's there, looking me over and talking to my three partners. Apparently, I was *out* for just a moment.

The trainer gave me smelling salts, which immediately woke me up. Then I noticed the pain in my nuts (obviously!), but mostly I was just trying to get my wits about me, because I wanted to walk this off and finish the game. Which I did. Nowadays there's not a chance in hell I would have finished; they would have taken me off the field to recover, no matter what I said.

Once in the locker room, I took out my cup, which was the old standard: a triangular, very uncomfortable chunk of hard plastic. It hadn't shattered, but there were a couple of large cracks.

In 2010 I took a nutcutter in Detroit that gave me a standing eight count, but I didn't have to leave. This was the last week of the season. Jerry Meals and I were working with two (at the time) call-up umpires, Scott Barry and D. J. Reyburn, neither of whom I had worked with much. I got nutcutted early and felt fine, but as a courtesy, the Tigers' team doctor, an African American gentleman, came in to check on me after the game.

"I just want to see how you're doing," he said after introducing himself.

"I feel fine, doctor," I said. "Just a little sore."

"Any swelling down there?"

"I don't think so."

"Well, let me take a look anyway."

He takes a look and feels around a little.

"Yeah, I don't think there are any issues. If you have any problems, though, here's my number."

"Thanks, doc."

Once the door shut, I said to the guys, "I haven't had a Black man so concerned about my nuts since I was in the Dominican."

Scott and D.J. looked paralyzed. Then Meals busted out laughing, and the other guys cracked up too. Scott said it might have been the funniest, most random thing he'd ever heard.

(By this point, I assumed everyone on the staff knew I was gay. This was the end of my second year with Meals, who definitely knew. The other two guys I barely knew, which made it even funnier, the shock value of me talking about the elephant who everyone knew was in the room.)

Only twice did nutcutters knock me out of a game.

Once was in Chicago, working the White Sox, so Rocky Roe had to come in from second base and strap it on. I'm in the locker room with the Sox's team doctor as Rocky is changing gear. The doctor left, and I'm lying on the couch, icing my traumatized soldiers, when Rocky pipes up, "Normally, I'd be really pissed that I have to put this shit on. But as I look at you with an ice pack on your balls, I'm just happy it wasn't me. That was a shot."

The other time I departed early was a getaway day game in hot and humid Baltimore. I took a wild pitch in the bottom of the second inning, and as the trainer and my crewmates were checking on me, I thought for sure I was going to throw up. Not wanting to see that embarrassing spectacle, Danny

Iassogna immediately said to the trainer, "Get him off the field." Followed by, "Bob [Davidson], go strap it on."

Although nauseous, I didn't actually lose my lunch. The Orioles' doctor poked around and said, "Listen, I don't think there's an issue here, but just to be safe, I'd like to take you to the University of Maryland Medical Center"—just a few blocks away from Camden Yards—"and have them check it out."

So off we went to the ER, where after about twenty minutes, they admitted me. I was wearing my T-shirt, plate shoes, and sweaty umpire pants that still, for some reason, had my ball bag attached. As I approached the intake desk, the administrator said, "So I heard you got hit by a foul ball at the Orioles game."

"Yeah, I got drilled."

"Where'd you get hit?"

"I got hit in the groin."

"Wow. Where were you?"

"Behind the plate."

His eyes got wider.

"Don't they have protective screens or something? I mean, I can't imagine—"

"No, I was behind the catcher."

"Right," he continued, "but don't they have that entire area screened off?"

"You don't understand. I was literally behind the catcher. I was the umpire."

Finally he notices what I'm wearing. "Oh. Well, that makes more sense."

Once I was assigned a room, the ER doctor came in. After a few questions, he asked me to drop my pants. After a quick visual exam, he then felt around like he was after the perfect tangerine in the produce section. Touching one, then the other, making sure of . . . well, making sure of whatever they make sure of.

"I'd like a urologist to take a look," he said. "I'll be right back." Ten minutes later he came in and said, "The urologist is on his way. And since we're a teaching hospital, do you mind if he brings in a couple interns?"

In Portland my primary doctor is at Oregon Health and Science University (OHSU), a teaching hospital. So I'm used to having an audience. Still, it can be awkward, or *really awkward*, when there's a gonads inspection involved. "That's fine," I replied.

Soon, in walks the ER doc, the urologist, and three interns as, once again, I'm taking my pants off. Now it was starting to feel like Underwear Night at the Eagle. As they intently examined my business while discussing blood flow and worst-case scenarios involving the bursting of various parts, I just stood there thinking, *Ah, how glamorous, this life in the big leagues . . .*

Taking a nutcutter might be the only time when every player on the field, no matter which team, actually sympathizes with you.

Well, with maybe one semiexception: Eddie Murray, who was not an umpire-friendly person. Once in Anaheim, he was batting and fouled one off my 'nads. I took a little time to walk it off. Once we got going, I called the next pitch a strike.

"Obviously you're not recovered yet," Murray snapped.

Trust me, Eddie Murray questioning a pitch is hardly front-page news. But shouldn't there be some type of ball-on-ball etiquette? A "feel your pain" exception? All I could do was shake my head and think, *Well, that's par for the course. If anybody's going to jump on a guy right after a nutcutter, it would be Eddie Murray.*

Fortunately, I umpired for enough years to enjoy real improvements in cup technology after decades of the same, tired thing. The old standard was the triangular cup. Then came the banana-shaped cup, which was a definite improvement (why so long to figure out what now seems rather obvious?). Eventually even that was improved upon, to where the cup and the cup holder were much more comfortable and snugger.

For most of my career, I wore a cup only when working the plate. I did have a few close calls on the bases, but not wearing one was never a regret. Even if I'd wanted to wear one, running around the bases with the old cup was too uncomfortable and too embarrassing, as you would have to constantly be making "adjustments." But when I first started working with Danny, I noticed he wore a cup for every game. So with the improved holder technology, I decided to give it a shot on the bases, and I soon got used to it. Boy, was I glad I did.

The very next spring, I was working first base at Phoenix Muni, then the A's Arizona home. Spring-training venues are more intimate, with fans sitting closer to the field than during the regular season. For this game, I reserved four tickets for Bill Kennedy, one of my closest friends and an NBA official, who came out publicly a year after I did.

Bill and his friends were sitting maybe thirty feet away from me when, with a runner on first, the pitcher attempted a pick-off. The throw wasn't errant, but the first baseman misjudged the ball, which glanced off his glove directly to my crotch, where it hit with a *clunk* and skittered toward shallow right.

This happened so fast that I had no time to react. Didn't even flinch. And it didn't hurt, but without the cup, I would have been beyond miserable. Both the runner and the fielder, hearing the thud and seeing the point of contact, didn't run or attempt to chase down the ball. They just froze and looked at me with the same wide-eyed look: *My God, are you okay?*

Meanwhile, there was a noticeable, collective gasp from the stands, with Bill and the boys holding their breath, staring, waiting for my reaction. I looked over and gave them a ME, TOUGH MAN sort of gesture, and with that, everyone exhaled and doubled over in laughter. That was the only time I remember actually getting hit in the cup while working the bases, and the look I got from those two players was priceless.

So that's *nutcutter*. One of the definitions, anyway. I'm sure you're glad you asked.

Kennedy loved coming to games. He also loved rattling my chain. Every spring, he would find out where my first plate game was, so he could show up and razz me after my first pitch in four-plus months. Once, I told him my first plate game was at Hohokam Stadium in Mesa, then the Cubs' spring-training home. So Bill drove the forty miles to Mesa, while my *actual* assignment was in Peoria, eight miles from his place in Glendale. Got him that time.

For that first game every year, Bill wouldn't ask for a comp ticket, so I could never be sure if he would show up or not. But then once the first pitch was called, the onslaught began.

If a strike, I would hear him bellow something like, "Really? Take the bat right out of his hands! Better be swinging; he's got a date!"

And if a ball, "Here we go . . . quit squeezing him! Call it both ways! Isn't belt high over the middle a strike anymore?"

Milwaukee catcher Martín Maldonado, after receiving the first pitch of the spring and hearing Bill scream about squeezing his pitcher, looked over his shoulder at me and said, "Wow, what an ass. First pitch of 2012 and that dick is on you?"

"It's worse than that, Martín; he's using my pass."

Same game. Jimmy Joyce, Alfonso Marquez, and Jim Reynolds were working the bases. They all knew Billy, but they weren't aware it was him sniping me. After the game, walking to right field and the entrance to the clubhouse area, Jimmy starts laughing, "Tough crowd, Scotty! One pitch and that prick was all over you!"

"That prick was Kennedy," I said, gesturing to where he was waiting in the front row. "Hey, Billy," I said, "hop over and come to our room."

The moment Bill hit the ground on the field side of the railing, I started yelling and pointing, "Security! Security!" A guard started to run toward Bill, and of course I didn't stop him until he was almost there. "It's okay—he's with me," I told the guard, laughing so hard I could barely talk.

When I first went to umpire school and for my first several years in pro ball, when you had a close play, it was called a *banger*. I don't remember when or why or how, but *banger* morphed into *wacker*. It seemed like it happened overnight and I didn't get the memo, but if you still called it a *banger*, you sounded like an old crusty veteran.

Similarly, you used to say a borderline strike *hit* (or caught) *the corner*. Now that same pitch has *caught the edge*.

I remember *polebender* from before I got into umpiring. Maybe nobody outside umpiring still uses it, but when I was a kid, that's what broadcasters called fair-or-foul home runs.

When you work the plate, you *strap it on*. Literally, you strap on the chest protector, but it really means working a plate game. But it also means you're heading into a game, as a crew, where you're expecting a lot of action, whether because the teams are out to get each other or out to get *you*. So you gotta *strap 'em on*, meaning your helmets, like you're going into battle.

Another umpire term is *working the stick*, which also means working the plate. Where it came from, I don't know. If you've got a three-game series without working the plate, you've got the *honeymoon series*. So if you get the *honeymoon series* in New York, you won't be *working the stick* and don't have to *strap it on* to call close pitches that *caught the edge*, although you may have a *wacker* or two, not to mention a *polebender*.

That brings us to a *shit series*. Yankees–Red Sox, Cardinals-Cubs, Giants-Dodgers are a few examples. Any big rivalry might be a *shit series*, usually with longer games, more bitching, and a higher probability of throwing at hitters and bench clearings. Yes, they're usually more exciting, definitely more intense, which you can feel in the air when you walk on the field. What's that? You have a *shit series* coming up in Yankee Stadium? Better get ready to *strap it on* (helmetwise).

A *cockshot* is exactly as it sounds—a pitch right down the middle, cock high.

If you eject a player or coach, you've *run* him.

Let me tell you about *the monkey*. A nutcutter game can be the entire game or just part of one. The game went smooth, not much going on until the eighth; then it turned into a nutcutter. Why? Because the score is close, and every half inning, runners got on base; or the team behind was constantly threatening but not getting that tying run in; or a save is blown and suddenly you're in extra innings.

This is when *the monkey* makes its appearance. Because every pitch, play, or decision, anywhere on the field, has the potential to turn the game upside down. The monkey was jumping on everybody's back, but if the game ends with no one on the crew having a controversial call—thus making it easy (and in most cases, incorrect) to blame the umpire—then *the monkey* never actually landed on us.

Oh, by the way, I never cared for the term *bad call*. I like to think none of us makes a bad call, but rather a *misunderstood call*. Sure, I called a runner safe when he was out, but you actually *misunderstood* when you thought I would call him out.

So that *nutcutter* game during that *shit series* had *the monkey* jumping all over the place. And when he landed? *Shithouse.*

I use this one a lot. Benches emptied? *Shithouse.* I called that guy out at third? Man, did that start a *shithouse.* That *shit series* had a bunch of *shithouses.* I knew that when *the monkey* landed, we would have a *shithouse.* What a *nutcutter*!

Granted, with replay, some of these terms aren't used as often as they used to be.

Even with replay, though, you can have a *honeymoon shit series*, where you don't have to *strap it on* but your partner *working the stick* had almost no *cockshots* but did have a ton of pitches *just off the edge*, all while surviving *wackers* and *misunderstood calls* on the bases, including that *nutcutter polebender* that landed *the monkey* and started a major *shithouse* that finally ended when you *ran* the manager.

Got it? Great! Now you won't have to buy *Rosetta Stone: Umpire*. Oh, and you're officially prepared for the rest of this book.

2

Eugene

I was born August 14, 1959, in Eugene, Oregon. My mom, Betty, had two sons from a previous marriage. It was the first time my dad, Jess, had been married. My two half brothers were Mike, born in 1951, and Keith, in 1953. My younger brother, Tim, was born in 1963.

Mike and Keith lived with us until 1968, and I always considered them full, not half brothers. They were both born in Potter Valley, California, about twenty miles northeast of Ukiah. They wanted to be back on the ranch, so when I was eight or nine, they moved back there to live with their dad and grandmother. After they moved, we drove every summer to Potter Valley to visit, since they and Dorothy, my mom's sister, also lived there, along with cousins and other family. We would share Thanksgiving and Christmas with Mike and Keith when we could, either there or in Eugene.

When I was growing up in Eugene—and for some years afterward—my dad worked for two linen and uniform companies: first American Linen Supply and then Eugene Linen Supply. He started at Eugene Linen in 1968 and retired in 1990. The business was shop towels and coveralls; soap and towel dispensers for gas stations, garages, and other businesses; tablecloths, napkins, and uniforms for servers and kitchen staff in restaurants. Pick up, wash, deliver; rinse and repeat.

Dad started out as a route driver. There's a great picture of him and me and his company truck, taken in front of our house on Crescent Street around 1962 when I was three years old. In the midseventies he was promoted to vice president of sales and service, a position he maintained until he retired.

My mom started working part-time at Kaufman's, a small chain of women's boutiques in Eugene, in 1961. They had three stores: Downtown, Campus, and Valley River. She advanced with the company and in 1972 was promoted to manager of the Campus store, moving to Valley River before retiring in 1981.

When I was born, we lived in a house on Crescent Street. In the spring of 1964, when I was four, we moved to 2660 Cheryl Street, where I grew up. When my dad retired in 1990, they sold that house and moved to Sunriver in central Oregon.

In 1971, a couple of months before turning twelve, I went to Potter Valley for my brother Keith's eighteenth birthday and high school graduation.

Two weeks later, he was killed in a car wreck.

It was June 27, a perfect Sunday morning in Eugene. Up Cheryl Street, around the corner, and about two blocks down Crescent was Norkenzie Christian Church. Now, I'm not from a hugely religious family. We're certainly not atheists, but we really didn't go to church, aside from a Christmas service or something. But my mom insisted that Tim and I attend Sunday school, and we'd either get a ride there or walk. And I'll never forget this sunny morning, just getting out of Sunday school. Of course, church starts after Sunday school, but we never stayed for that. Seems odd now.

Tim and I walked out after Sunday school, and my dad was there to pick us up. That was strange because we'd walked to church, and this was a beautiful summer day, the sort of day you spend all winter in Oregon thinking about. I immediately knew that something was going on, as there was no normal reason for him to pick us up. Then I saw the look on my dad's face, which I will never forget.

We got in the car, and he went the long way home, down a different side street to go around the block. "What's up, Dad? What's going on? Why did you pick us up?" He started crying and said that Keith had been killed in a car wreck that morning.

I'd never seen my dad cry. And when we got to the house, my mom was a wreck; it still hits me hard now, fifty-odd years later, when I talk about it. We drove to Potter Valley that day, and it was the longest ten hours of my life. It was devastating, just awful. I was old enough to understand what was going on. Tim, not as much.

At the time, I was told about a Saturday-night dance at the Potter Valley

Grange. Keith played the drums. He wasn't actually in the band, but I guess they egged him on to come up and play a little bit. He was having a great time.

They told us he fell asleep driving home, and his car swerved off the road and hit a tree. Along this country road where it happened, the tree he hit was the only tree for about a hundred yards either way.

As I got older, I realized he had been drinking. But they didn't tell us that then. It was tough. My mom has never gotten over it. The funeral, the whole thing, it was just so, so sad.

Otherwise, life in Eugene seemed pretty simple. We were typical middle class. As a kid, I felt like I got pretty much whatever I wanted. A baseball glove or a bat or a bike, whatever. I do realize now, as I've grown and talked to my parents, how hard they worked to manage all the finances, getting us through school. But it was a very happy childhood.

I was always a huge, huge baseball fan. I liked football and was never big on basketball, but baseball was the sport I loved. We would have sandlot games, and sometimes there would be literally four kids per team. You gotta cover a lot of ground playing four on four. I started playing baseball when I was in fourth grade. I tried real hard, but it was tough, because I couldn't run, hit, field, or throw, which is kind of important. I just wasn't very good.

Still, to me it was obvious I was destined to be the first baseman for the Dodgers. That was a foregone conclusion. My grandfather, my mom's dad, lived in the Los Angeles area. He was a Dodgers fan, so I was a Dodgers fan. The first Major League game I ever saw was August 9, 1973, five days before my fourteenth birthday. Driving up to Dodger Stadium, with my dad and my older cousin Jim, it was like Mecca, this shining star overlooking all Los Angeles. It happened to be Willie Mays's last year, playing with the Mets. We were in the right-field stands between first base and the foul pole. Pretty good seats, lower level. Willie didn't start the game, but he did pinch-hit in the ninth, grounding out to third. What a thrill that was, to see him in real life.

Dodger Stadium was (and still is) just so grand. For someone like me, who grew up living and breathing the Dodgers, it was sacred territory. The first time I actually worked a baseball game there—and yes, now we're getting way ahead of our story—I was still in the American League, but the Dodgers were playing the Angels in the annual preseason Freeway Series.

I remember going out on the bases and looking around the stands, going, *Wow. How did I get here?*

Because, again, I was supposed to be the Dodgers' first baseman. Finally, though, it did become obvious that that wasn't going to happen. As much as I loved baseball, I just wasn't very good at *playing* baseball.

So I had some tough moments in organized ball. In fifth grade, which was my second year playing for a real team, for some reason I signed up late. There were A and B teams composed of fifth and sixth graders, and undoubtedly, I should have been on the B team, because (a) there weren't too many fifth graders on the A team and (b) I was horrible. But for whatever reason, the coach put me on the A team. That was the worst thing that could have happened.

League rules said you had to start every other game, and if you didn't start, you still had to play at least two innings. So of course, when I did play, they tried to bury me in the outfield. I remember fly balls being hit to me and me misjudging them, dropping them, all those things. At bat I was intimidated, because the pitchers threw the ball really hard. I was on a team I should not have been on. I wasn't good, and the other kids on the team weren't real happy with me. It was just an awful experience.

Conversely, the very next year, when I was in sixth grade—and for some reason I still wanted to play—they put me on the B team. That might seem demoralizing, but I wound up being thrilled, because I actually had the best year of my baseball career. Trust me, my batting average was probably around .200 or whatever. But I got some hits, including a couple of triples, and made a diving catch for the last out of a game. Granted, I misjudged the ball and ended up having to dive for it, but still. It was the first year I really had fun playing baseball, and I played three more years. But going into high school for my sophomore year, there was either varsity or junior varsity teams. And there was not a chance in hell I was going to make one of those. So my baseball career as a player was over. And that's when I started umpiring, the spring of my sophomore year, at fifteen.

Growing up, I also was fascinated by radio. I listened to 1600 KASH Radio Eugene, a top 40 station. That's why I wanted to be a disc jockey. The Eugene School District had four high schools, each with a remote facility for KRVM-FM, the district radio station. Each high school had an allotted time, Monday through Friday, where students broadcast live from school. So I started doing that at my high school, Sheldon, and really loved it.

Right across the street from Sheldon was a commercial radio station: KBDF-AM 1280. They and KASH were the top 40 stations in Eugene. In the summer of '76, right after my junior year, I walked over to KBDF with a tape I had from some of my KVRM shows and asked if any jobs were available. Pure cold call. My thought process was to just get in the door doing *anything*; I had no expectation of getting on the air but wanted to be in that environment and learn whatever I could.

I'll be damned if they didn't hire me. They needed somebody for Sunday mornings, to play the thirty-minute PSAs and religious shows. So my very first shift was on Sunday, July 4, 1976, the bicentennial. I wasn't on the air, just playing tapes from four in the morning until nine. But I was thrilled—I'm in a radio studio! I had thought maybe I'd be a gopher or something, anything to get inside the station. Yet there I was, actually in the studio, playing these half-hour tapes, and I was thrilled.

I did that for one Sunday. That week, they called me in and said, "Listen, we're changing everything up. We want you to work from 3:00 a.m. to 9:00, a six-hour shift."

From 3:00 to 4:30, they said, you're live on the air. From 4:30 to 8:30, you're playing four hours of all this crap, and then for the last half hour, 8:30 to 9:00, you're live again. I couldn't believe it. There I was, not even seventeen yet, just trying to get a foot in the door, and suddenly in week two I'm actually broadcasting? That was the start of my radio career, and I loved it. Absolutely loved it.

So all through my senior year, I worked at the station. I also started officiating basketball and then football the next fall.

As a part-time guy in radio, basically you're working weekends. You might have one, two, maybe even three shifts over the weekend. You might fill in during the week if somebody needed a day off, that kind of thing, but that's basically the part-time gig in a radio station. So it didn't interfere with school, because it was mostly weekends. I also worked a shift playing *American Top 40* with Casey Kasem. Every week, it was on three albums, since every radio station had turntables. So *American Top 40* was all vinyl, which blew me away. I mean, the sheer number of records they pressed and shipped to stations around the world was incredible.

They also gave me the Sunday night shift from seven to midnight. Just me, no tapes or anything. Monday morning, I would show up at school, and as I was walking down the hall, "Hey, Dale, I heard you last night!" "Hey, I called in last night and asked for Shaun Cassidy!" I couldn't help but think, *I'm pretty damn cool, aren't I?*

This was right at the end of top 40 on AM stations being kind of a thing. FM was really making inroads, with the audio obviously much better. But in the spring of '77, KBDF was Eugene's number one station in the eighteen-to-thirty-five demographic. That was huge, and I loved what I was doing.

I was umpiring, too, but at this point, I hadn't yet thought about umpire school. I enjoyed umpiring and tried to get better and move up locally. The other sports too. But really, what I thought I was going to be when I grew up, so to speak, was a disc jockey. Because I enjoyed it so much and there was an obvious career path.

I graduated from Sheldon in '77, and that fall, I started at Eugene's Lane Community College. I took television broadcasting, because I thought that was the next natural step. You know, I was already in radio, so maybe I'd go into TV.

I enjoyed television broadcasting and my two years at Lane. We had our own color studio, with a live, fifteen-minute cable newscast every Monday, Wednesday, and Friday. I was one of the four anchors who rotated. We would write copy, run cameras, do the lighting and audio, work as technical directors and floor directors; you had your hand in everything.

I think five people actually watched it. But it was live and really cool. I reported stories about the Jonestown massacre in Guyana and the murders of Mayor George Moscone and supervisor Harvey Milk in San Francisco. Those stories remain fresh in my memory.

But when I graduated in May of '79 with my associate's science degree, I realized I had no real desire to go into television.

When I was doing my show on the radio, it was just me. I was running the commercials; I was running the mic. I wasn't relying on anybody. In TV, you're relying on everybody. You can flawlessly direct a program, but if the technical director screws up, or the camera guy or the floor director . . . if one thing goes wrong, the whole thing can be a bust. That frustrated me. I liked being in control of what I was doing. So I enjoyed radio more, because I wasn't depending on a lot of people. When I graduated, I went full-time at KBDF.

My first shift as a full-timer was Monday through Friday, 10:00 p.m. to 2:00 a.m. Eventually, they promoted me to 6:00 p.m. to 10:00 p.m., Monday through Friday. I was loving life, umpiring or refereeing (depending on the season) and working a great time slot at the station.

A year or so earlier, I'd been told about umpire school by an umpire friend, Kurt Kruger, who had gone in 1975. He didn't get a pro job afterward, but he absolutely loved the experience. "You're a pretty good umpire," he told me, "and you've got a lot of potential. You enjoy the intricacies of umpiring, so when you come back to Eugene, just having been to school, you'll get college games and be working higher levels." At the time, I was working high school games, occasionally junior college.

"And you know," Kurt said, "you *could* do well enough to go into the Minor Leagues."

But that wasn't my motivation for going to umpire school. My motivation, after talking to Kurt, was that I really liked umpiring and wanted to advance locally. Honestly, almost everybody goes to umpire school hoping to get a job in professional baseball. You do have some who are older—and when I say older, I mean thirty-five and above—too old for professional baseball to consider hiring. There are also guys who just want the experience, want to learn, but have no desire to go pro, nor do they expect the opportunity. I went with the thought of getting the experience that Kurt had described. But in the back of my mind? Sure. *Hey, if you ACE this, if you do really well, there is that shot.*

This all started in 1979, the year I turned twenty. But I thought to myself, *Why go to umpire school now? I just got out of Lane. I'm working full-time in radio and loving the gig. And more importantly, umpire school starts the day after Christmas, which means I'll be there for New Year's Eve and, at twenty, couldn't go drinking with everyone else.*

So let's review, shall we? Apparently, my priorities at that time were centered on getting into bars and clubs on New Year's Eve rather than what was best for me and my future. I'm sure my parents were very proud.

So I waited a year. In the spring of 1980, I went to management at KBDF and said I wanted to go to umpire school and give it a shot. Because my shift was from six to ten at night, I wouldn't have been able to work many games outside of weekends. I told them I'd like to scale back to part-time so that I could work a lot more games. Then after umpire school, I'd come back to the station and work full-time, whatever shift they could give me.

They told me, "Listen, we think you're insane, but we know you have a passion for this. You've always got a job here. When you come back, we're not going to fire somebody to put you in full-time. But we'll certainly want you back, so we'll work it out."

Right around this same time, the Eugene Boys Athletic Association started incorporating girls' sports and changed their name to the Eugene Sports Program. They came to me with a job offer. "We're looking for a commissioner of officials. You would recruit, train, and assign officials for all our sports: football, volleyball, and soccer in the fall; boys' and girls' basketball in the winter; baseball and softball in the spring."

I wasn't exactly desperate for more work, but how could I turn this down? So now I had my own office at ESP, and while I didn't have my own secretary, I did have *a* secretary. And that great title: commissioner of officials. I still worked part-time at KBDF, and I still umpired and officiated.

Living the dream, right? I felt rich, so I bought a new car—a gold '79 Toyota Corolla hatchback with AM/FM-cassette stereo, which I connected to a pair of speakers encased in wood blocks in the back of the car. Get too close and I would literally drive that late-seventies top 40 music right into your brain.

I would umpire a game at four o'clock on Friday afternoon, at Spencer Butte Junior High. Then, that evening, KBDF PERSONALITY DALE SCOTT IS YOUR DISC JOCKEY FOR THE SPENCER BUTTE JUNIOR HIGH DANCE. So I'm onstage, playing the tunes, and these baseball players would point toward me and say, "Hey, you're the dude that struck me out today!"

At the Lane County Fair, KBDF would have a booth where every night from ten to midnight, one of the KBDF personalities would DJ—*the 1280 Dance at Lane County Fair*. You'd be up onstage, with everyone dancing and clapping. That was when they started calling me the Umpire with the Golden Voice. Yes, I was having a ball.

In the summer of 1980, I was planning to finally attend umpire school that winter. At the time, Bill Kinnamon had two schools, one in

Florida and one in San Bernardino, California; the other school was Harry Wendelstedt's in Florida. The Kinnamon school in San Bernardino started the day after Christmas, and it would run right to the first week of February. The California and Florida schools would overlap for a week, and part of the staff would shift from one to the other.

In the fall of '79, I finally moved out of my parents' house. I'll never forget hauling a load of stuff—and it's not like I had a shit ton of stuff—to my new roommate Terry's apartment. About three hours later, I came back home to pick up more, and my dad had already started renovating my room for his den.

"Hey, wait a minute. What's the etiquette here? You can't wait a week, just to see? Is there no mourning period now that your oldest son is gone?"

My parents laughed, "Here's the rest of your shit. Go. Have a good time." I lived with Terry through that winter of '79 and into '80. Later I got my own place on Coburg Road, a couple of miles from my parents' house, just before I turned twenty-one. I was there until December, and then I moved back in with my parents.

Because later that month, I was finally heading to umpire school.

3

Playing the Game

People ask me, "When did you know you were gay?"

I always was. I just didn't know it. There are little things, as I look back now, that were certainly clues. Or should have been. I remember when I first got into junior high—before I really began labeling anything, because I didn't have the label yet—but there were a couple of guys in the seventh grade I had a crush on. It wasn't like I wanted to write them love letters or anything; it wasn't necessarily sexual.

But I was drawn to them more than I would be to females, and it was certain guys, not everyone. I remember one time—this was when I was about fourteen, probably ninth grade—when my dad pulled me out of school for a week to go deer hunting in eastern Oregon with my uncle Leamon and a couple of family friends.

Getting supplies in Burns, the nearest town to camp, I was between my dad and my uncle in our pickup, stopped at a red light. In the crosswalk before us was a couple in their midtwenties.

Leamon piped up, "Wow, check *her* out. You see that, Dale?"

Looking right at the guy, I said, "Yeah, I do see that."

Secretly, I'm laughing, thinking of both my dad and uncle, *They have no idea who I'm looking at*. But it was totally natural for me; that was what I would automatically do, check out the guy.

I knew I was attracted to and felt more comfortable around guys—to me it was completely normal. There was no shame or remorse; I didn't define or label it. I wasn't thinking, *Oh man, you must be gay*. But I also knew, *This isn't something I can talk about or tell anyone.* It wouldn't be until a couple of years after graduating high school that I figured it all out.

In July 1979, a few weeks before my twentieth birthday, I finally discovered, or at least acknowledged, my true self. That's when I met Chuck, a gay man twenty years older than I, with whom I remained friends until he passed away some twenty-five years later. Chuck opened my eyes and educated me about the gay world, a world that until then I didn't realize I was actually a part of.

Up to this point in my life, I hadn't put a label on my sexuality, since it felt normal to me. It wasn't something I thought about, kind of like being right-handed—I just . . . was. So why overthink it?

Things changed that summer, though. I figured it out. I was gay.

Chuck told me that Skinner's Butte Park in Eugene, the park where my brother Tim and I played all the time when we were kids, was known as a gay cruising spot. Guys would drive between two parking lots at each end or just park and watch the cars go by. I had never heard of anything like that, but yeah, I was curious. What's this all about?

On a beautiful July night after playing a charity game with the KBDF softball team and having a couple of beers after the game (illegally, since I was only nineteen), I headed toward my parents' house. As luck would have it—actually this was totally on purpose!—I drove by Skinner's Butte Park.

It was about 10:30 when I entered the park, curious to see what Chuck had described . . . *I'll just drive through once and then head home . . . you know, just to check it out.*

I couldn't believe what I saw. There were several cars cruising back and forth between one lot and the other, like we did on a Saturday night on Willamette Street; we called it "cruising the gut," like in *American Graffiti*. A few years later Doug, my closest gay friend in Eugene, called Skinner's Butte "the yacht club." He would call and say, "Hey, let's go yachting. Meet you at the yacht club!"

To this point, I had met only a few gay men, all of them forty or older and nobody I was attracted to. With the exception of Chuck, I would meet them once and never see them again. I *wanted* to meet guys eighteen, nineteen, twenty years old—guys I could relate to. Frankly, I didn't believe they existed.

And if they did, where were they? Was I somehow the only nineteen-year-old gay dude in Eugene, Oregon?

That night, I found out I wasn't.

Among the cars at the park that night was a convertible with three young men, all near my age. After passing each other a few times, I parked, and they drove up beside me. We started chatting and laughing, and once again my eyes were opened. It felt like yet another awakening. Just a few days earlier, Chuck had begun my accelerated education about a world I knew very little about. Now I was getting a master's degree from three guys my age.

At the time, I had a girlfriend, Leslea, who was a year younger than I was. We started paying attention to each other when I was in ninth grade, and for most of high school, we were a couple. I lost my hetero virginity with her a year after I graduated. We were sexually active; I was young; and yes, it felt great. But it wasn't me. It wasn't what flipped my switch. This was the late seventies, disco was king, and being bi was kind of cool . . . so I must be bi.

At least I kept telling myself that. Except, I would also think, *If by* bi *I mean "just guys" . . . Uh, I think there might be a conflict here.* Now I joke that I was bi for about twenty minutes.

A few days after my Skinner's Butte awakening, I told Leslea, "So I met a couple guys the other day, and . . . well, I think I'm bi."

Yes, I knew I was gay, but I wasn't yet ready to go there with her. So I thought I'd tell her I'm bi, she'd drop me like a rock, and I could move on in my new reality.

"Really?" she said. "You're bi?"

"Yeah. I think so."

There was an awkward pause, and then . . . "The thought of you with another man is hot."

If I had been drinking something, I would have done a spit take; this was not the response I anticipated! But like I said, it was the late seventies.

Leslea and I gently went our own ways after that. I still see her once every couple of years, when I'm in Eugene for a Duck football game and I drive through the old neighborhood. She still lives in the house she grew up in, a block or so from my childhood home. We laugh about it now. She was always very cool about the whole thing and is a wonderful woman.

When I figured everything out, coming out to myself was pretty cut-and-dried and played right into the mentality of an umpire. When I have a call on the field, it's either out or safe, ball or strike. You don't have time to overthink it. *Well, he did slide, but his hand came up, and that throw was pretty good, but he had to go up to catch it, the runner isn't that fast, and the outfielder has a great arm . . .* Nope. I don't have time for all of that. I have to react to what I see and make a call.

The day I came out to myself (it wasn't actually *one* day, but it seemed like it, as my true awakening all happened so fast in those few days in July), I looked in the mirror, and it suddenly became clear. *Whoa, now I get it . . . you're not bi, dude. You're gay. YOU'RE GAY.*

So now my thought process, like when making a call on the field, was not to fret and overthink it but, instead, to just react: *Okay, you're gay. Now that you know who you are, how are you going to deal with it?*

This was who I am, and the realization was a relief. At the same time, I understood that I had to "play the game." Society hadn't evolved to where I could come out by telling friends and family, "Hey everybody, I'm gay," and then have everyone say, "Cool, Dale! No problem!" I would need to continue being the guy all my family and friends have known for years but *also* create my own space, just for me.

I had to play the game, which meant *I may have to lie my ass off, but I'll be damned if I'm going to look in the mirror every day for the rest of my life and lie to myself. I know who I am, and I'm happy about it.*

That's when I broke through my blissful ignorance of who I was. And I was not only okay with it, but I was actually excited to see where this new path would take me. I wasn't going to include someone like Leslea within some lie to cover for my sexuality. I've met many gay guys who did that, even got married and started families because of religious reasons or family pressures, and fundamentally were not true to themselves. So many paid a painful price, whether it was cheating on their wives, bitter divorces, broken families, or dealing with the mental anguish and guilt of living the lie in their personal lives. I swore I would never do that, and I'm grateful that I didn't.

I'm all too aware that coming-out stories for many are difficult, can be suicidal, and often include awful experiences with friends and loved ones. I don't dismiss those experiences at all. I'm fortunate that I was able to decipher all of this when I was nineteen and move forward from there without the inner turmoil. Granted, it would be years before a lot of my friends knew (although several of them figured it out before I actually told them). I didn't want them to know, not because I was ashamed—quite the contrary, as I loved being gay—but because I knew society wasn't there yet.

Outwardly I've always shown a lot of confidence and self-assurance. John McSherry, our lead instructor at umpire school, berated me in front of the class after I screwed up some drill we were doing.

"Scott, goddammit, you're better than that! You stand out there and act like you're Mr. Cool, like you got everything under fucking control. Well, guess what? It's not under fucking control, so quit acting like you're so damn cool!"

I certainly try to exude an *air* of being in control, confident. That said, internally there were *plenty* of times when I wasn't. Times when I was weary of the challenge or the buildup to it. Ninety-nine times out of a hundred, the buildup to a big game is worse than the game itself, and sometimes that buildup rattled the shit out of me, internally.

Many times before big games, I was a nervous fricking wreck. I tried to channel those nerves positively but was a mess in my room all day before a World Series plate job. But when I walked out of that hotel room, I looked like the most confident, let's-go-get-'em, not-a-care-in-the-world guy.

Where did I get that? Where does it come from? I'm not sure.

Maybe I got that show of confidence because I was so good at living a double life. From a young age, I became really good at portraying myself as someone who's straight. Just one of the guys. I've had so many people say, "I can't believe you're gay," not only because of my profession, but also because I didn't match people's stereotype of someone gay (and yes, stereotypes are ridiculous since there are gay people in all walks of life).

Remember that moment in Burns? I'm looking right at the *guy* while my uncle is telling my dad, "You better watch out with this kid. He might be giving you a grandson soon." It's how I portrayed it. Like I had it all figured out. Perception is reality.

All the travel in baseball helped me lead that double life. I could be completely different at home than on the road, and vice versa. I easily transitioned between the two, filling in the gaps between the straight and gay worlds, so there was little suspicion among people who knew me largely in my umpiring life.

I would tell guys in instructional league that a girl from Portland just moved to Tempe, so I was going to hang at her place tonight, or whatever story I came up with (and I came up with plenty of them). All my stories seemed to work (why would he lie?). When someone asked why I didn't bring her out somewhere, I came up with something else, like she worked a swing shift and was tired, so we were meeting at her place. Yeah, it was all a fricking lie, but it was one to protect my identity, not to hurt anybody or gain some unfair advantage. And it created my own space so that I could then check out a gay bar and live my other life. I did things like that all the time and could do it seamlessly.

Does this make me some sort of a psychopath, that I can lie so easily about those situations? I don't know if what I was doing should be complimented or condemned. What I do know is that it helped me keep my sanity to be able to live my gay life while working my baseball one.

4

"You Were Terrible!"

So off I went, finally, to umpire school. It was December 1980, and I was twenty-one years old.

There were only twenty-seven students at the Bill Kinnamon Umpire School in San Bernardino, California, with the top five moving on to Bradenton, Florida, for a one-week advanced school in March.

After a week or two, I had a pretty good handle on my competition. Out of the twenty-seven, in my estimation, maybe ten had a shot at making the top five. There were six or seven who weren't trying to get a job anyway; they were older or were there just for the experience, treating it like an umpire fantasy camp. Then there were a few who wanted pro jobs but physically weren't up to the task. As we went through drills on the field and worked in the cages calling pitches, I could tell some didn't have the physical attributes—the movement, the instincts, the footwork—and couldn't pick it up. Then there were those whose judgment was horrendous.

Thinking that I now had a shot at Bradenton, the light went on: *You know what? I think I could make the top five. I think I can do this. I might have a chance of getting a job.*

I figured that after umpire school I would go back to Eugene, where I'd resume my duties as commissioner of officials and still have my radio gig at KBDF and my officiating in football and basketball. I would also have all this knowledge and experience from umpire school helping me advance into working college baseball. Before school started, I asked myself: *If the chance comes up where I'm offered a Minor League job, am I willing to let* all that go? My answer was yes. An opportunity to umpire in professional baseball is a once-in-a-lifetime thing. I didn't want to look back years later and regret passing it up.

I could always go back to radio if baseball didn't work out—if not KBDF, then somewhere else. At this point, it was really what I thought I would be doing anyway. But now I was thinking, *There are some guys here who are definitely better than I am, but to grab one of those five spots? I think I have a shot.* That motivated me even more.

Umpire school is damn near a twenty-four-hour thing, or at least it seemed like it. Monday through Saturday for five weeks (yes, we had Sundays off), you're up for breakfast between seven and eight; then you're in the classroom with rules, tests, or lecture sessions from eight to ten. After that, it's outside to the field or the batting cage, learning the two-man system, working drills, or calling pitches on right- and left-handed hitters from a pitching machine until dark. In January that happens around five o'clock, with a thirty-minute lunch break well behind you. After dinner, you've still got two or three classroom meetings every week, or studying the rulebook on the nights you don't.

The school was housed at the Western Region Little League Complex, north of downtown off I-215, at the base of the San Bernardino National Forest. We stayed in barracks named after the various states that competed there every summer to represent the Western Region in the Little League World Series. I was assigned to the Colorado barrack. With bunk beds, shared shower and toilet facilities, plus an assembly-line type cafeteria, it had the feel of a military installation.

Many think of California as a mecca of sun, beaches, and warm weather. It certainly has those things, but not many people rhapsodize over winter in San Bernardino. The average high and low temperatures that time of year are sixty-eight and forty-three degrees. Now, sixty-eight in January might sound nice. But the school was located in a natural wind tunnel. With the windchill, that sixty-eight amounted to a very chilly, penetrating midfifties (or worse) . . . every day. Maybe that's why the Florida schools were so much better attended?

Usually every Saturday night and Ladies Night Wednesday, several of us would go to a club in downtown San Bernardino to unwind, have a few beers, and listen to some of the most pathetic pickup lines known to man: "Ever go out with an umpire?" "Umpires cover all the bases!" "Know how to use a clicker?" (I know I'm gay, but please tell me these don't work?)

Of course, I played the part of an interested and *straight* twenty-one-year-old. Trust me, I wasn't. But it was fun to watch, laugh, and have fun away from the complex. Plus, at that age, I could rebound quickly after a late night and a few drinks. (Not any more. I used to time my hangovers with a clock, and now I time 'em with a calendar. These days, it's usually a two-day event. That's why I don't drink much now.)

After the five-week course, it was graduation day and the announcement of where we finished. I had absorbed more about the umpiring profession than I ever knew was possible. I was happy with my progress, week to week. Looking around at my fellow students, I thought I was anywhere from third to seventh . . . which would put me on the bubble, with only five going to Florida.

The list was announced, and I'd finished . . . fifth, just *barely* making the cut.

The number one student was Kip Arnold, from Los Angeles, followed by J. B. Hance (Lubbock), John Jankowski (Omaha), and Danny Toal (Tucson).

Danny had never umpired in his life. That doesn't happen often, but maybe more than you think. One thing about going to umpire school and having never worked a game? You have zero bad habits. When I was committed to going to school, Kurt Kruger told me what they'd be teaching and what they wanted to see from students. All the basics. So in the summer of 1980, knowing school started in December, I concentrated on that and tried to eliminate what I suspected might be my bad habits.

When I started school, I thought I was a pretty decent umpire. I'd done well for the five years I had been working, with a lot of positive feedback from other umpires and even a few coaches. I was at least semiconfident that I could hold my own.

Once I got there, I realized I knew nothing. It's so detailed and specific.

You're taught everything known to man about the two-man system. You learn to communicate, really communicate, with your partner. You're taught not only the rules inside and out but also *why* the rule is in the book. In many instances that will help you understand how, coupled with good judgment and common sense, you enforce rules either by the letter of the law *or* within the context of how the game is played.

I was taught, really for the first time, about situations and arguments.

About proper angles, distance, and timing. Footwork for pick-offs, steal plays, double plays, passed balls and wild pitches. On the bases in a two-man, you're covering a lot of ground in a hurry, and you can't afford to waste steps.

None of this is to fault the local guys I learned from. Rarely are you going to have local instructors who know, have worked, and can teach pro mechanics. As soon as I got to San Bernardino, I threw out what I'd been taught and doing in Eugene, and I started over.

Although I never served, umpire school felt like what I imagined boot-camp to be, or at least some similarities. The camaraderie, pulling for your partners all while competing against them, clapping and cheering when someone nails a rotation or masters a drill. That mentality lasts throughout your career—you and your crew, you and fellow umpires versus the world it seems. It also transcends to officials in other sports, a fraternity. It's a bond that's hard to understand until you're in that situation.

So I learned quickly that I didn't know shit. And I was like a sponge, which was the other thing Kruger told me as I prepared during the months before school: "Be a sponge, man, soak it all in. They're gonna teach you stuff you never thought of."

After graduating and learning I wasn't done, I had four weeks before reporting to Bradenton. A short "vacation" in Eugene, and then on the road again to start a new experience. Except for Kip, the other four of us Florida-bound graduates decided to drive, picking up each, one by one, on the way east.

Umpire Development—the department that hired, supervised, and assigned all Minor League umpires—also ran the advanced school. All fifty umpires from the three schools received $75 plus two meals a day (breakfast and lunch) and lodging for the week. That year, the top thirteen in the class would be hired and assigned a Minor League spring-training camp and issued a check for round-trip airfare from home to Bradenton. Depending on the volume of openings in the Minor Leagues (the number varied each year, depending on how many umpires quit or were released), many of the other thirty-seven would be hired but receive just the $75 for the week.

I was excited to drive coast-to-coast. Previously, I had only been to the four states that border Oregon, plus Hawaii. First destination: Tucson and Danny Toal. After a night of checking out a couple of Tucson's finest drinking establishments, we left the next day for Lubbock, picking up J.B. and switching from my car to his, a four-door with much more room. J.B. gave us a whirlwind Lubbock tour, and then we headed east the next day for the Dallas–Ft. Worth airport and added John Jankowski, who'd flown in from Omaha, to our Florida-or-bust pilgrimage.

Along the way, as we crossed into each new state, we pulled over and took a picture of the "Welcome to" freeway sign. Yeah, we were those guys. Danny was the oldest at twenty-six, J.B. and John were twenty-four, and I was twenty-one. We were carefree, not knowing what was ahead or how much our lives would change (if at all) when our time in Florida was over, living in the moment and having a blast on our road trip.

We arrived in St. Petersburg during finals week of the Kinnamon Florida school. Bill Kinnamon invited us to spend a few days there, staying in the barracks, to participate in drills and cage work, since we had been off for a month. The advanced school in Bradenton, only twenty-five miles south, would begin immediately after finals week.

As you would expect, just a few days before graduation, the atmosphere was very intense and competitive. By this time, Kip Arnold had arrived, and we were looked upon suspiciously as the "California Five." Yes, there's a brotherhood, but at this point, we were not part of theirs. They were still fighting for Bradenton slots, while we already had ours. There were close to 120 students in St. Pete, almost a hundred more than at San Bernardino; only the top twenty joined us for the advanced school.

Of the fifty umpires in Bradenton, twenty-five came from Kinnamon, and twenty-five from the Harry Wendelstedt Umpire School. It was an intense week, competing with the top fifty students that year, the best of the best. It was no longer a matter of *I think I can do this*. Like the other forty-nine, I wouldn't be here if they didn't think I had a shot at moving on. And as things went along, I thought I was doing well, at least holding my own.

Anticipating the next morning, when names would be announced, the tension building up all week finally peaked on evaluation day.

On the field, various situations were being set up, with different umpires called to step in and work the drill, all seemingly at random. While that was going on, the main focus was the action in the cage, calling pitches. That's where the top supervisors were most of the day. Some umpires were sent to the cage once; some were called twice. A few guys were called five, six, seven times as the day continued. It was obvious that those with multiple cage callbacks were on the bubble.

I was never called to the cage. Not once. My fate was apparently sealed, the decision made. They already had me in . . . or out. Either way, they didn't need to see me. There were only a few who didn't go to the cage. Very few. I didn't have a clue about the decision but thought I'd had a decent week. Maybe I didn't? I would find out soon . . .

Earlier in the week, we'd been told to call a travel agent and get an airfare quote. In 1981 a round-trip coach ticket from Eugene to Sarasota was just short of $1,000, a boatload of money at the time and a hell of a lot more than $75. Later I found out that mine was the highest fare of the entire class. But then again, I lived the farthest away.

Barney Deary was head of Umpire Development, with Dick Nelson (West Coast supervisor) and Mike Fitzpatrick (East Coast) on hand. Also at Bradenton were retired MLB umpires Al Barlick, who represented the National League, and Johnny Stevens, American League.

Barlick and Stevens were there all week, essentially working as scouts for their respective leagues. Although they taught some, most of the time they were in the cage, observing. All the instruction was done by Nelson and Fitzpatrick.

Decision morning, they were all in the room you enter when your name is called, one by one, alphabetically. Finally, it was my turn to go in.

As I sat down, Barney asked, "So, Scotty, how do you think you did this week?"

"I think I had a pretty good we—"

Stevens cuts me off midsentence: "*You were terrible! You had a horrible week. I don't know why you wasted your time coming here. Awful!*"

Holy shit! A retired American League umpire and current supervisor is burying me.

Barney jumped in, "Now, Johnny . . ."

Obviously, I can write off the American League! I'll never go there. This guy is blackballing me, and I haven't even kicked a pitch yet!

Johnny was a strange man. I didn't know him for shit, but he was going off on me like I burned down his house or something. WTF?

29

Everyone else was a bit taken aback, almost apologetic: "Johnny, come on now. You're rough on everybody."

Finally, Barney said, "Scotty, we actually thought you did okay."

The entire time, I'm thinking, *I'm done. They'll hand me my $75, and I'll be on my way. Eugene's not such a bad place.*

Barney and the others start telling me how they thought I did, pointing out a couple of things I should work on. To be honest, I didn't hear what was being said. I already knew, after the eruption of Mt. St. Stevens and not once being called to the cage during evaluations, that I must have fallen short. Meanwhile, Barney was writing something on the other side of the table—a $75 check was my guess.

"Dale, I'm pleased to give you this check. You'll be getting a spring-training assignment in Arizona." Barney handed me a check for $980.

What? Seriously? I couldn't believe it!

I've called my parents a million times; a few of those calls remain unforgettable. One was a few weeks earlier when, from a pay phone in San Bernardino, I told them I finished fifth and was moving on. The call from Florida that day with the news I finished in the top of my class, would be working in the Minor Leagues, and had a spring-training assignment was another one. The call five years later with the news I was hired by the American League is also on that list. The joy and excitement on those calls, my mother crying—she was so happy for me—that's something I will never forget.

When I attended Lane Community College, I paid for my tuition. I could afford it, as I was making good money, between umpiring and working at KBDF. My parents saved what they could for my education while I was growing up, and since it wasn't used for my two years at LCC, they paid for umpire school: $880, including room and board. I was happy to tell them their money hadn't gone to waste.

Of the four road warriors, J.B., Danny, and I all got spring-training assignments and airfare. John was the only one of us who didn't, and he flew home. Kip Arnold also got hired, but he stalled in Class Triple-A a few years later. On our way back west, the three of us spent two nights in New Orleans celebrating. We ate and drank like we hit the lottery, and in a way we had.

After dropping off J.B. and picking up my car in Lubbock and then dropping off Danny in Tucson, I drove to my cousin Linda's house in Cerritos,

California. With only a few days before reporting to Yuma and Minor League spring training with the Padres, going to Eugene didn't make sense.

I was soon on my way to Yuma. Being a pro rookie, I had no idea this was considered *the worst spring-training camp in Arizona*. Yes, I knew Yuma is close to . . . well, nothing. *But I was thrilled to death.*

My camp partners were crew chief Terry Luhr (Triple-A); Randy Knuths (Double-A), from Shedd, Oregon; and Bill Spooner (A), who's now been an NBA official for more than thirty years. Those first two shared a room, as I did with Bill. When I checked into our hotel, he was already in the room and opened the door wearing workout shorts and a T-shirt, holding a beer.

"Hey, Bill. I'm Dale Scott."

He stared at me, glanced down at my shoes, and then slowly brought his gaze up, scanning me all the way. After this (what seemed like forever) once-over, he stared at me again.

"You like beer?"

"Yeah."

"Good answer," he said, and stepped aside to let me in.

The Padres put us up in the same place they housed their Minor League players: Motel 6. With no in-room phones, if you had a message, they would tape your room number on the inside of the office window. So at least twice a day, you'd walk by the office to see if there was a message. If you needed to make a call, there was a bank of four pay phones that were constantly in use by players, most of whom didn't speak English and had a tendency to speak loudly. *You* try having a private conversation at the Yuma Motel 6.

Worst camp in baseball? Hey, who cares! I'm just thrilled to be here!

Since Yuma was 180 miles from the nearest spring-training camp, the teams played each other, Triple-A versus Double-A, and their two Class A teams squaring off. Bill and I worked the same two A-ball teams. Every day. For two fricking weeks. And lucky us—because they are camp games and coaches want to see every pitcher who needed work that day, rarely did we play just nine innings. Usually, we went eleven or twelve. Or more.

Hmmm, yeah. I'm starting to process this "worst camp" narrative, but it's still an assignment.

On March 30 we were on the field when we got word that President Reagan

31

had been shot. The camp director shut everything down for the day. Bill and I went back to our room and watched the news coverage for hours.

The next day, we were informed that because of yesterday's shutdown, they hadn't seen everyone they wanted, so we would be going a "little bit longer."

That day, we went seventeen innings.

Okay. I really am thrilled to have a Minor League assignment. But, yeah, Yuma is the worst camp in Arizona.

Now when Bill Spooner comes to Portland to work the Blazers, he usually arrives the day before. My husband, Mike, and I take Bill to our favorite Chinese restaurant or get takeout and sit around for hours at the house, laughing and drinking. Our beverage of choice? The "good answer" I gave him all those years ago: beer.

That was the beginning of a great friendship and my thirty-seven-year career in professional baseball.

5

"He's That Blind SOB"

There's a funny quote in Ken Kaiser's book. In umpire school, he said, "we were taught to always refer to managers, players, and coaches as rats. They weren't good guys or bad guys. They were rats, all of them, rats. But after my first few years in the big leagues and really getting to work with them, I thought that was a pretty unfair comparison. Unfair to the rats."

Kenny joined the American League staff in 1977, just a few years before I went to school. But he'd spent thirteen years working in the Minor Leagues, so he'd actually gone to school nearly twenty years before I did. By the early eighties, some of the more derogatory terms for players, coaches, and managers were starting to fade out. And I don't think any of that is "taught" now.

But yeah, when I went to umpire school, the players were called rats. This was just ingrained in you. Hey, it's just *you and your partner against the world*, which a lot of times it really is. Or seems like that, anyway. And *you don't trust a rat*.

I learned that the hard way my first year in pro ball, in the Northwest League. Yes, I'd theoretically learned that in school. But it was one of those things I had to find out for myself.

This was very early in the season, in Bend, Oregon. Our locker room was basically a closet, and it was really hot in there. So my partner, Keith Meastas, and I set up chairs outside the room. I had the plate that night, so I was rubbing up the baseballs. This outfielder for Bend—believe it or not, his name was Kent Keiser—saw us out there, and he'd never seen baseballs getting rubbed up. So he started asking questions about that and where Keith and I were from, just making pleasant conversation for five minutes. He was just a kid, a couple of years younger than I was. And afterward I thought, *He seems like a nice guy. There's a lot of players who wouldn't come up here and talk to us like that.*

Well, in the eighth inning that night, I called Kent out on strikes. I ended up running him and the manager, and he went apeshit crazy. (I soon realized, Kent operated under the common philosophy that if he didn't swing at the pitch, it must be a ball.)

So I thought, *Dale, you were taught this in umpire school. Don't get lured in by some guy who seems really nice and talks to you like you're old buddies, because the first chance he gets to stick it up your ass, that's exactly what he'll do.* On my own in central Oregon, I finally learned something they'd told us for five weeks in school.

As an aside, believe *this* or not, more than forty years later, I still have my ejection report from that evening. So just to give you some idea of life as a rookie umpire, about two weeks into this exciting phase of my new career, here's an excerpt:

> In the eighth inning with one out and the score 8–4 in favor of Salem, I called Keiser out on a third strike. He told me that I was "horseshit" so I ejected him. Manager Carey asked me what he said. I told him and his reply was, "You are horseshit." I ejected Carey. He then told me that I was "horseshit and full of shit," and made visual reference of the strike zone with his hands at his knees. Finally he left. Please note that earlier in the game, both Keiser and Carey said I was "full of shit" and I did not eject them.
>
> In the bottom of the 9th I called Gomez out on strikes to end the game. He then tossed his bat and helmet at my feet in obvious disrespect of the call. The bat or helmet did not strike me. I told Gomez that his actions would be in a report to the league office since the game was over.

Seventeen days later, again in Bend, I called Keiser out on a play at the plate, and manager P. J. Carey, who at the time was not much older than I was and who wound up managing twenty-four years in the low Minors, came out to argue. When he kicked dirt on the plate, I ran him.

Oh, and our amiable young friend, Mr. Keiser? From my report to North-west League president Bob Freitas: "Right after I had the call, Keiser jumped up to argue and did brush up and lean against me. I told him not to touch me. That's when Carey got there. I *should* have ejected Keiser, but did not."

Now let me add context to those ejection reports, which make me cringe now, reading them for the first time in decades. The Northwest League is a rookie league. I made rookie mistakes, and those reports show it.

First, according to my report, both P.J. and my buddy Kent had earlier in the game "said I was 'full of shit' and I did not eject them."

Those were mistakes. Why? It's rather obvious. If I had ejected them then, they would not have been around to do *the exact same thing* in the eighth inning. I had allowed them to cheap-shot me with no consequences, so why *wouldn't* they do it again later?

Second, and even more cringeworthy, in that second game, the same culprit from earlier that month brushed up and leaned against me to argue a call at the plate . . . and I didn't run him? But I did report that contact to the league president? WTF, Dale?

I'm so thankful there wasn't a supervisor at the game, or this might have been my first *and* last season in professional baseball!

Granted, there was a lot going on in Bend. It was Beer Night.

Let me explain Beer Night. Not only was the beer cheaper, but they also sold a whole bucket of beer, like KFC but way less chicken and way more alcohol. Bend's beer bucket contained 150 ounces, or just more than a twelve-pack.

The bucket sold for $15. But if Bend hit a home run, for the rest of that half inning it was half price . . . $7.50 for a twelve-pack, basically. The key to that sentence is "for the rest of that half inning." After a homer, you would look into the stands—they would always be full on Beer Night—and they'd be empty before the hitter rounded first. Because once the third out was recorded, even if you're in line, the bucket goes back to full price.

So instead of cheers as their hero rounded the bases, you heard the sounds of a stampede as fans exited like a DEFCON 1 alert had just been issued. Now imagine how drunk the fans could get after three or four Phillies home runs as the game went along. Well, now imagine this particular Beer Night was a doubleheader, with Bend hitting multiple home runs in game 1. I was working the plate in game 2 when the incident I'm about to describe happened in the bottom of the sixth of a seven-inning game.

The Eugene Emeralds were ahead 9–3 when I called my BFF Kent out at the plate, which ended a Phillies rally. By this point, Bend had hit four or five home runs in the two games.

So Keiser jumps up, brushes against me, and is still leaning on me when his manager Carey arrived, who then loaded the plate with dirt and was ejected. While arguing with P.J., out of the corner of my eye I saw something fly by. Then another, and I quickly realized I was in the middle of my own DEFCON alert. The beer-bucket drunks were throwing all kinds of objects onto the field in general, and at me in particular. Carey figured he'd already done his best work and abruptly stopped screaming and headed for his dugout, and safety.

Fortunately, the beer-bucket brigade had horrible arms, and most of their projectiles weren't that close to me. Of course, it helped to recall a tip from a few months earlier at umpire school: when bombarded by thrown objects—in this case, the usual cups and wrappers but also some empty buckets, batteries, and partially eaten hot dogs—make your way to the mound area, as rarely can anyone launch something that far. So that's where Keith and I migrated while Greg Riddoch, Eugene's manager, ordered his team to stay in their dugout.

Oh, and the kicker? Also in the stands were my dad, Jess, and Mark Farley, a longtime friend from junior high and high school. Happily, I can report they were not part of the beer-bucket brigade and did not throw anything at me. They were, however, regretting the conversations they had throughout the evening with various fans revealing who their son and friend was. Now both were subtly looking for the nearest exit.

Finally, the bucket brigade either lost interest, threw out their arms, or had to hit the urinals. We started the last inning right around the time that four Oregon state troopers showed up. And once the final out was recorded, I was happy to see them as Keith and I walked off the field to our closet—er, locker room.

One of the troopers stayed by our door while we showered and dressed. My dad and Mark arrived ten minutes later. "Sorry that was so boring," I said. "Usually, a lot more happens. What took you so long?"

My dad smiled. "Mark and I weren't sure we wanted anyone to think we were with you."

We all laughed, and then they both walked several feet behind me and Keith to our car.

The Northwest League opened toward late June, and I wasn't scheduled to work back home in Eugene until August 14. Salem, about sixty miles north, was the nearest team to Eugene. So our first time there, July 3, my parents drove up to watch me for the first time as a professional umpire. Salem played at Chemeketa Community College, with maybe 2,500 seats. On this night they were full, with fireworks scheduled for after the game. Of course I got tickets for my parents directly behind the plate and five rows back, to watch me work.

The Senators, affiliated with the California Angels, were hosting Bend. In the top of the first, I called a balk on Salem's left-handed starter, which brought their manager, Rick Ingalls, out to argue. While he and I went at it, the couple sitting next to my parents were yelling at me (along with about 2,500 other fans): "You suck! Get a real job! Try using your good eye!"

My parents sat there quietly, showing no emotion.

The third inning ended when I called out a Salem runner at the plate, which once again prompted a visit from Ingalls and a rather loud critique from the crowd, including the couple next to my parents. "What a joke! You're not only blind but an idiot! You're a blind idiot!"

My parents sat quietly, calmly.

The top of the fifth was when things really got fun, as I once again balked the lefty, this time with runners on first and third, scoring Bend's first run. This was too much for Ingalls, even though his team still led, 4–1. He prolonged his argument and threw his hat, so I ejected him. This enraged the capacity crowd, including my parents' neighbors.

"YOU SUCK, YOU BLIND IDIOT! DID YOUR MOTHER HAVE ANY KIDS THAT LIVED? YOU'LL NEVER GET TO DOUBLE-A! YOU'RE HORRIBLE! WHAT A MORON!"

The composure displayed by both my parents was commendable. Not challenging this guy or making a snide remark, they once again remained seated and sedate.

At the next lull in the action, the excitable fan had calmed down and started up a conversation with my dad.

"I couldn't help noticing you're not rooting for Salem. Are you a Bend fan?"

"No."

"Just a baseball fan out to see a game?"

"No, actually our son is out there on the field."

"Oh yeah? Is he the bat boy or ball boy?"

"No, he's that blind son of a bitch you've been screaming at for five innings."

Surprised, the now-embarrassed seatmate replied, "Well, you know . . . I don't really know what a balk is? I get kind of excited. I'm sure he was right." And a moment later, he left for the concession stand. After returning, he was rather quiet for the remainder of the game.

So that was Mom and Dad's first professional game.

Almost two months after opening day, I finally worked in Eugene. It was also my twenty-second birthday, August 14. Excited to call a game in Civic Stadium—the same field where I'd worked several high school games the previous couple of years—I left as many tickets as I could for family and friends, plus there were at least ten members of the Lane County Umpires Association, my fellow umpires over the six years since I started doing this.

The *Eugene Register-Guard* and TV station KEZI both interviewed me before the game; KEZI actually had me wear a microphone to start the game, for audio they would use during that evening's eleven o'clock telecast. Most young umpires probably would have found this strange, but with all my radio and TV experience, it wasn't strange at all.

Medford was in town, with me working the plate in the opener. This was the second Northwest League game for my mom, third for my dad. Maybe they'll see a smooth game this evening! (Or not.)

After the Emeralds finished warming up and I crisply brushed off the plate, my mom commented loudly to everyone around her, "That's the most cleaning he's done in years." Thanks, Mom.

With two outs in the top of the first, a Medford runner tried to score on a passed ball. Close play: *Out!* Medford's manager, Brad Fischer, coaching third, charged me, screaming that I'd missed the play. After getting in my face, he kicked dirt in disgust. It wasn't in my direction, but it was still enough for me to eject him.

Let's review! With a bunch of family, friends, and local umpires in attendance for my hometown debut in professional baseball—all captured on video and audio!—we had a bona fide shithouse and ejection before the home team even batted. At this point, no doubt, my parents were convinced that this was simply a routine game for me.

After the game, my mom said, "When they get in your face like that, I don't know how you don't just hit him!" Yes, Mom, that would go over really well with the league president.

I was *not* promoted after that first pro season. Rather, I was simply heading back to the Northwest League, which was disappointing, but at least I'd be close to home. My evaluations were all positive, so I'd been hopeful about a promotion. But I also realized that half the NWL umpire staff were in their second year, so not moving up didn't strike me as unusual. And since I wasn't promoted to a Long-A season, I also wasn't assigned to Minor League spring training in 1982.

However, I *did* get an assignment that I never in a million years expected. Dick Nelson, one of two Minor League supervisors who covered the area west of the Mississippi River (yes, that's a huge territory, but somehow Dick managed to see every Minor League umpire twice during the season, putting nearly sixty thousand miles on his car every year), called me in late February.

"What are you doing April 3?" Dick asked.

"Nothing scheduled, Dick. What's going on?"

"You think you can work an exhibition game at the Kingdome? Atlanta and the Mariners?"

"Of course!" I replied, hardly believing him.

Atlanta was opening their season in San Diego and wanted to play a breakout game somewhere out west. Seattle, who opened in Minnesota on the sixth, agreed to host the game after they broke camp in Tempe. A three-man crew was assigned, with Ted Hendry working the plate, Rick Reed on the bases, and the third assigned by Umpire Development. That meant me, purely by virtue of being the closest Minor League umpire at that moment.

Really, though? I was going to work a big league game after just one season in rookie ball? I drove up I-5 to Seattle with my parents. I'm sure they were hoping their streak of seeing me in the middle of at least one big-time argument and ejection would end. But not as much as I was.

In the locker room, as Teddy was rubbing up the game balls, I asked what I needed to know about working a three-man crew. Sure, I'd worked a few three-man amateur games, but never professionally, let alone on an MLB field. Umpire school taught the two-man system, with little or no mention of more.

Teddy nonchalantly responded, "Oh, just your regular three man." That meant absolutely nothing to me. Fortunately, Rick saw the look on my face and chimed in, "Well, there are a few things we can go over," and then relieved my anxiety by reviewing the fundamental mechanics of the three-man system.

Happily, my argument-ejection streak with my parents in attendance did end that night in Seattle. The game went smoothly, and I didn't screw up our rotations too badly.

After my Kingdome experience, I had more than two months until my second Northwest League season started, so I worked high school and college games back home. But then two weeks before the NWL opened, I got the call I'd hoped for . . . because of a horrible tragedy.

On June 6 American League umpire Lou DiMuro was struck by a car in Arlington, Texas, and passed away two hours later. You never know when a promotion will come (if it comes at all). An umpire might have a season-ending injury or medical condition or retire during the season, but nobody wishes for a promotion under such circumstances.

The grim reality, even while mourning the loss of a fellow brother in blue, is that the games must go on. Lou's death started a domino effect: Rocky Roe was named as DiMuro's full-time replacement, which opened up a Triple-A spot, which opened a Double-A spot that went to my Yuma roommate, Bill Spooner, moving from the California League to the Texas League. And that Cal League opening went to me.

Immediately, I went from preparing for a second, short 70-game season to a 140-game season that started two months earlier. Without much warning, I was now driving to Modesto (where the umpiring staff had two apartments) to meet up with Tim Tschida, my new partner. The Cal League had ten teams, and half of them were so close to Modesto that we could commute. But the day after I arrived, Tim and I drove to Salinas, 107 miles from Modesto and 60 miles south of San Jose.

Joining Tim for my first season in a league that had already played sixty-plus games, I was fresh meat to managers and players. And one Cal League manager was just consistently tough on me—Chris Cannizzaro, who'd been a backup catcher in the big leagues for many years and was sorta famously hard-nosed. He managed in Rohnert Park—home of the Redwood Pioneers—and was just a prick to umpires. He knew Tschida from the year before and seemed to respect him, at least compared to me. We'd have a run-in, and Cannizzaro would look at Tschida and say something like, "Tim, I'm sorry you're stuck with this guy."

One time, Tschida had a steal play that went against Redwood. The shortstop and second baseman ganged up on him, arguing the safe call as Cannizzaro comes charging onto the field. As taught, I came out from the plate to peel the players off, so Tim can go one-on-one with the manager. When I arrive, Cannizzaro looks at me and says, "What are you doing here?"

"I'm trying to prevent your players from getting ejected."

"You don't have a clue what's going on. We don't need you out here."

"Okay, fine," I responded. "I hope they both get run."

That was our relationship. Chris either didn't believe me, didn't like me, or both. He also, unlike some of the younger managers in the league, wasn't learning how to argue; he knew exactly what he was doing. Whenever we had Redwood on the schedule, I thought, *Oh, God, here we go.*

I gotta say this, though: In a lot of these towns, there weren't many places to go. Toward the end of the season, Tschida and I went to a bar for a drink or two after the game. Cannizzaro was there with friends, and when he saw us, he had a couple of drinks sent over. We gave him a nod and raised our glasses.

As he was leaving, Cannizzaro swung by our table and said, "It's been a long year, huh, fellas?"

Yeah. Sure has, Chris.

"I just want to let you know—you guys have done a great job this year." Maybe, just *maybe*, after all those arguments those last three months, I had earned Cannizzaro's respect?

At the All-Star break, I'd had a couple of days off and drove to LA for an overnighter. I also took an overnight trip to San Francisco when we had an off day in August. I claimed to be visiting an uncle or cousin, but the truth was that I needed to step away from baseball and visit West Hollywood or Castro to *be with my people*. Those quick trips were twenty-four-hour opportunities for me to get away from "playing the game" and be myself. As awkward as these dishonest getaways were, they kept me sane.

One more Cal League story: Games in Visalia rarely had much of a crowd. But there was a man and woman with season tickets who sat behind the plate every single night. This was not central California's most attractive couple; we called them the Addams Family.

Every time you were there, no matter what crew, they were all over us. Any call that went against Visalia, they had something to say, and you could *hear* everything because there was nobody else there.

When we saw other crews—a common occurrence, since we all worked out of centrally located Modesto—we would joke, "Hey, how was the Addams Family?"

"Oh, they were miserable."

One afternoon in Visalia, Tschida and I went to a local ice-cream parlor. As we walked in, we looked behind the counter, and then we looked at each other. It was Mr. Addams from the Addams Family. Turns out, they owned the shop.

He didn't recognize us out of uniform, so we went ahead and ordered our ice cream—rocky road for me, pistachio for Tim—and sat down. There were two guys behind us, and as they started ordering, I looked at Tim and whispered, "Let's have some fun with this."

Mr. Addams started putting a scoop on a cone for his next customer, and I said, "You call that a scoop? C'mon, you gave us a bigger scoop than that."

Tim said, "Man, I'd be embarrassed calling that a scoop."

Everyone now stopped and looked at me and Tim, wondering what the hell's going on. Mr. Addams was carving out another scoop, when I said, "*That's not a scoop.* C'mon, you're *better* than that."

Mr. Addams had heard enough.

"I'm sorry, but you'll have to leave."

"Oh, I'm sorry," I said. "Were you upset that we're yelling at you while you're working?"

"As a matter of fact, yeah, I am."

"Okay, well, that's sorta how we feel when you yell at us. We're the umpires. See you tonight!"

Tim and I left feeling pretty good about ourselves. As umpires, you have that dream, but of course, you never have that opportunity. Just this once, though, everything fell into place. And the Addams family? The rest of our games in Visalia, we didn't hear a word. Church mice, both of them.

We finished the season in San Jose with a Sunday afternoon game, during which Ted Giannoulas—better known as the Famous Chicken—was performing. Tim and I wanted a picture with Ted after the game. But he'd just showered and never posed for pictures without his chicken costume. So Ted, with nothing but a towel and his chicken head, took one with us.

Tschida and I were thrilled that the season was over. Neither one of us had been assigned the playoffs, and we weren't surprised, since we'd led the league in ejections. Joe Gagliardi was president of the Cal League and not friendly to umpires. His office was in San Jose, so he attended our last game and stopped by the locker room afterward.

He had barely sat down when he started with his year-end assessment of the Tschida-Scott crew.

"Tim, I'm so disappointed in you," he said. "It's your second year, and your ejections are up? It's like you've learned nothing."

Then Gagliardi turned to me. "Dale, you're just a copycat of Tim. Not even a full season, and you did exactly what he did. That's very disappointing, and I can tell you both right now that neither of you will be back in the Cal League next year. Because I will not have you. And I'm not sure if either one of you has a future in professional baseball."

Many Minor League presidents feel that an ejection is a failure by the umpire. Either you missed a call or your game management is poor, which leads to ejections. This is far from the truth. Ejections are part of the game—a tool that's *necessary* for good game management. Don't get me wrong. You can have a bad ejection. But ejections are generally not evidence of an umpire's failure.

I'm sure that Tim and I stood out to Gagliardi because we'd led the league in ejections. By a lot. There were several nights during the summer when we'd get back to the apartments in Modesto, compare notes with other crews, and find that we had an ejection or two that night while none of the other guys had any. In my half season, I had ten ejections, while Tim finished with fifteen. Meanwhile, the second-place crew combined for only twelve all season.

Gagliardi firing us was deflating, especially for me. After two years in the Cal League, Tschida wasn't planning to come back for a third and *was* planning on a promotion to Double-A. If not, the odds were that he didn't have a future in pro ball anyway. For me, though, I figured I'd come back next year since I hadn't spent a full season there. Now I was thinking, *Oh my God, maybe this is the end of my career. I could be done.*

On the other hand, about a week before that last game, we'd seen Dick Nelson in Rohnert Park, and he told us both we were heading to instructional league in the fall. That was good news, because it meant they still considered us prospects. But now Gagliardi was telling us we wouldn't be coming back to the Cal League, which had me thinking, *Okay, so where can I go next year?*

A few days *after* our league president's stirring pep talk, Nelson called both me and Tim and told us we weren't just going to instructional league. He told us to ignore Gagliardi, because we were getting promoted to Double-A in 1983. After both Tim and I were hired by the American League just three seasons later, the joke circulating among A-ball umpires was, "Hey, if you're lucky, you'll get fired from the Cal League like Tschida and Scott . . . just look where they ended up."

That fall, I went to instructional league in Phoenix, a pivotal point in my career, as I learned a lot in those six weeks. Dick Nelson saw us work more during those six weeks than during the entire Minor League season. And every day after our games, we would all sit around together and review any odd plays or situations we'd had.

In March 1983 I was assigned spring training in the Mariners' camp and then drove to Tulsa for the start of my Texas League season. My new partner was Terry Mann, and by our fourth game, I figured out we had absolutely nothing in common. Terry was thirty-six, married with children, and starting his third season in the league. I was twenty-three, gay, certainly *not* married with kids, and a Double-A rookie. Terry was thirteen years older than I was, and it seemed like thirty.

I was our driver, which meant we were using my car for the whole season. We had never met when I arrived in Tulsa, the night before opening day. Today, you get your own room in the Minor Leagues, but then we shared a room. Between the car and the hotel, you spent a *ton* of time in close quarters with your partner.

So we quickly got to know each other, and I just as quickly realized we were nearly complete opposites. After night games (and they were almost all night games), we might get a beer together, but Terry was content going back to the room, watching a little TV, and calling it a night. He loved to get up early, play golf, grab lunch, and then come back to the hotel for an afternoon nap before heading to the ballpark. Meanwhile, I liked to go out for a while after the game, have a few drinks. I wouldn't be tired until two or so in the morning. Then I loved sleeping in, not getting lunch until one or two in the afternoon.

Being a good partner, he would join me after games for a drink but was ready to leave after one. At the end of our first week together, I said, "Hey, you like staying in, getting up early, and playing golf. I like going out and staying up. If you want to get a beer or something after a game, great. But it's no problem if you want me to drop you off at the hotel while I go out. When you get up in the morning, take the car, go do your thing. By the time you get back, I'll be up and ready to go do *my* thing."

This was the middle of April, and we wouldn't be done until Labor Day, so I didn't want to try to make us something we weren't. It wasn't that we didn't get along. We were just two completely opposite people on completely opposite paths. It was his third year in the Texas League and ended up being the last of his pro career.

Terry agreed, and the arrangement worked out great for both of us. It gave me the freedom to go wherever the hell I wanted after work. In some Texas League cities, I would find a gay bar and be who I was, rather than who I was *supposed* to be. I didn't *always* have to "play the game."

One great thing about Terry was that he knew all the hotels, all the ballparks, all the restaurants, all the bars in each city, which was awesome for a Texas League rookie like me. Plus, everybody knew him and, for the most part, respected his work, which made my time on the field a little easier.

In the big leagues, if you're with somebody on the crew you don't get along with or have some sort of personality clash, it's so much easier to navigate. There were MLB crews who literally stayed at four separate hotels and flew four different airlines; the only time they saw each other was at the ballpark, and not necessarily because they didn't like each other. Maybe one guy wants his Marriott points; the other, Sheraton. The same with airline miles. Then again, there were also times when guys stayed in different hotels because they couldn't stand each other.

You can get away with that in the big leagues. You're making enough money and per diem that you can stay where you want, and you don't need your partners to get around. In the Minor Leagues, it was completely opposite, especially before you got to Triple-A (when we got our own hotel rooms). So you were rooming with the guy you were working with, *and* you're spending ungodly amounts of time in the car with him.

Terry and I worked the Texas League All-Star Game that year. Not as a reward for a stellar first half of the season, but because the game was in El Paso, where we were scheduled to work right after the All-Star Game. After the season, I was again assigned to instructional league in Arizona.

The next spring (1984), I was chief of the Giants' Minor League camp in Phoenix, before heading back to the Texas League. However, I went back knowing I'd be the first umpire promoted when there was a Triple-A opening, which I assumed meant the Pacific Coast League. I knew a lot of the umpires in the PCL, many of the cities were reasonably close to home, and of course, the PCL included Hawaii, where just about every umpire wanted to work.

When Barney Deary called in mid-May, I was in San Antonio.

"Dale, I want to congratulate you," he said. "You're being promoted to Triple-A. You're to report to Des Moines, Iowa."

I kind of laughed and said, "Barney, I didn't know Des Moines moved to the Coast League." (Bizarrely, that city *would* move to the Pacific Coast League. But that was years away.)

"Well," he said, "you're not going to the PCL. You're going to the American Association."

I was thrilled to be promoted but disappointed I wasn't going to the Coast League, close to home.

But hey, I was going to Triple-A! And as it turned out, getting the call to the American Association was the best thing that could have happened to me. At the time, International League and American Association umpires were seen a lot more by big league supervisors than the Coast League umpires were. Simply because the supervisors were all based in the East or Midwest.

Until the nineties, when it was abolished, there was something called an "option," which allowed the American League or the National League to pay a fee to a Triple-A league and essentially lock up an umpire from that league. Basically, you then became the property of that Major League and thus unavailable to the other. Options didn't guarantee a job, but being optioned was a major step forward in your career.

When Marty Springstead became executive director of umpires for the American League, he lobbied to get rid of the option. He argued that the best Triple-A umpire should be hired when there is an opening in either league. That is hard to argue *against*, logically.

In Des Moines I joined crew chief Larry Young, Matt Fairchild, and (as luck would have it) Tim Tschida. I was thrilled to be working with Tim again and didn't know the other two. We worked the series there, drove to Omaha for another series, and then flew to Louisville.

Working in Louisville felt like the big leagues. Cardinal Stadium, home of University of Louisville football, had artificial turf and a capacity just short of twenty thousand for baseball. In 1983 the Redbirds drew over a million fans, a first for any Minor League club.

Dick Butler showed up in Louisville, as the AL already had Larry under option, plus an interest in Tim. Mike Fitzpatrick was in town also, evaluating for Umpire Development. Our rotation had Larry working the plate Friday night, me with Saturday night's game, and Tim working Sunday afternoon. For Butler to see Larry and Tim, he also had to watch my game in between.

My plate job, my third since being promoted, went fifteen innings and exactly five hours. Fitzpatrick told me later that somewhere around the four-hour mark, Butler asked, "Who is this behind the plate again?"

"Dale Scott. He just came up about ten days ago."

After the game, Butler told me he was impressed with not only my consistency but how I looked the same in the fifteenth inning as I had in the first—same energy, same hustle, same enthusiasm. Just like that, I was on the American League's radar.

The American League sent supervisors to our next two series, with Larry Knapp in Evansville and Bill Haller in Indianapolis. A few days later, both Tschida and I had our options bought. I went from being disappointed about not going to the Coast League to being in Triple-A for three weeks, working five plate jobs, and suddenly knocking on the door to the Major Leagues.

Like I said, being promoted to the American Association was the best thing that could have happened to me. I worked the first round of the Association playoffs and then was assigned to winter ball for the first time. And therein lies a tale. A few of them, actually . . .

6

Only in the Dominican

In 1984 there were four winter ball destinations for the National League's and the American League's Triple-A umpires: Columbia, Venezuela, Puerto Rico, and the Dominican Republic. When promoted to Triple-A and considered a prospect, often you'll be asked if you want to work winter ball.

I say "asked" as if you've got the option of declining the opportunity, but let's be serious . . . There is only one correct answer: Yes, sir, and my bags are packed already.

I'd been promoted to the American Association that May, and after my fifth plate job, the American League bought my option. Now after working just three and a half months in Triple-A, I was asked by the AL if I wanted to go to the Dominican Republic. ("Yes, sir.")

Suddenly, this baseball thing was happening at a much quicker pace.

I felt both excited and ready for the experience the *next* three and a half months would bring. You always heard stories about winter ball, both on and off the field, and now I was going to find out in person. I would be joined by another winter ball rookie, Mike Felt, plus Tim Tschida and Tom Hallion, who had both been there the year before. I was especially happy that Tim was going back, since we'd been in Bradenton together, as well as the Cal League, the Arizona instructional league, and the season we'd just finished in the Association. Oh, and he spoke fluent Spanish, which would prove invaluable.

The Dominican League started October 20 and ended in late January, playing a sixty-game schedule with Monday and Thursday off every week.

There were six teams: two in the capital city, Santo Domingo, where we had an apartment, and the other four in San Cristobal, San Pedro de Macoris, La Romana, and Puerto Plata.

With four teams outside the capital, I had the opportunity to see various parts of the country. The Dominican Republic has a diverse topography, with three mountain peaks over ten thousand feet dropping all the way down to those beautiful Caribbean beaches. I also saw, firsthand, depths of poverty that made a deep impression that stays with me to this day. Shanties and lean-tos of wood or corrugated metal with no electricity or running water. Children selling chiclets or shining shoes out on the street, late at night.

At Estadio Quisqueya, the stadium in Santo Domingo where we worked thirty of our sixty games, there were three brothers who sold roasted peanuts and chiclets inside and outside the ballpark. They were ages thirteen, ten, and eight, and they were the cutest, sweetest kids. I chatted with them before every game and was told by the oldest, Miguel, that they were not permitted to go home until they made a certain amount of money. He didn't seem sad or depressed about this but rather matter-of-fact, as if this was normal for the kids I would see around at all hours.

All of us would give the brothers money or hand out a baseball or two they could sell for a lot of pesos, or at least a ton more than the many bags of peanuts or boxes of gum they spent hours trying to sell. All three brothers were around during both seasons I worked in the Dominican, and they reminded me again and again how privileged and lucky I had always been.

Yet you wouldn't hear about any hardships from them. Their smiles, positive energy, and enthusiasm were infectious and enduring. Every once in a while, I still think about those three brothers and wonder how their lives went since I saw them last in January 1986.

The Dominican League consisted of the best Dominican players, many of them on Major League rosters, with nearly all of them playing professionally in the States, as well as a certain percentage of non-Dominicans allowed on each roster. Major League teams sent down prospects, plus current Major Leaguers who for whatever reasons (injuries, usually) needed some playing time to prepare for spring training.

The league would not let Dominican umpires work the plate—quite frankly, they just didn't think most of those guys were good enough—so every game day had one of us strapping it on in each of the three games. There was always a game in Santo Domingo, so that one had two American umpires: one on the plate, the other at first. The other two games had the American working the plate and three Dominicans on the bases.

So with a sixty-game schedule, in just three months we would each work forty-five behind the plate and fifteen at first. During a full season in the big leagues in the mideighties, you only worked about thirty-five plate games in *six* months. That is one of the reasons umpires were assigned winter ball, to get a ton of plate work in . . . and boy did we.

To make this system work, we had an American partner with two Dominican umpires in every other Santo Domingo game—Tschida and Hallion as one crew, Felt and I as the other. Meanwhile, outside Santo Domingo, in every other game, one of us worked the plate, with three Dominican base umpires. And that's where the fun began!

All our games were 8:00 p.m. starts, except Sundays, when first pitch was at 4:00. One of our three Dominican drivers would collect us at our apartment anywhere between 3:30 (11:30 on Sunday) if going to Puerto Plata (a four-hour drive) and 7:00 (or 3:00 on Sunday) if working in the capital. San Cristobal was an hour drive, San Pedro an hour and a half, and La Romana two hours. Obviously, I spent a lot of time in the car, most of it with our driver and three Dominican umpires. Very few spoke any English at all. These cars were not exactly roomy sedans, let alone SUVs. More like a '73 Oldsmobile Cutlass Supreme that was barely street legal. I never loved my Sony Walkman, along with the many cassette tapes I made before leaving the States, more than during those winters crammed in a small car for those long drives.

Of course, the Cutlass seemed like a limo compared to Publicos, the multipassenger taxis we would wave down for a shopping trip or a favorite restaurant. They would stuff a couple of passengers in the front seat, with four or even five in back. These cars most definitely were not street legal, and the number one criteria for buying one certainly wasn't the engine but, rather, how loud the horn was, since that was more important and in constant use.

The seemingly endless rides to the ballpark were adventures in themselves. You would go dressed, since the "locker rooms" at the stadiums were not fit to shit in. Literally. They made the restroom at a busy truck stop look like a gentlemen's lounge in a five-star hotel. My equipment bag always carried a roll of toilet paper, since (1) just about any facility and certainly the disaster they called a locker room rarely if ever had TP and (2) at any time during my two tours of duty in the Dominican Republic, there was a possibility I could have, oh let's just say, a gastroenteritis episode.

Not to bring this book down to the sewer (too late?), but even taking all the obvious precautions—don't drink the water, be careful of what you eat—living in the Dominican for several months meant I would at some point get the runs.

It was one of the things the American players, managers, and umpires had in common. One night working the plate (seemingly, that's all we did!), I felt an episode coming, so right after a third out, I beelined toward the dugout of the team that had just hit, to use their facilities. As I passed the American pitcher coming out to warm up, I told him, "Take your time. I need to—"

Seeing the look on my face and my skin color, he cut me off, saying, "I got ya; I spent a lot of time in there yesterday!"

On these trips to and from the ballpark, especially after games, our driver would stop at random roadside food stands in the middle of nowhere. Under the light bulbs were chicken, fish, and beef. Or so I was told. The food looked less like a hearty meal and more like a gathering place for flies, and I noticed there were never any dogs around. That led me to second-guess the "beef" category. Even though I was hungry after working a game, I always waited to eat until getting back to the apartment.

I would, however, order a cerveza. And not just any cerveza, but a *Presidente*, the best beer in the Dominican. As sketchy and unappealing as the food looked at these roadside stops, they always had a chest refrigerator and the coldest Presidente in the galaxy. I do not think you can possibly get a beer any colder than the beers that every one of these places served. One night early in the season while leaving the park, we ran into the Licey team owner. Making small talk, he asked how things were going and if we needed anything? Not knowing what to say, I joked that I had already had my Presidente, so I was good. From that night on, a driver delivered two cases of Presidente to our apartment every Monday, compliments of Licey. And no, as much as we appreciated our weekly delivery, that club didn't get favorable treatment on the field.

After a game in Puerto Plata, we were rushing to start our four-hour trip home. Our driver, who may have had . . . okay, *did* have a few belts of rum as he waited for us to finish, pulled out and promptly hit an open car door, knocking it completely off. He stopped, jumped out, went face-to-face screaming with the driver of the sedan, and jumped back in, and off we went. I asked one of the Dominican umpires, What just happened? He said our driver chewed the guy out for denting his fender with his door and told him he was lucky we were in a hurry or he would have kicked his ass. Only in the Dominican.

Yes, all the plate work was great training for young umpires. But our bosses also wanted us dealing with various situations, on and off the field, many of which would never come up in the States but still needed to be handled quickly and under pressure. Basically, they wanted to see what we were made of.

Manny Mota, the longtime Dodger, is a hero in the Dominican. He played many years for Licey and had managed them to consecutive Dominican League championships the two previous seasons. Mota switched teams the season I arrived, managing San Cristobal, while Terry Collins took over Licey. This didn't sit well with Licey's owner, so one night when Felt and I had these two playing each other in the capital, Collins walked up to the pregame ground-rules meeting with an unusual demand.

"Manny is out of uniform. You have to eject him."

Mota, who had remained in the dugout and sent a coach to the plate meeting, was, like most Dominicans and ballplayers generally, superstitious. He'd won championships the last two years with Licey, and now he still wore his gray Licey uniform pants, even though his new team wore white pants.

"You want me to do what now, Terry?"

"Look, Dale, my owner told me to do this," Collins explained. "I couldn't care less, and I have too much respect for Manny to do something as chicken-shit as this. But I have to. It's a pissing match between him and Manny, and I don't want any part of it." Both Manny and Terry were actually part of the Dodgers organization, and Terry was obviously uncomfortable bringing it up.

Technically, Terry was right: Manny was out of uniform. Terry was also correct that this was a petty, bush-league request for retaliation disguised as a rule violation. I couldn't ignore it out of hand, since I wouldn't be backed by the rule book, but I also refused to be a pawn between Manny and his former boss, with their third-grade tit for tat, by ejecting Mota before a pitch was thrown. So I came up with a compromise.

"Terry, I'm not going to eject him, but I will let him know that if he steps onto the field for any reason—pitching change, injured player, to argue a play, anything—he will be ejected. He has to stay in the dugout the entire game."

"That's good enough for me, Dale. Let's just play the damn game!" Collins replied, and headed back to his dugout.

When I walked over to tell Manny what was up, he nodded with a sly smile. "That wasn't from Terry," was all he said. As I thought, this had nothing to do with his damn pants.

Felt later said he was glad I was there. He would have just run Manny for being out of uniform, but my solution to this internal spat was thinking outside the box. Just one example of the situations we would have "only in the Dominican." In fact, that's exactly what Collins said one night a couple of weeks later.

Working with some of the Dominican umpires was a challenge. There were a handful who were quite good, and you'd always be happy to work with them. Several of the others, you had to be ready for just about anything.

Licey (founded in 1907) and Escogido (1921) were the Dodgers and Yankees of the DL, both teams playing in Santo Domingo and sharing Estadio Quisqueya. When these teams played each other, you never knew what might happen, on the field or in the seats. Almost without fail, there would be a fight in the stands, usually in one of the betting sections. Every game had at least one section where fans would place bets with each other on, well, just about anything. Some literally bet what the next pitch would be. I would call a strike on the first pitch of an inning and hear both cheers and boos from just one section. For the longest time, I couldn't figure that one out, until someone finally told me what was going on.

I was working first base during one of these contests, when Escogido had runners on first and second, with nobody out. A sure double play ball was hit to the shortstop, who flipped the ball to the second baseman. As he attempted to pivot and throw to first, the Escogido runner barreled into him, with the ball dropping and all runners safe. Interference for sure . . . except my second-base umpire had . . . nothing.

Terry flew out of the dugout and sprinted to second, and I started moving that way myself while knowing this probably wouldn't turn out well. Terry then changed directions, coming straight at me and yelling, "Dale, that's interference! You saw it! That's interference!"

This was one of the joys of working winter ball: any time an American player or manager had an issue with a Dominican umpire's call, they almost always went directly to you. In part because of the language difference, but mostly because they could not believe some of the calls they were witnessing. At times, neither could I.

I told Terry to hold on, let me talk to him. The umpire at second spoke some English, so I asked him what he had. He looked rather shell-shocked with the chaos going on around him, not to mention the packed stadium in an uproar, and replied that he had nothing: the fielder dropped the ball, and all runners were safe.

Okay, let me rephrase my question: "Did you see the runner do anything? Was his slide to the base legal? He didn't interfere with the fielder?"

"No, all legal," he replied, looking as confident as I would flying a jumbo jet.

I went back to Terry and said, "He's got nothing, Terry."

"That's bullshit, Dale, and you know it!"

"Look, Terry, I can't start running around to every base, changing calls. We might as well work a two-man."

He looked at me with a combination of anger and disbelief but seemed to understand, kind of, what I was saying. "Fine, but only in the Dominican! That is the only reason, right? Only in the Dominican!"

"Only in the Dominican, Terry."

Fans in the Dominican could get, shall we say, a bit rabid during games. At most of the parks, we had to walk a short distance in the concourse from our "locker room" to the field and again from the field after the game. Going to the field usually wasn't a problem, but the walk through the unsecured area after games could often be rather exciting.

First, we would serve as target practice, with those in the bleachers throwing ice. Next came the verbal abuse, not to mention threats of physical abuse, directed at us in the concourse. Although I do not speak Spanish and wasn't sure what they were saying, I definitely didn't like their tone. We had one police officer escorting each umpire back and forth, but there were times when I wasn't sure which side mine was actually on. Also, the police wore helmets and carried rifles and ammo belts, looking more like soldiers.

It didn't take me long to get my police escort on my side, though. Baseballs were like gold bricks, worth a lot of money in a country with so much poverty. When you worked the plate, you had a ball man (not boy), who brought you the game balls on the field. He knew exactly how many balls you started with and counted every single one hit out of play or thrown out. The moment the game ended, he would run up to you and collect the balls in your bag, knowing exactly how many you should still have.

Knowing this and knowing how coveted a baseball was, when we got to the top or bottom of the ninth (depending on who was ahead), I would subtly slip a couple of balls through the front of my button-down shirt and hide them between my chest protector and body. I also prayed I wouldn't take a foul ball to the chest, as that might well prove rather painful.

I then signaled to the ball man that I needed two more baseballs. He would give me a confused look and gesture that I already had my allotment. I would show him my ball bag, indicating I was a couple short, and signal aggressively to bring two more out. He would prance out and investigate my bag, seeing I was indeed two short. Now his mind was blown. His count had been exactly right for the entire game, and now suddenly I was two short? How?

As entertaining as this was every night, I had a reason for the sleight of hand. The moment the game finished, as usual, the now-confused ball man ran out, and I gave him the remaining baseballs. I met the officer who was going to escort me off the field, smiled while looking him in the eye, and stealthily slipped him one of the baseballs I was hiding under my protector, saying, "You, me . . . amigos, sí?"

Now I was confident he was with *me*. Worked every time.

"Only in the Dominican" didn't just happen on the field. During my second tour of duty, in 1985, Felt and I were back with newcomers Steve Kriz and Tom Owen. Like the year before, we had a three-bedroom apartment next door to the Sheraton Hotel Spa and Casino. It wasn't unusual for our power, water, cable TV, or any combination of the three to blink out on any given day for any amount of time. Once, we had no water for a week, which drove us crazy but seemed rather common to everyone else living in the complex.

So being next to the Sheraton was a godsend, not only because we were able to use their spa and shower facilities during our outages, but also because we would lounge by the pool during the day and kill time there after games in the casino at night. We befriended the two American managers who ran the place, and although we rarely gambled, they let us hang out and have a few drinks while they chatted us up about baseball.

One night, I was abruptly awakened at about three in the morning by a bloodcurdling scream that sounded like it was coming from the kitchen. I jumped up and ran into the hall, meeting Mike and Tom, who also were suddenly awake. In the kitchen, Steve was standing in his boxers, white as a ghost, hyperventilating.

"What the hell happened?"

"OH MY GOD," he yelled, trying to breathe normally. "I came out to get a drink of water. I didn't turn on the light, just opened the refrigerator door. With just the light from the fridge, I saw some movement, and a rat, which must have been a foot long, jumped down from the top of the refrigerator, bounced off my arm, hit the floor, and ran onto the back porch!"

There was a brief pause before the three of us had to bend over from laughing so hard. Finally getting over the shock, Steve started laughing with us. It also started the habit we all adopted of never, *never* going into the kitchen at night without turning on the light. Several of them, actually.

Then there was the time I saw a doctor. Growing up, for whatever reason, I was always getting strep throat. So, naturally, I came down with it while working winter ball. I told one of the team trainers, who set up an appointment with Licey's team doctor.

I arrived at his clinic, and the receptionist showed me right to his office . . . literally an office. This wasn't an examination room like I was used to but, instead, a rather large office, with his desk and chair in front of a big window with the shades drawn, a couple of chairs facing the desk, and a large couch and sitting area behind them, all upholstered in leather. There were paintings on the walls and a table in the corner, with glasses and two full liquor decanters.

As I walked in, the doctor, dressed in street clothes, exhaled a plume of smoke as he turned to greet me, smoking an unfiltered cigarette. It was rather apparent that I was about to experience one of the most unique doctor's appointments ever.

"Welcome, Mr. Scott. Please come in, sit down. Now, what can I do for you?"

"Well, I think I have strep throat," I said. "It's really sore and hurts to swallow, and I'm having trouble eating or drinking."

"I see," he replied, pulling a tongue depressor from a jar on his desk. "Say, 'Ahhhh,'" he commanded. I opened my mouth, and he placed the wooden depressor on my tongue, doing all this, mind you, while still taking drags off his Pall Mall.

"Oh, yes, I see—not a problem," he said, taking the depressor out of my mouth and yet another drag. "I'll take out your tonsils."

"What? Seriously? My tonsils?" I said, trying not to cough up a lung with the lingering smoke all around.

"Yes, I'll take your tonsils out. No problem!"

"Um, yeah . . . That is a problem," I said, now wondering if this was someone's hidden-camera comedy bit. "If I need my tonsils taken out, I'll fly back to Miami."

He took another hit off his now very short cigarette, smiled confidently, and pointed to a framed University of Miami diploma on the wall.

"I went to medical school in Miami, so no need to go there. I can take care of it right here!"

"Look, doc, I'm pretty sure this is just strep throat, and I can knock it out with antibiotics. Let's try that first, and if it doesn't get any better, then we can figure out where to go from there."

By "where to go from there," I meant *off this damn island and far away from Dr. Nicotine and his tonsil obsession!*

"No problem—if that's what you would like to try, I'll write you a prescription. But if this fails, be sure to let me know. I'll be happy to take out your tonsils." Yeah, you've made that abundantly clear.

I got the script, thanked him, and could not escape that building fast enough.

As I thought, the antibiotics worked. But toward the end of my second tour of duty, I was sick again. And that night would, in my mind, guarantee me a spot in the big leagues.

I was in our apartment at four in the morning, sitting on the toilet, holding a paper bag, and using both. I had salmonella, an inner ear infection, another sore throat, and scabies.

Yeah. Scabies.

As I sat there in my disoriented, fevered state, I thought, *If I don't get hired by the American League after this, I'll sue them for the job*. After hearing the story of what I went through that night, I figured there wasn't a jury in the world that would rule against me!

Only in the Dominican.

7

Getting the Call

A couple of weeks before I left for Florida and my first American League spring training, two fitted AL hats and four uniform shirts arrived at my parents' house. The American League powder-blue, button-down shirt came with the league patch and my number: 39 (during my first two years, I was 39, and then before the 1988 season, I switched to 5, which I would keep for the next thirty years). My dad took a picture of me in uniform. It was such a thrill to wear it, with my own number.

Fort Lauderdale in 1985 was my first real MLB experience, and everything was so different from working Minor League spring training. I was getting paid big league money, both per diem and game fees. I had my own rental car (a convertible!), my own hotel room, and . . . *off days?*

I got used to the freedom quickly, like the moment I walked into what would be *my own hotel room* for the next twenty-five days. It was a complete change, and it all happened so fast! *My God, here I am! A year ago, I was in Arizona, getting ready for my second year in Double-A Texas League. Since then, I was promoted to Triple-A, within three weeks had my option bought by the American League, worked the first round of the Association playoffs, and spent the winter in the Dominican Republic, and now I'm working big league spring training in Florida!*

I made the most of my first trip to Florida's Gold Coast. My parents visited for a few days, my dad beaming as he watched his son umpire the big boys. On one of my off days, we checked out the Everglades, solidifying in my mind that I would never want to live that close to massive reptiles and snakes.

While my parents were there, I worked an Expos-Yankees night game on the plate, with Ken Kaiser as one of my partners. The game went extra innings, and in the bottom of the tenth, the Yankees' lead-off hitter tried to stretch a double into a triple. Let's just say from my vantage point—hell, from everyone's vantage point—he looked out. Keiser screams SAFE while throwing up his arms. The entire Expo dugout erupted, and Kenny, not missing a beat, yelled at them, "What, you want to be here all night?" Watching from the plate, I thought, *You can do that?*

One day when walking into the hotel lobby, we ran into my colleague Al Clark. I introduced my parents, and Al said, "I'm so happy to meet both of you. Your son is impressive—really, one hell of an umpire! He's going to have a long career."

Al continued on to the parking lot, and my mom said, "What a nice thing to say. You must have made quite an impression when you worked with him!"

"Mom," I replied, "I've never worked with Al; we just met yesterday." Al was great at building up a young umpire's confidence, though. We ended up working together a lot that spring and during the first several years of my career, and we remain good friends to this day.

Later in the month, I had two consecutive days off, so I drove the convertible to Key West for a couple of nights. Key West was a gay mecca, with several bars and guesthouses, a mythical place I'd heard about for years and finally got to experience. Just to have two days away from baseball, *to be myself,* was both a blast and a relief.

With spring training over, I was off to the American Association, which opened on April 12 and finished September 2. For the entire season, we had *one scheduled day off* . . . August 29, four days before the end of the season. Meaning, if we didn't have any postponements for rain or whatever, we would work 136 straight days. That day off seemed like tipping someone a nickel. Why bother? As it turned out, we did have a rainout in May. So we got two days off.

My partners that year were crew chief Phil Janssen and Mike Felt. Janssen never reached the Major Leagues but later worked with Marty Springstead in the American League office and, starting in 2000, for Major League Baseball. In 2003 Phil was hired as executive secretary for the union and still holds that job today.

I'd worked with Felt in the Dominican the winter before and would again after the 1985 season. Mike, who is now a Minor League supervisor, is a good guy—very sincere and hardworking. His expertise in the two-man system makes him a perfect fit as chief of instruction at Minor League Baseball's Umpire Training Academy, teaching and evaluating in the Minors. However, back in the eighties, I felt that Mike was overmatched when I worked with him.

As an instructor at umpire school and for the advanced week at Bradenton, Mike was known as Mr. Fungo, as he'd mastered hitting the ball wherever needed for the various situations set up for teaching students.

Al Barlick, who was a National League supervisor *and* in the Baseball Hall of Fame, took a liking to Mike. So when Mike was promoted to Triple-A, the NL put him on option soon after. In retrospect, that may have been a disservice to him, because basically he wasn't ready. That option put a lot of expectations on Mike; plus, he leapfrogged over several senior Triple-A umpires, creating even more pressure.

Mike was a goof—a nice guy but a goof. With two Dominican winter balls bookending the '85 American Association season, I spent thirteen out of sixteen months with him. Spending that much time together, I joked that if I had Mike committed because he was making *me* insane, there wouldn't be a jury in the world that would fault me.

Phil Janssen was another story. He wanted to kill Mike practically every day. Phil didn't drink—although that season could have pushed him over the line—but you'd swear Phil was drunk half the time because of his inane and kooky personality. With these guys, though, I was the peacemaker. "Phil, just go over there in your corner. Mike, you'll be fine; he's not going to kill you today." Mike drove me crazy too. But Phil was constantly losing his shit.

That season, Phil had something like sixteen ejections, while I had fifteen and Felt had . . . three. This wasn't because Mike was such a superior umpire. It was because he wouldn't fucking throw anybody out.

John Boles was Buffalo's manager (and later managed the Marlins in the Majors). Mike was around five feet nine; John about the same. Boles was not a bad guy—pretty decent with umpires. But one day, Felt called something, and here comes Boles flying out of the dugout. We've got a full-fledged shithouse going, so Phil and I are peeling off players, to let Mike and Boles go at it.

Boles is *pissed*, and he's beaking Felt with the bill of his hat. And Felt's saying, with his high-pitched voice I'll never forget, "Don't do that, John. I'm telling you right now, don't do that." And Boles beaks him again.

Phil and I are looking over our shoulders as we're trying to corral a shortstop, a second baseman, and a right fielder, who are all screaming. We make eye contact and are thinking the same thing: *Fucking run him. Run him!* Meanwhile, Mike's over there saying, "I'll tell you—if that dugout is on fire one more time, I may have to run you."

Goddamn.

In another game, having finally heard and seen enough, I stepped in during one of Mike's arguments. "That's it. Get the fuck out," I told the manager.

In the locker room after the game, Mike said, "I probably should have run him."

You think?

In defense of Mike, it wasn't his fault the NL slapped an option on him prematurely. He wasn't ready for Triple-A and the unusual season you endure in winter ball.

Once and future MLB managers Jim Fregosi and Gene Lamont also managed in the league. Oh, and Felipe Alou. Felipe managed Indianapolis, and he hated me. One time when I'm working the plate, his pitcher is surveying, his catcher is holding pitches, and they're screaming from the dugout. It's just one of those fun nights. Finally, Felipe comes flying out, supposedly to talk to his pitcher, but I know exactly what he's doing. So on his way out, I said to myself, *I'll just get this over with.*

"All right, let's go Felipe."

"Where the *fuck* were those pitches?"

"Felipe, we're not gonna talk about pitches."

"I can't believe you're calling those pitches."

"Felipe, we're not talking about pitches. You want a new pitcher, or are you done?"

"Those pitches—"

"Get the fuck outta here."

"You are the worst umpire in the world! There is nobody worse than you. Everybody in the league has told me, and I know everyone thinks the same thing: You're the worst umpire in the league."

"Well, that's funny! Because I polled the umpires, and you're the worst manager who has ever walked the earth!"

Felipe and I had our good times in winter ball too. I ran him on one of those Dominican days when I not only was homesick but also had the shits all day. And now, right on cue, he's going off, blasting me with the same song: you're terrible, you're the worst in the league, blah, blah, blah.

"You know what, Felipe?" I said. "I don't give a fuck. I don't give a fuck about you, I don't give a fuck about this league, I don't give a fuck about this country." Obviously, the day I'd been having before the game was now being expressed rather bluntly.

Down there, you could get away with saying a lot more, which I certainly did that night. Many years later, I had Felipe when he was managing the Giants. I never ran him in the Majors—don't even remember any arguments. I think we'd both shot all our bullets back in the American Association and the Dominican.

Every umpire dreams of "getting the call," that magical moment when you're told to report to a big league city, to umpire a big league game. Very few pro umpires actually receive one. Most times, that call is a nighttime surprise, often waiting for you in the locker room after finishing your Triple-A game. Example?

"Dale, Vic Voltaggio got hurt tonight. You need to be in Detroit tomorrow afternoon for a one o'clock game."

I got that call on May 16, 1986. But I'd already been hired by the American League and knew I'd be going up sometime that season. So that wasn't *the call*, the one sending me to my first regular-season game in Major League Baseball.

That call had come nine months earlier, in August of '85. Then, I had no idea when *the call* would come, if at all. There were (and are) no guarantees in professional baseball. Sure, I was under option with the American League and had worked my first AL spring training, but until you actually receive the news and work in the big leagues, you haven't.

A couple days after my twenty-sixth birthday, Dick Butler called me in Louisville and let me know that on August 19, I would be working third base in Kansas City. This was a makeup game from the Royals' earlier rainout with the Tigers, who were the defending world champions (while the Royals, as things turned out, were a couple of months from winning the World Series themselves).

I would be with Jim Evans and his crew: Ted Hendry and Dan Morrison. Both teams and Jimmy's crew were flying into KC that Monday (which had been a scheduled off day for everyone) just to make up the game and then leaving KC to resume their original schedules. Nick Bremigan, the fourth member of the crew, was coming off his two-week vacation. So instead of Nick rejoining his crew for the one game in Kansas City, Butler told him to be in Oakland on Tuesday, as planned, with me being sent in his place.

That was *my* magical call, long dreamed of.

I was going to work a Major League game. Whatever happened after that, even if I never got the opportunity to work another one, nobody could ever take that away.

Butler told me to take my base uniform only, including my AL hat and number 39 shirt, which I'd been carrying around all season, just in case—no need to bring my Priesmeyer, though.

Back then, the Priesmeyer Brothers Trunk Company was the sole provider of our umpire trunks. Those trunks were big enough not just for our plate equipment but also for *all* our other uniforms and gear: plate and base pants, shirts, shoes, and hats; warm-, cold-, rainy-weather plate and base coats and windbreakers; for the American League, base sweaters; and all warm- and cold-weather undergarments. Priesmeyers were big, heavy, and bulky *and* a major pain to travel with. So not having to drag mine to Kansas City for the one game was nice.

On the morning of the nineteenth, I flew first-class (a big league perk we cherish) from Omaha to Kansas City. That flight was all of what, twenty minutes? The umpire crew met in the hotel lobby at 4:30 for the thirty-minute drive to Royals Stadium. As we approached the exit off I-70 east, we passed the stadium, on our right, and what a beautiful sight it was. Opened in 1973 (and later renamed Kauffman Stadium), today it remains one of the most beautiful ballparks in professional baseball.

Once in our locker room, I, like every umpire (except Bill Miller), took off my street clothes to keep them fresh and clean and then lounged in work undergarments before donning my uniform fifteen to twenty minutes before walking onto the field. (Later in my career, I worked with Bill for several seasons. Bill would stay in his street clothes until ten minutes before we left the locker room, when he quickly changed. Several times, he also decided to shave during those ten minutes, and more than once, Bill walked to the ground-rules meeting trying to stop the bleeding of a razor cut or two. I razzed him all the time: "You have twenty-one hours to shave, yet two minutes before we walk is the perfect time to do it?")

Since meeting the crew in the hotel lobby, I'd been trying to project calm, to give the impression that I saw this as just another game. Of course, inside I was bursting with excitement, plus a few butterflies. As I pulled my base uniform from the small bag I'd brought from Omaha, Jim asked me if I was nervous.

"Not really. Just excited," I replied, as I put my T-shirt on.

Jim, who has a very dry sense of humor, looked at me and said, "I'm glad you're not nervous. So do you always wear your shirt backward?"

"Of course, Jim. I set the trends . . . Okay, maybe I'm a little nervous."

A few minutes later, we were on the field. When the managers, Detroit's Sparky Anderson and Kansas City's Dick Howser, came to the plate for the usual lineup cards and ground rules, they both shook my hand and said, "Dale, good to see you."

Wow, they knew my name! I was impressed, until later when I realized they had all four of our names on the large lineup cards posted in their dugouts.

After we covered the ground rules, I ran past third base and settled in shallow left, looking around this beautiful park and taking in everything I could. In your whole career, you get just one of these. It had been only ten years since I'd worked my first baseball game, anywhere.

Suddenly, I heard a voice—

"Hey, Dale!" It was George Brett (*Damn, he knows my name too!*).

"Hey, George," I tried to say calmly. Because, you know, I talk to future Hall of Famers every day.

"First game?"

I looked down at my pants—fully expecting to find a wet spot—and then looked back at him.

"Yeah. How could you tell?"

Laughing at my panicky glance, he said, "I hadn't seen you around, that's all. Congratulations, and welcome to the American League."

"Thanks, George," and with that, the ball was thrown around the horn, and the game began.

Kansas City won in ten innings: 2–1, in a crisp 2:42. My night at third was quiet, with only two calls. Coincidentally, one of them went against Brett. With the score 1–1 in the sixth and a runner on third, George checked his swing; on appeal, I said he went around for a strikeout. In the tenth, I called Steve Balboni's line drive fair. He wound up on second base, and a few moments later, a pinch runner scored the winning run.

That was it. My first game was in the books. That would be my only AL game before getting hired on the staff eight months later. When I tell that story, that I worked only one American League game before they hired me on the full-time staff, I joke, "Yeah, but I had a really good game!"

I flew back to Omaha the next day, rejoining my Triple-A crew. Although I landed in Omaha on Tuesday, I don't think my feet hit the ground until the weekend.

The next spring, the AL had me in Sarasota, where Marty Springstead lived. Tim Tschida and I were both assigned to that area so Marty could watch us all spring.

There were two American League openings that year. Marty had retired from the field and gone to the front office, and Jerry Neudecker retired (he'd been the last guy in the Majors to wear the outside chest protector). I had worked one game in the big leagues in '85. Tschida had worked twenty-seven. The two guys above us—also Triple-A umpires who had worked as AL fill-ins—were Tom Lepperd and Rich Humphrey. They hadn't worked a ton of big league games either, with Lepperd appearing in forty-six games and Humphrey in thirty. Tim and I were about ten years younger than they were, with less experience. So we naturally thought the two staff jobs would go to them, and then we'd be one and two on the fill-in list.

So we were working in Florida, doing our thing. Near the end of spring training, Tim and I both were told we had appointments to see a doctor in Sarasota for a physical. This didn't seem unusual, since we figured to be working a lot of AL games the upcoming season.

On April 1 I was working the plate in Sarasota, a White Sox home game. No cell phones in 1986. About twenty minutes before game time, a clubhouse attendant walks in and says, "Hey, Dale, you've got a call. You can take it in my office."

It was Dick Butler, who never called right before a game, so I was pretty curious. With his slow Kentucky drawl, he said, "Dale, ah . . . gittin' ready for thuh plate today?"

Well, Dick, you made the schedule and called me here at the stadium. Obviously, you know I'm getting ready for the plate. I replied, "Yes, Mr. Butler, I am."

"Well, ah certainly hope you have lead in your plate shoes."

Okay . . .

"Just wanted to let you know, as of right now, you are officially on the American League staff."

I was amazed. Flabbergasted. Had not seen this coming. I thanked him, and he said good luck. But it was a pretty brief conversation, because I had a game. I don't remember whom I was working with, and I'll be honest—I don't even remember the game. What I do remember is that Dick was right—I did feel like I was floating.

It was official. I was hired on April Fool's Day, and yes, there were some managers and players throughout my career who did think it was a joke.

I'd always had Minor League spring training in Arizona, so Florida was mostly a new animal for me. That night in Lakeland was the annual dinner for all the Minor League umpires in Florida. It was a chance for Barney Deary and the Minor League staff—Dick Nelson, Mike Fitzpatrick, and a few others—to address all the guys in one place. It was also a chance for everybody to get together and have dinner and a few cocktails. I hardly knew any of the Minor League guys in Florida. I knew a ton of the names, but I'd always been a West Coast guy. And you just didn't cross over that much back then.

So I went to this annual meeting the same day I got the news that I was hired by the American League. I had already jumped over a bunch of guys who were there, Triple-A guys, names I knew but mostly hadn't met. Now I'd not only jumped over those guys as a Minor Leaguer, but all of a sudden I'd just gotten a job. *The* job. So it was a very strange situation.

I knew that there was probably animosity toward me already. I mean, *Who the hell is this guy from out west who's all of a sudden getting MLB spring-training games?* So the last thing I wanted was to meet these guys who had more years in the game with, "Hey, good to meet you! Oh, and by the way, I just got hired by the American League."

I had this unbelievable excitement of getting hired . . . but I really couldn't tell anybody. Plus, I didn't know who else was hired. I just knew I had one of the two available jobs. I didn't know if they had hired Lepperd, Humphrey, or Tschida.

When I saw Tschida there, he was going through the same thing; he'd been hired that afternoon, too, but didn't know about me. So both of us were afraid to say, "Hey, I got hired." Because that might lead to, "Oh, you didn't? Gosh, sorry."

So we were kind of talking on the fringes, because, at the time, neither of us knew. And then there were all these guys I didn't know. Tschida knew a lot of them and introduced me around, but both of us were silent about something we wanted to scream about. Finally, there was sort of a lull, with Tim and I apart from the rest of the gathering. Tim said, "Did you get a call from Butler today?"

"Yeah. Did you?"

"Yeah! Whaddaya know!"

We were both thrilled and surprised that it was the two of us.

Even though it was Springstead's first year in the front office, we were really Butler's picks. Marty had input, having watched us the last month during spring training, but he hadn't seen us over the last couple of years. What they decided—as Marty told me later—was that while both Tschida and I were green, with very little experience, our youth meant we had more potential.

It was so strange, being at this banquet, meeting all these people, and having this news you really want to burst out with because you're so proud and happy. But you can't. Right before I was leaving for the drive back to Sarasota, I was talking to a couple of guys, when someone came up and said, "Hey, I heard a rumor that you and Tschida were hired today."

I wasn't going to lie to them, and of course they were extremely congratulatory. But I knew that some of those guys, as I was looking them in the eye and shaking their hands, were very disappointed. These were guys who had spent more years in baseball and had not gotten the chances I was fortunate to have. You empathize with them, knowing openings don't come along very often, and when another one is filled, that's one more opportunity now closed to them. This happens all the time in professional baseball; with each season, you find out that, one by one, many of your friends have either quit or been released.

That day was like winning the lottery, and once again things were happening fast. All of a sudden I was getting a ton of mail from the league, signing W-9s, getting packets about insurance and other benefits, getting mail from the Major League Umpires Association (MLUA), being fitted for my uniform. It was a flurry of stuff going on.

The pay bump was nice too. Not only would I be getting a big increase in pay, but now I'd be getting paid year-round. I'd be done in the fall, but those checks would just keep coming. *Yeah, this is pretty awesome. I like this a lot.*

8

When Sparky Quit Chewing

So that was April Fools Day 1986. Tschida and I were now full-time American League staff.

But as low men on the seniority list, we were among four staff umpires actually designated as vacation relief. So if everyone stayed healthy, our first games wouldn't be until Memorial Day, because, at that time, the American League umpires all took their two-week vacations between Memorial Day and Labor Day. As vacation relief, you would essentially be guaranteed to work in the Majors from June through August. You were also subject to a call-up in the other months if someone got hurt or otherwise needed to be off.

And then, believe it or not, the league still owed *us* two weeks of vacation, because that was in the contract for all full-time staff, even those of us working vacation relief.

Well, someone always went down with *something* before Memorial Day. On the seventeenth of May, I got the call to work my first AL game.

My Triple-A league was again the American Association, not the Pacific Coast League (my preference, of course). So as the season started, I would be a fourth guy for a three-man Triple-A crew, traveling with them until I got called up. All while making big-league salary and per diem.

As an aside, after the '86 season, I said to Marty Springstead—because I figured to be working vacation relief for a few years: "Listen, instead of the Association, can I work the Coast League?"

"Actually," he said, "that works out well, Scotty." He had three other guys who needed Triple-A slots, and I was the only one who really wanted to work in the Coast League. Plus, he wanted us spread across the country, so if somebody in the Majors went down on the West Coast, for example, I could get there more easily. So that worked out great, and I started the season in the PCL every year from 1987 through 1990. It was awesome. Bill Richardson, the league president, told me, "Listen, I don't care where you go. Just let me know."

So I made my own schedule. Portland would have a home stand for ten games, and I worked ten straight Portland games, sleeping in my own bed every night. Then when Portland would go on the road, I either went to Las Vegas or Phoenix. Or Tacoma, so I could just drive up. And I'd go to Vancouver, because I love Vancouver. The one thing Marty said was, "You cannot go to Hawaii. I'll be damned if you're in Hawaii and I need you in Kansas City."

Unless I was working in Portland—more on my adopted hometown later—I'd stay where the regular Triple-A crew stayed. Well, except Vancouver. There, the crew stayed at this kind of shithole near the stadium. I'd stay at the Hilton downtown, because I was on that big league per diem.

A lot of guys said the greatest job in umpiring was the vacation-relief job. And why not? You had it made! I worked that first year in the Association and then the next four in the PCL. Then the AL hired Jimmy Joyce, who also worked in the PCL. "Jimmy, dammit," I joked. "I had the perfect setup, with all the Portland home stands. And now I gotta split 'em with you."

That was the only time, besides eight games in Eugene back in '81, when I worked where I lived. You'd be doing stuff at home and notice, "Oh, it's 4:30, 5:00—I'd better get to the ballpark." Then you'd be home thirty or forty minutes after the game. All that ended in '91 when we got a new contract, but it was a great gig when I had it.

End of aside.

On Saturday, May 17, I came up for Vic Voltaggio, who had a medical issue (after my first game, the crew visited him in the hospital). I'd been called late the night before and told to report to Detroit for the next day's afternoon game. I had first base, with crew chief Dave Phillips on the plate, Tim Welke at third base, and Larry McCoy at second. This was NBC's national *Game of the Week*, with Bob Costas and Tony Kubek in the booth. Davey and Costas were friends, both from St. Louis, so after the game, Costas came by the locker room to say hello and chatted with all of us.

In the bottom of the sixth, we had a rotation play. Dwight Evans was on first with two outs when Dave Bergman hit a shot down the left-field line that Welke went out on. That pushed Davey from the plate to third base, with Larry picking up Bergman as I rotated to the plate. (That all might sound complicated, but rotations happen in just about every game with hardly anyone except us noticing.) Evans continued around third, as the throw to Angels catcher Bob Boone came in from the outfield. There was a play at the plate, and I got it . . . *OUT!*

I didn't know this until seven months later, but there was a great action shot of me calling Evans out. Boone had just made the tag, and with dust hanging in the air, I'm in profile really selling the out. The following winter, the picture was in a *Sports Illustrated* story about Boone's free agency. I have a framed, blown-up copy in my office that the Lane County Umpires Association, where I started in 1975, presented to me at a banquet in 1987.

If you count everything in my career—regular season, postseason, and one All-Star Game—I worked exactly one thousand plate games. Officially, anyway. Because my very first plate game doesn't actually show up in the records.

Because I'd worked first base in my debut, I had the plate the next afternoon, with future Hall of Famer Jack Morris starting for the Tigers. In the other dugout was Angels rookie first baseman Wally Joyner, who'd hit six homers in his last seven games and was on his way to a great nickname (Wally World) and the All-Star Game.

As I'd find out later, Detroit was one of the worst teams to work, for many reasons. One of them was Jack Morris.

But my first MLB game behind the plate turned out not to be a game at all. I was tight and struggled, with Morris surveying several times. (When a pitcher surveys, he stares in, intently examining you, the moment after you call a close pitch a ball, like a land surveyor on a road crew.)

Early in the game, we had a two-hour rain delay. Then in the third inning, with the rain pouring down, Joyner launched a two-run homer off Morris. But none of that counted, because three pitches later we had to stop the game again, and after thirty-four minutes of looking at a horrible forecast, Davey called it.

That night, Dave and I had dinner in Windsor, Canada, just across the river from downtown Detroit. "I didn't want to tell you before your first plate game, but Morris is a prick. When we saw it was you coming up, we thought, 'Well, I guess he's going to learn about Jack early.'"

You never forget your first big league ejection. Mine came eleven days later in Anaheim.

Working the plate, I called Doug DeCinces, the Angels' third baseman, out on strikes in the seventh inning. He got in my face, yelling that the pitch was inside and then slammed his bat down close to my feet. I ejected him.

Gene Mauch, the Angels' manager, strolled onto the field and approached me like a professor or a grandfather.

"Son," he said, "that's not how you handle these situations. You're going to have to learn that in the big leagues."

I thought, *Well, maybe that's not the best way for DeCinces to handle his situation, either. So we'll just agree to disagree.*

My second ejection was a couple of weeks later. It was getaway day, Detroit at Toronto, on a Sunday afternoon in front of a big crowd. Lance Parrish was catching for Detroit, with Sparky Anderson managing.

With a young umpire, Sparky was old-school: *I'm going to attack him, just to see what he's made of.* And this was a situation where the Tigers didn't like my strike zone, with pitchers surveying and Parrish showing me up by holding pitches an extra beat. In the fifth, Sparky beelined to the mound for a visit . . . with absolutely no intention of actually talking to the pitcher. The only person he wanted to visit was me, and it was obvious. Instead of putting off the inevitable, I immediately headed straight to the mound, knowing we were gonna go at it.

As I approached the mound, Sparky started in. "Where in the hell are those pitches? Those are good pitches."

"Sparky, we're not going to talk about pitches. You know that's not going to happen."

"The hell we aren't. You missed every one of 'em."

I ejected him, which is what he was there for, and he immediately tore into me: how it was a horrible strike zone, how I was terrible, how I've always been terrible, and how it's a disgrace that I'm even on the field. He's really letting me have it, screaming in my face the entire time. Finally, the rest of the crew came in, with Dave escorting Sparky back to the dugout. I'll never forget how, once Sparky was finally away from me, Larry McCoy pulled out a handkerchief and said, as discreetly as he could, "Here, wipe your face. He sprayed tobacco juice all over you."

I looked down at my light-blue shirt, and there was tobacco spray everywhere. It was all over my face, too, as I wiped it with the handkerchief that looked like someone had spilled coffee on it. While Sparky was screaming, I hadn't noticed the spraying.

After all of that, I walked back to the plate, and Parrish said, "The worst thing about this is that he's gotta leave, and you get to stay."

It was a hot day on that artificial turf. "Well, maybe he got the best of that deal," I said.

"We'd all get the best of the deal," Parrish said, "if you left."

I'd had Parrish in spring training, and he's got the personality of a U-boat commander. And not during the so-called Happy Times but toward the end of the war, when things weren't going as well for those guys. An inning later, after holding another pitch when I'd warned him to stop, I said, "Well, Lance, maybe you should leave too," and I ejected him. I think he was relieved. I know I was.

Several days later, Marty called, telling me Sparky would not be suspended for spraying me with tobacco juice. I was upset, as there's not too many more degrading things you can do to someone than spit or spray in their face. Marty said that Dr. Bobby Brown—the president of the American League my first eight years—wasn't suspending Sparky, because the Tigers, after reading my report, told Dr. Brown that Sparky had quit chewing.

So, of course, there was no *way* he could have sprayed tobacco in my face, right?

I told Marty that Sparky sprayed me with *something*, unless his saliva is naturally brown. What the hell did I wipe off my face that stained Larry's handkerchief? Bronzer?

Early in my career, I learned a good lesson: If it was an umpire's word versus a manager's or a player's, guess who Dr. Brown was going to believe?

9

"Mike, Your Mom Is Blasting Me"

Through the course of a long baseball season—or for that matter, a long career—you cannot overestimate the importance of having someone close who's your biggest fan, who always has your back, who keeps the home fires burning. For me, that someone—and he's been with me since just after my first year in the American League—is Michael Rausch.

Sure, you have your crew—your brothers on the field and off, day in and day out. You lean on them when things aren't going well, when you're having an umpire slump, or when everyone is just plain tired because the season never stops but your off days have.

In the big leagues, I had a few thirty-one-day months in which I worked thirty days, traveling every two or three days. Sometimes, from Sunday to Sunday, you're in five cities and four time zones. In 1985 my American Association schedule included one off day . . . four days before the end of the season. Thanks for nothing. So your crew is critical if you're going to stay positive and just keep moving forward.

But you need more than just your crew. Or at least I did. That was Mike.

I finished my first American League season in Arlington, Texas, on September 21, 1986. This would be my first off-season with no baseball since my first season, in the Northwest League. After the 1982 and '83 seasons, I headed to Arizona for instructional league. After the 1984 and '85 seasons, I worked in the Dominican winter league; from March of '84 through September of '86, I worked twenty-eight out of thirty months. That's a lot of foul tips!

To say I was excited on my connection from Dallas–Fort Worth to Eugene would be a serious understatement. I was now under contract with the American League, getting paid year-round and rolling in dough, with my W-2 going from $3,000 in 1985 to $38,000 in 1986. And now I was facing, head-on, five straight (or should I say *gay*) months off.

My first order of business was getting a place of my own. Although I was technically living with my parents, I hadn't lived in Eugene for more than a month at a time in three years. No disrespect to my parents, but let's be serious: I was twenty-seven, making money, and free until March. Oh, and gay. *Yeah, I really need to get the hell out of my parents' house!*

But where? I considered three options: Eugene, Portland, and Seattle.

Eugene? I grew up there and had a ton of friends and family there. But as I experienced in my first big league season, getting in and out of Eugene was a pain in the ass. Many off days, if I had lived in a bigger city, I could have flown home. Living in Eugene and trying to get to my next assignment after an off day was usually impossible. And the gay scene in Eugene? Yeah, no.

Seattle? I considered moving there, because with the Mariners in the American League, I would actually be *home* during the season when working their games. Plus, transportation wouldn't be an issue, as you could fly nonstop to just about any AL city from SeaTac. But I didn't know anyone in Seattle and really didn't know the city very well either, except downtown and Capitol Hill.

Why Capitol Hill? Remember what I said about the gay scene in Eugene? Seattle had a thriving gay neighborhood called Capitol Hill, so big points for a Seattle move.

Portland? Actually, the Rose City was the odds-on favorite all along, so my decision wasn't difficult. I loved Portland (and still do). I had been coming to Portland a lot, escaping the gay desert of Eugene ever since I came out in 1979. The airport, while not as big as I would have liked, was big enough to get me to and from American League cities. In a city a hundred miles from Eugene, I would be close enough to family and friends yet far enough away, as a single gay man who (finally) could live on my own without looking over my shoulder, afraid that someone I knew might see me leaving a gay bar or notice that 99 percent of my friends were guys.

So that day in early October, as I drove north on I-5 to Portland, I was reflective but also stoked. *Only eleven years ago I was a sophomore in high school working my first game; it's been just nine years since I graduated. Less than six years ago, I was getting ready to attend umpire school, with no idea of what would happen after that. Now I've quickly climbed through the Minor Leagues, spent the last two winters in the Dominican Republic, and just finished my first year in the big leagues.*

I was living a life that I could only dream about not too long ago.

Now I was getting my own place in a new city, knowing I could finally live openly gay, or at least in my nonbaseball life. All I could think about was what was in front of me . . . so many men, so much fun. I mean, come on. I was twenty-seven and felt like a caged animal who had just been freed!

So naturally, that night, I met Mike.

While in Portland, I would stay with Terry, my old roommate back in Eugene. My plan was to check out a couple of townhouses for rent that I found in the paper (it was 1986, so there was no internet—barbaric, I know). Terry and I grabbed a bite to eat and decided to swing by CC Slaughters, a bar in the West End (Portland's version of Capitol Hill). This was a Monday night, so I didn't expect much of a crowd.

It was early, around 8:30, and like we thought, hardly anyone was there. A couple of bartenders, two guys sitting at the bar, and a rather sketchy lesbian going solo on the dance floor. Although *Seinfeld* was still a few years from going on the air, she was doing what later would be called "the Elaine": half goose step, half seizure.

About this time, two guys walked in, ordered at the bar, then stood about twenty-five feet away from us. When they walked in, I could not take my eyes off one of them. He had a clean-shaven baby face, dark eyes, and a beautiful smile. Terry was chatting about something, and though I tried to pay attention, I kept looking toward this guy and noticed that he was looking toward me.

He would watch that solo dancer, smile at me, then look down. I would do the same thing. We both did that several times, which (for the uninitiated among you) is the ancient gay ritual of cruising. I was mesmerized by his smile! Finally, I walked over and offered to buy him a drink. He said yes, so we went to the bar and ordered, as I introduced myself.

His name was Mike, and he'd stopped by Slaughters with his friend Randall to grab a quick drink before heading home. Just like me and Terry. We chatted about—oh who cares? I was in love!

I know, I know: love at first sight. Doesn't happen, right?

I mean, seriously. I'd arrived in Portland just a couple of hours earlier, excited about being *free* for the next five-plus months and about all the new people (*translation: guys*) I was going to meet while having my own place and getting paid good money to do absolutely nothing until March. So now this is happening? I'm falling in love with the first guy who walks into a deserted bar on my first night in the big city? Have I totally lost my mind?

Perhaps.

But I couldn't help it. That smile! Those eyes!

We chatted and sipped our cocktails. Randall was getting restless and wanted to leave. Later I found out why. Before he and Mike walked into Slaughters, Randall had said, "I'll go in, but don't leave me hanging when someone starts talking to you. You always end up doing that!"

So Mike left him hanging when I started talking to him.

I told Mike I'd give him a ride, but after Randall said he was leaving and took Mike's coat with him, Mike followed Randall out. Before he did, though, he invited me to lunch the next day at Macheezmo Mouse, a local Mexican restaurant he managed. I said lunch for me was at two o'clock, which was perfect since by then the lunch rush would be over.

The next day, I met Mike for lunch and then went to look at those rentals. Before I left the restaurant, we made plans to meet when he was off and grab a drink. The first place I checked out was all I needed to see; I put down my deposit and got the keys. So not even twenty-four hours in, I now had my own place in the John's Landing neighborhood, three miles from downtown.

At five, I met Mike and was both surprised and disappointed that he'd brought along Heidi, a coworker. Little did I know, she was there to give Mike a second opinion. We went around the corner to the Virginia Cafe, a Portland staple since 1914. Mike was ordering a second round when I excused myself and went to the restroom. When I got back to our table, Heidi was gone. I asked where she went; Mike said she had to get home. Later he told me the truth. When I left the table, Heidi looked at Mike and said, "You don't need me here. He's awesome. If you don't fuck him, I will!"

Mike had his second opinion.

We went to dinner at Hobo's, a gay restaurant in Old Town that at the time had the best prime rib in the city, then checked out my newly rented, completely empty townhouse. Having no furniture wasn't a problem, except we both ended up with rug burns.

Yes, it really was love at first sight. For both of us.

Mike was living in a run-down rental house with two straight roommates, Dave and Rob. I would hang out there once in a while, they'd pass around a joint, and we would shoot the shit. Dave and Rob were baseball fans and loved my war stories. But they couldn't figure out how Mike and I were friends, or even in the same orbit. Finally, before Mike moved out, he told them we were gay and a couple. Rob, who was pleasantly stoned when hearing this new puzzle-solving information, replied, "Wait a minute, you're serious? I don't care, but really? Dude, you're humping the ump?" Classic!

In December, Mike officially moved in, although we'd been practically inseparable during the two months since we met anyway. He is the youngest of five, and during this time, I met Dick and Elita, his parents, and his oldest sister, Elisa, and her family, all of whom lived in Portland. His brother, Rick, lived in Florida, and his other two sisters, CiCi and Mary, lived in Arizona.

Several times, we had dinner or cocktails at his parents' house, so I got to know them fairly well. They, like his roommates, just couldn't figure out how we would have met. Here's Mike, who's not at all into sports and for the last couple of years had been drumming with the Social Zeros, a local punk band. And here's me, just moved up from Eugene, four years older, conservative looking, and an umpire in the American League. Two guys who don't seem to have a whole lot in common. Or anything, really.

Not that it was a problem, far from it. His parents loved golfing and were avid sports fans, and Elita was a huge baseball junkie who grew up in San Francisco and bled Giants orange. Considering that during their annual trip the next spring to visit CiCi and Mary in Phoenix, she'd be getting comp tickets to Giants spring-training games, Elita couldn't care less how Mike and I met!

Now that Mike was moving in with me, though, he wanted to come out to his family (or more accurately, the rest of his family, as his three sisters already knew). The entire Rausch family was very Catholic, especially his mom. In fact, we joked that she was the female pope, so coming out to her would be interesting. He decided to take her to lunch for the big moment so that when he broke it to her, they'd at least be in public and she wouldn't cause a scene. Or at least, that was the theory.

At lunch, Mike told Elita he was moving in with me. She seemed thrilled, as she hated the run-down rental where he had been living. Plus, she really liked me and thought I was such a good influence on him.

"I'm glad you think so well of Dale," Mike said, "because, you know, his place has only one bed."

"Doesn't he have two bedrooms?"

"He does, Mom. But just one bed."

"Michael, what are you trying to tell me? You're moving in with a gay man?" Mike laughed. This was classic.

"No, Mom. I mean, yes, Mom. He's gay. I'm gay. We're both gay, and we're together."

After a few seconds of silence that seemed much longer, Elita—who suddenly wasn't nearly as thrilled—let loose: "Who else have you told? You haven't told your father, have you? Your brother? I mean, it's almost Christmas! Please do not ruin Christmas, Michael! You know you have always gone through phases. I'm sure this one will pass too. You can change! You know that, right? Who else have you told?"

Ultimately, Mike's strategy paid off, as Elita didn't cause a scene. And Christmas wasn't ruined either. He told his dad after New Year's, followed by several weeks of radio silence as Dick and Elita worked through this revelation about their son. That silence was broken in March, when they spent several weeks in Phoenix and I was leaving them tickets to about 75 percent of my spring-training games.

That brought up another delicate situation.

Spring-training stadiums are much more intimate than home ballparks, with capacity around ten thousand. The tickets we leave for friends and family are usually good seats behind home plate or one of the dugouts, close to the action. I always knew where they were, and shortly after walking onto the field, I would acknowledge whoever was using my tickets.

I left Dick and Elita tickets to a lot of games during the '87 Cactus League season. But I quickly realized that they—or more specifically, Elita—weren't aware of CTE (comp ticket etiquette).

What is CTE? One, you don't sell your comp tickets. Two, you don't ask for comp tickets and then fail to actually show up. And three, *you don't yell at the guy who leaves you the comp tickets.* Or for that matter, the rest of the crew either.

They had no problem with the first two of those, but the third was a challenge. During the first couple of games that I worked the plate, Elita would occasionally voice her opinion on my ball or strike decisions. And not with the rest of the crowd. She would wait just a second until the usual noise had calmed down, so that I—and everyone else near the plate—could hear her. Not only that, but often she would personalize her criticism. "That was low, Dale!" "Come on, Dale, that wasn't a strike!" "You've been calling that all game, Dale!"

Yes, friends, my sweet, kindly future mother-in-law was blasting me, by name, from the free seats I left her. Of course, that allowed others in the stands—who hadn't had a clue what my name was, but now did—a wonderful chance to join in with their own personalized critiques.

One evening, Mike called me in Phoenix to say hello, just to see how things were going. I told him that things were fine, yet he sensed that something was bothering me. So I told him.

"Mike, your mom is blasting me."

"What? Seriously? Are you sure it's her?"

"Yes, Mike, I'm sure. I know where they sit, and besides, half the time, she uses my name."

"I'll call you back!"

Mike called his mom.

"Oh, honey," she told him, "we're having such a wonderful time! Dale's been leaving us tickets, and the seats are great!"

"Great, Mom. I'm so happy for you. Now, I'm going to tell you this just once: Stop blasting Dale. If you still want free awesome seats, knock it off!"

"It's part of the game to yell at the umpire."

"Not when the umpire is your son's boyfriend who's leaving you free tickets so close to the field that he can hear every word you scream at him! Got it, Mom? Either the yelling stops, or the tickets do."

Pause. Then Elita said, "I will stop heckling him, Michael. But I have one more thing to say."

"Be careful, Mom . . ."

"I would think a man of Dale's stature, in the position he's in, would have a thicker skin. Goodbye!"

Elita never yelled at me again.

Yes, getting blasted from the stands comes with the territory. If you want to bitch about my calls, though, buy your own damn ticket!

The good news? Comp tickets and great seats apparently override Catholic antigay sentiment. Mike and I are sure that if I'd been working in an office somewhere, the radio silence would have lasted a bit longer. Regardless, I was accepted by his entire family and love them as my own to this day. I'm forever grateful for that. Dick left us in 2008, Elita in 2017, and I miss them both.

10

Sophomore Slump

My second year in the American League was a borderline disaster.

As a rookie in 1986, I'd been one of four rovers. "Vacation umpire" is what we were actually called, and we were the four umpires hired by the league most recently. The other three were Mark Johnson, Larry Young, and Tim Tschida. The way our collective bargaining agreement (CBA) was set up, the nonrovers got two consecutive weeks off during the season, sometime between Memorial Day and Labor Day. Four umpires were off every week, and we would fill their spots. If everyone on staff stayed healthy all year (spoiler alert: that never happened), the four of us would start in Triple-A (while earning a big league salary and per diem), fill in for vacations from late May to early September, and then go home the last month of the season, since by then the Triple-A leagues were finished. Of course, if there were umpire injuries in April, May, or September, we filled those slots as well.

For the four vacation umpires, this meant no continuity working together. Bouncing from one crew to another meant you rarely stayed in rotation. You might work the plate on Sunday and go to a new crew the next day, where the chief would put you at second or first; there were some chiefs who would put you right back behind the plate. Not being on a regular crew could also mess up travel, if, for example, you were on a crew in Toronto that was going to nearby Detroit next, but instead you get sent to join a crew in Oakland.

After 1986 Marty Springstead did away with having the newest members of the staff be vacation umpires. He put us on set crews when we came up in May, and he had more senior guys fill in for vacations. Why have young umpires, who were trying to establish themselves and learn the cities and teams, bounce around like that? Instead, he decided to give them stability by placing them on a crew with a regular rotation, giving them the opportunity to work with the same guys. A great idea that made a lot of sense. Too bad it didn't do much good for me.

For the 1987 season, I was assigned to Don Denkinger's crew, with Larry McCoy and Drew Coble. All three were great guys but not really instructors. Some guys are not just outstanding umpires but also outstanding instructors. They see things you do or don't do on the field, notice how you take a play or handle a situation, can sense when you may be lacking or unsure, and are able to communicate those observations constructively, building your confidence. Richie Garcia and Joe Brinkman were two of the best at that.

Make no mistake—Don was an *outstanding* umpire. Most people remember the one missed call in the 1985 World Series, but this guy had a tremendous résumé, with huge games throughout his career. But Don, Larry, and (to a lesser extent) Drew were not great instructors and maybe shouldn't have been with young guys as much as Garcia or Brinkman. At least not young guys who needed plenty of help. Like I did in '87.

That's why I went with Garcia the following three seasons. But in '87 I would come off the field after a plate game where both dugouts had three-alarm fires, and I would hear the standard, "Hey, Scotty, nice job! So guys, where are we going tonight?" Meanwhile, I was sitting over in the corner, shell-shocked, and thinking, *Did you not see what the fuck just happened out there?*

They saw it. They just weren't the right guys to sit down with me and say, "Okay, let's figure this out." All three of them tried, but it just wasn't their forte.

I struggled the entire season and was still considered a rookie even though it was my second full year, and the managers, coaches, and players were more than happy to pile on. I had my problems on the bases but especially on the plate. Balls, strikes, inside, outside, it didn't really matter. My confidence, fragile at this stage of one's career anyway, was plummeting.

For any official in any sport, if your confidence is shattered, everything else just implodes. It's a horrible feeling. Each time you think you have a decent game, you'll turn around the next day and something will happen. That whole season, *they weren't believing me*. Frankly, I wasn't believing me either.

Oh, and it seemed like "umpire luck" kept coming my way.

What's umpire luck?

1. When an umpire makes a mistake that is then magnified by a subsequent play or plays, compounding the mistake made. For example, if a 2-2 pitch should have been strike three but the strike wasn't called and later in the at bat, the batter hits a home run or if a batter-runner is erroneously called safe at first on what would have been an inning-ending double play and then the offense racks up several hits, walks, and runs after the missed third out, those would be umpire luck.

2. When an umpire is having a tough game or series (or in my case, season) yet (a) keeps getting a majority of, if not all, remaining close plays for that game or series or (b) gets plays that don't happen very often. Some examples include obstruction; any one of the many possible interference calls; and a "time play," where you have to decide if a runner scored before a tag play was the third out.

When your confidence is as low as mine was and spiraling . . . I felt like I was getting *all* those plays. Not that the other guys didn't get some, but when they did, the teams *believed them*. And as the season went on, it got worse and worse. And worse.

I felt like I was treading water, and the water was winning. On any given night, anyone else on the crew would have a wacker force play at first or a close steal play at second, and once in a while, I would think, *Ohh, I'm not sure if he got that right*. Yet in most cases, there would be no real reaction from the team. I would have the same close play . . . and the bitch gates would open up! I know you're going to be challenged and tested when you're a young umpire, but this was beyond that. Calls that weren't that close got over-the-top reactions. So it became a habit for me to hesitate after every close call, looking for the manager to come flying out of the dugout.

On July 1, I had the plate in Fenway with the Orioles in town. Baltimore had runners on second and third, two outs, and second baseman Rich Burleson batting. With two strikes, he swung and foul tipped the pitch to catcher Rich Gedman, who came up with his glove like he caught the ball. I called Burleson out.

The ball had actually skipped off the ground into his glove, which would make it a foul ball.

Umpire luck.

The Red Sox ran off the field while the Orioles went crazy, jumping around and screaming. This was Cal Ripken Sr.'s only full year as the Oriole's manager, and what a peach he was. One of the worst I ever dealt with.

Old Man Ripken was a true umpire hater. When he was the O's third-base coach, one of his favorite lines when he was arguing about . . . well, he'd argue about anything, was, "I'm wearing this uniform—that means I can say something!"

To which I always thought, *You do realize I'm wearing this uniform, which means I not only don't have to listen to you, but I can also dump your ass?* Anyway, he was going crazy and refused to leave the field: "Ask for help! You gotta ask for help!!"

Until 2000 we rarely would ask for help or have a crew consultation on a call. Right or wrong, you died with your decision. I'm not saying that was a good philosophy; that's just how it was done. But this time, I was unsure if I got the call right—kind of a theme for me that year—so after quite a performance by Mr. Ripken, I went to Larry McCoy (who was then our acting crew chief, as Don was out with an injury). Larry, who didn't realize the ball had been tipped, reluctantly confirmed that, yes, the ball *had* hit the ground.

So now we have to bring the Red Sox, who were all in the dugout, back on the field, and boy, they sure loved that. Now *they're* pissed off and screaming, while slowly returning to their positions. They knew we got it right; they just wanted to let me know personally, and the crew generally, how completely horseshit we were.

Once again, I was shell-shocked as I walked into the locker room. One of my lowest points in a season full of them.

But not *the* lowest. That came later.

Like the entire staff, every season, I looked forward to the All-Star break. It was usually three days, but for some crews four. The way my season was going, I needed the break even more than usual. So naturally I got a shorter one than normal.

To start the break, I was coming home from Toronto, arriving in Portland around midnight (or three in the morning, body time) Sunday. For some reason, Milwaukee scheduled a 1:00 p.m. start for their first game after the break. That meant my four nights home was reduced to three, since I'd have to leave Portland Wednesday afternoon and make a connection in Minneapolis to get to Milwaukee that evening, in order to be ready the next morning to head to the stadium. With a normal evening start in Milwaukee, I could have left either very late Wednesday night or early Thursday morning.

This might not sound like a big deal. But like all umpires, I cherished my visits home, and not just every day but every hour counted. Add to that how the season had affected me mentally, and missing that fourth night at home seemed like a personal affront. When you're drowning every day, that's how you think.

A couple of weeks after the break, I was in New York with an off day before our weekend series at Yankee Stadium. We stayed at the Summit, at Fifty-First and Lexington, just a few blocks from the American League office on Park Avenue. Marty Springstead called me and said, "Hey, Scotty, I want you to come into the office today."

When I arrived, Marty seemed very serious, not his usual engaging self.

"Scotty, how do you think you're doing this year?"

Of course, my performance wasn't worth a shit, but I wasn't going to tell my boss that.

"Well, Marty, I don't think I'm having an All-Star year, but I think things are going well."

He shook his head and said, "Scotty, things are not going well. The reports I'm getting, *they just do not believe you*. If we don't make a change, Scotty, if things don't start to rebound, I'll have to let you go."

That was devastating, without a question *the* lowest point in my career. We umpires had a three-year probationary period—actually, it might have been five back then—and at this point, I was only a year and a half in, which means it would have been a lot easier for them to let me go, for practically any reason.

Hearing this, I was extremely low.

"Look, Scotty, here's what we're going to do. When you're done after Labor Day, I want you to go for a week of instructional league in Sarasota. I'll be there to work with you. We need to get you off your knee, Scotty. Nobody believes you behind the plate, and we need to change that."

Starting in Double-A and all through Triple-A, I worked behind the plate on my knee, which a lot of guys did in the eighties, especially in the American League. It's totally out of vogue now, but it had worked for me in the Minors.

Now it definitely wasn't working for me, as I was fighting with the outside corner. Also, working the knee, you had a tendency to look lazy, laid back. With the problems I was having this season, the resulting lack of confidence, and the entire league not believing me, looking lazy wasn't helping.

"You need something that looks more aggressive and confident," Marty said. "In Sarasota you can work on different plate stances and mechanics without the pressure of trying to change in spring training. Find what works; then you can practice it next spring. So when the season starts, you'll be locked in."

At least he wasn't washing his hands of me. Clearly, he wanted me to succeed and was willing to help. But a two-year MLB umpire going to instructional league was unheard of. The only time a big league umpire goes to instructional league is if he's been hurt and needs to get back into game shape.

So, yeah, that was a blow to my ego, my pride. But I totally got it, because I knew something had to change. As much as I wanted to think Marty was being overly dramatic, bottom line? He was telling me the truth—this was not working.

The Sunday before my birthday, in August, I had a getaway day in Cleveland, with the next day off before going to Minneapolis. It had been a month since my shortened All-Star break, but flying home late Sunday night, only to leave at the crack of dawn Tuesday for the Twin Cities, wasn't ideal. Mike wanted to celebrate my birthday, so we decided to meet in Denver, with both of us arriving Sunday night and not needing to fly out so early on Tuesday, for a much-needed (by me) two-night break. We had a great time walking around the city, driving up into the Rockies to marvel at the scenery, and enjoying an early birthday dinner with a spectacular view of a full moon rising over the city. Tuesday morning, Mike flew home, and I was off to Minneapolis.

The Metrodome's locker room was more like a closet really. After the dome was built, they realized they'd forgotten a room for officials, so they gave us the auxiliary coaches room, which was barely large enough to fit the four of us with our bulky Priesmeyer trunks. And when I walked in, I saw

Don Denkinger rubbing up the game balls. Drew Coble was scheduled to work the plate but, for some reason, hadn't made it. That meant I had the plate, since I'd been at second base in our last game.

I didn't have any choice but to strap it on and try to focus. Of course, internally I started stressing. It had been just ten days since Marty dropped the "I'll have to let you go" bomb in his office, and that cloud was still hovering over me. Darkly.

Don, who had witnessed my daily struggles since April, must have realized how screwed up I was.

"I'm working the plate tonight, Scotty," Don said. "I had a short trip"—he lived in Des Moines—"and you've been on a plane all day. You just go to first."

It was a kind gesture, especially since I actually hadn't been on a plane all day, having made the easy flight from Denver. It was Don's way of handling a crewmate who had been drowning all year, without embarrassing him. There's no way to sugarcoat this, though: I felt like a failure and doubted if I would ever get out of this deep hole.

A couple of weeks later, Dick Butler was in Oakland for our series. Although Marty had Dick's former job as the league's supervisor of umpires, Dick stayed on to help with the transition and would still evaluate us.

Before the game, Dick came in and said, "Marty wanted me to give you a message."

"Yeah? What's up?"

"Well, you know you're going to instructional league. Marty also wants you to work winter ball in the Dominican. In Sarasota you can just work on your stance. And then in the Dominican, you can actually work games, again with no pressure, to perfect your new stance, call a lot of pitches. So when you get to spring training, you'll have a fresh look, and hopefully we'll get this thing turned around."

I was stunned. *Are you kidding me? I'm a mental wreck, and now you want me to work all winter?* I had been looking forward to those few months off after instructional league, if for nothing else but my sanity.

I flew home after the game for a day off, depressed. I told Mike I didn't think I could survive another Dominican winter. Not only because of all the work. I'd lived down there for three months at a time, and it's a challenge. Bottom line, I needed some time *away* from the game.

I decided to give Marty a call.

"I got your message from Dick about winter ball. I understand why you're doing this, and I know things have to change. But I'm not sure if you understand how the format works down there."

So I ran through the math with him, how if I were down there for the whole sixty-game season, I would work forty-five plate games. Then I was brutally honest: "Marty, I just don't know if I can do it, mentally. After the season I've had, going there for another three-plus months . . . it's too much."

"I didn't realize all that," Marty said. "I'll tell you what. Go down to winter ball"—which started around the twentieth of October—"and I'll have you home by Thanksgiving. I'll come down for a week, so we can see how things are going."

I could live with that. Yes, it would be a challenge; yes, I needed to suck up my pride. But I absolutely understood what Marty was doing. Dick Butler never would have come up with that solution. He would have written me off as a bad hire. Dick never umpired, and although he learned a lot about our profession, he could never fully relate, because he had never been on the field. Plus, he didn't have Marty's imagination. Dick played mind games with you, reverse psychology or whatever. That was his way of making you better. There was no way he would have thought of instructional league and a short tour in the Dominican.

Mind you, sending a two-year veteran Major League umpire to winter ball was unprecedented. And I took some flak the next spring at the umpires' union meeting. *Why didn't you tell him to go fuck himself? He can't do that!*

"I'll tell you why," I said. "Because he was right. When you have a supervisor telling you that if things don't change, we're going to have to let you go, and when you know, in your heart, that he was absolutely right, then something has to change."

Marty saved my career, and I told him that several times. He realized, *I've got a kid here who's got a ton of potential but is struggling. I need to help him figure this out.*

For that entire 1987 season, I was swimming against the tide, trying to make headway but steadily drifting out to sea. Marty knew something had to change and then came up with a concerted plan to make that happen. Then he put me with Rich Garcia's crew for four of the next five years. In fact, when Marty came to the Dominican, he brought Garcia with him. Marty wanted us to get to know each other, and Marty and I both valued Richie's talents as an instructor (bonus: Richie spoke Spanish and could help Marty get through a week in the Dominican Republic).

It all worked out perfectly. I was home by Thanksgiving, in time to watch my Oregon Ducks demolish Oregon State, 44–0. I got the mental breather I so desperately needed. That winter I got a call from Marty: "Scotty, we have numbers that have opened up in the American League."

My first two years, I was 39; Tim Tschida was 38.

"Tschida just took number 4," Marty said, "so I have 5. Do you want it?"

"Yes!"

"You don't want to think about it?"

"No, I want 5."

"Why are you so quick to take 5?"

"I'll tell you why, Marty. First of all, it's obvious I need to be in the umpire protection program because of the year I had. I need a fresh number, and I want people to call me Sean. Maybe they won't notice who I am, and with this new stance, maybe I'll fool these bastards into thinking I've had a good year. Second, I'm not a math major, but there are only thirty-two guys on the staff and I'm number 39, which says something. And three, let's be honest, 39's not on the roulette wheel."

He laughed his ass off. "Oh, that's great, Scotty. I can't wait to tell Dr. Brown that you want number 5 'cause it's on the roulette wheel."

Marty saved my career, got me back on the right track, and placed me with Garcia to help me both mentally and mechanically. My career took off after that.

My first World Series, in 1998, was a four-game sweep. I worked Game Three on the plate in my red American League shirt, making me the first of only two umpires to wear red in a Series game (Derryl Cousins was the other, in 1999). A couple of days after I got home from San Diego, Marty called and said, "I just want to let you know, of the four plate games, you had the best one. We got you there, Scotty, didn't we?"

"Marty," I said, "it's only because of you. You got me there."

He was so proud that we had done this together, that he'd seen that potential in a young umpire who had now worked in his first World Series and done well. That's another phone call I'll never forget.

So that was 1987. Tough, tough year. By far my worst in thirty-seven years of professional baseball.

My struggles made me not just a better umpire on the field but also a better teacher, mentor, and crew chief. One of the best compliments I've heard from young guys, both while I was working and since, is that they were thrilled when assigned to my crew. Some crew chiefs have reputations for working well with young umpires—others not so much. I was a better crew chief because of all I'd gone through during my second season.

I have a lot of empathy for young umpires who may lose some confidence during the first years of their career. When I tell them stories about the disastrous season I had, many can't believe it. They're used to veterans saying something like, "Hey, kid, we've all been there."

After listening to me, they know I'm not just saying that.

11

For the Last Time

Memorial Day, 1988. First game of a three-game series. I was at first base, and crew chief Rich Garcia was working the plate, with Rick Reed at second and John Hirschbeck at third.

Walt Weiss, Oakland's rookie shortstop, led off the bottom of the third and hit a liner right at the feet of Yankee second baseman Bobby Meacham. Did Meacham catch it? Or did it skip off the ground into his glove?

Rick, who was behind Meacham, immediately signaled no catch. Meacham, however, didn't look for a signal. He believed he'd caught the ball and started throwing it around the horn. Even if Rick was 100 percent wrong, a quick glance Rick's way would have left Meacham plenty of time to throw Weiss out by thirty feet.

From my angle, I thought it skipped. But it wasn't obvious, one way or the other. If we had replay as we do now, from what I saw on the field, I would have said *stands*. No matter what Rick's call had been. I didn't have it 100 percent either way.

So Meacham doesn't look, Weiss is safe at first base, and *then* Bobby realizes what was called and starts arguing, which brings Yankees manager Billy Martin flying out of the first-base dugout. Running by me on his way to Rick, he yells, "YOU SAW HIM CATCH IT. YOU SAW HIM CATCH IT."

"No, Billy. He trapped it," I responded, although I'm not sure if he heard me.

Garcia arrived from the plate and quickly got me and Rick away from Billy, to see what we both had. I told them I didn't have anything different.

So Richie let Billy know we weren't changing the call, as Hirschbeck joined the festivities. I was now on the periphery, watching and listening.

Suddenly, Billy whips around Rick, looks at me, and says, "You saw him catch the ball."

"He didn't catch the ball, Billy. He trapped it."

"You're full of shit," he said. "You are full of shit."

Boom. I ejected him.

A player, manager, or coach can basically cuss all they want (with a few exceptions), but when they *personalize* their comments, they risk being ejected. Starting a complaint with *You're*, as Billy did, is often all it takes. In other words, he might think and say the call is full of shit, but when he says I am? Buh-bye.

Of course, that really set him off, and he tried to kick dirt on me, which ended up being more difficult than he anticipated. The dirt was still damp from the usual pregame watering, so he couldn't get it airborne. The dirt was just clumping up, and *Billy really wanted to kick dirt on me.*

He took two good whacks at getting some damn dirt to fly, and with the first one, his shoe nicked my knee. It wasn't intentional, and it wasn't a solid hit. He just grazed me.

"You just kicked me, Billy! You kicked me!" I screamed, while pointing to my knee several times.

During his entire failed Rockettes impersonation, he was yelling his chant of the day: "You're full of shit! You're full of shit!" Failing to kick dirt on me, Billy then bent down, scooped as much as he could with both hands, and shoveled it right on my classy American League sweater.

Now Billy and I were going at it over Richie's shoulder, as he and John attempted to stay between us. Billy continued to tell me what I was full of, while I made sure he knew I wasn't happy about being kicked, which would be in my report.

Richie finally got Billy pointed in the right direction (his dugout) and slowly walked him that way as Billy continued to plead his case. The game ended up going fourteen innings, although (as I found out the next day) Billy barely made it halfway through.

Yankees pitcher Tommy John, a true gentleman, usually came by once every series to say hello to the crew. Before the next night's game, he walked into our locker room, pointed at me, and said, "You really pissed Billy off yesterday."

We all laughed as he continued, "That was the third inning. Around the fifth, I went to the clubhouse, and Billy was there with a Big Gulp cup, drinking vodka on ice. I think it was the seventh when one of the clubhouse kids took him back to the hotel. He was *blotto*. I've seen him pissed off before, Dale, but you *really* pissed him off."

We finished the series with a day game Wednesday, followed by an off day, so I flew home for a couple of nights. The video of Billy's ejection and dirt toss was getting plenty of air time, with lots of speculation about whether he'd be suspended and for how long.

This was hardly Billy Martin's first go-round. Just three weeks earlier in Texas, he'd been ejected and *successfully* kicked dirt on Tim Welke. And late that night, he'd gotten the holy hell beat out of him in the bathroom of a topless nightclub.

Billy had *not* been suspended for kicking dirt on Tim, and his fine was reportedly just a few hundred bucks, which, especially considering his rap sheet, seemed less than sufficient. Especially to umpires and *especially* to Richie Phillips, our union's general counsel.

While I was still in Portland, AL president Dr. Bobby Brown called with a few questions about the ejection, having already read my report and presumably seen the video.

"Billy says he never kicked you."

(Not that Dr. Brown was biased or anything, but he'd been Billy's teammate on the Yankees back in the early fifties.)

"Well," I said, "he just nicked me."

"Is it possible that what nicked you was maybe a little bit of dirt or something?"

"To be honest, Dr. Brown, the reason he wound up *picking up dirt* is because he couldn't get any when kicking, since it was still damp from being watered down. Is that *possible*, though? Sure, I guess. Anything's possible.

"All I know," I continued, "is what I felt when he kicked. That's why I pointed at my knee and kept saying, 'You just kicked me, Billy. You just kicked me.'"

Swear to God, it was just like two years earlier, when I ejected Sparky Anderson and got—I mean didn't get (?)—sprayed by tobacco juice.

You're taught in umpire school—and it's emphasized—to *never lie in a report.* Explain what happened, what you heard, what you saw, and if *you yourself* did anything improper. If I told a player to go fuck himself, I'm supposed to put that in there too. Or if you don't put that in *exactly,* you certainly don't say *I never cussed him* if you actually did cuss him.

The league office gets your report. So do the teams, and of course, the Yankees told Dr. Brown, "Billy says he didn't kick him."

And nine times out of ten, Dr. Brown would come back to us and say, "Well, they said he didn't kick him, so I guess he didn't."

So the employee (me) who works for the American League—Dr. Brown signs my checks—and represents the league on the field, with millions watching . . . it's the employee who's not telling the truth. That was so frustrating. Let me be clear—Dr. Brown and the American League weren't alone in this. In the Minor Leagues it was even worse, at least in the Cal and Texas Leagues. In the American Association, on the other hand, I had Joe Ryan. He was one of the greatest league presidents ever and would back his umpires 1,000 percent.

Joe was reminiscent of the cartoon character Mr. Magoo. He sort of talked like him, with a soft mumble, but his eyesight was pure Magoo. He wore thick glasses and was legally blind. As president of the Association and the guy handing out fines, he was an umpire's dream, and his player fines and suspensions were legendary.

Once, Joe was sitting at a game with Umpire Development supervisor Mike Fitzpatrick in the first row right behind the plate. There was a close steal play at second, with the runner called out. The runner jumped up screaming and bumped the umpire, who immediately ejected him. Joe, who couldn't see anything as far away as second base, heard the reaction in the stands and asked Fitzy, "What's up?"

"Runner called out at second jumped up and bumped him," Mike replied.

Joe jumped up and screamed, "That's three games and $500!"

So that off day phone call with Dr. Brown was frustrating, just getting the not-so-subtle message that my report wasn't truthful, that what I wrote didn't happen. That is, according to Billy . . . the same guy who just a few weeks earlier had kicked dirt on another umpire and then was beat up in a topless nightclub at two in the morning. But I was the one who couldn't be trusted. Got it.

Shortly after we spoke, Dr. Brown levied a three-game suspension and a $1,000 fine.

"There is no excuse sufficient enough to warrant dirt being kicked and thrown at an umpire," Brown said. "I have warned Billy that this type of action must cease and that, if repeated, it could result in harsher penalties."

Three games and a thousand bucks didn't seem harsh at all, considering that this was Billy's second dirt-kicking episode in three weeks. The union and Richie Phillips didn't find it harsh, either, and immediately announced that after serving his suspension, Billy would automatically be ejected upon leaving the dugout and entering the field, for the rest of the season.

According to the *New York Daily News* a few days later, "Martin, who remained in the dugout throughout Monday night's game, his first since serving the suspension, countered with a threat of a lawsuit against the union and its rep."

It took no time at all for this to turn into a shitstorm. If you had *any* sympathy for umpires—and I'm not saying anyone did—but if you had any sympathy after Billy's tirades against Welke and myself, now that was thrown out the window. In the eyes of most everyone, umpires and the union were being unreasonable. You can't just eject Billy every time he steps on the field.

Sure, technically you could. But there would be unbelievable repercussions. And guess who would be in the middle of it all?

Once I'd filed my report and talked to Dr. Brown, the penalty was out of my hands. It's not that I didn't appreciate Phillips and the union having my back. I absolutely did. This was my third season, but it was my first experience as the center of a major controversy. To me, a tactic that risked whatever goodwill we had, and was immediately condemned by just about everyone, didn't feel like a winning strategy.

Meanwhile, it was hard not to follow the drama. The first time I read Billy's quotes that I'd changed my story with him and lied in my report, I told Richie Garcia, "That is not what happened. That's not what I said." Once again, it reinforced a lesson I'd learned in Double-A five years earlier about umpires and what shows up in the media.

Working the Texas League in Jackson, Mississippi, I called Kevin Mitchell out on strikes. He didn't like it, and I ejected him. Well, the next day in the Jackson paper, Mitchell was quoted extensively: "The pitch was obviously low, so I just told him there's no way you can call that pitch a strike." He went on from there to paint me in the worst possible light, like he'd been calmly discussing pitch location and I was an autocratic jerk just itching to throw him out.

He'd made up the entire conversation.

What Mitchell really said was the pitch was fucking low, I'd been fucking him all day, fuck you; so I ejected him.

But reading this in the newspaper, I thought, *I know what happened out there, and that's what I wrote in my report.*

I learned a lesson in Jackson, that it's probably best to avoid the local press and whatever bullshit gets printed. Most of the time, reporters won't bother to get the umpire's side of a story, and even if they did, it's tough to win a he said, he said between myself and a player. Guess who most readers (fans) are going to believe. If I'm tempted to track down the reporter to tell my side of what happened, it gives the story a fresh set of legs and another news cycle. Plus, as an umpire, you can rarely beat the power of the pen or the microphone.

Media's hard to avoid, especially in the big leagues, but don't let your guard down and think they're your friend. Facing reporters after games when there was a controversial call or ruling is part of your job as a crew chief. I've had situations where I explained what took place from our perspective or explained a rule and then I'd read the story and see my words taken out of context; the rule I explained would be missing a key element or only partially quoted; or I, my crew, or both would be misrepresented entirely.

In my career, there were only a handful of national and beat writers either who were introduced to me by more senior umpires as someone you can trust or whom I learned to trust on my own. John Lowe, Gerry Fraley, and Bob Elliott were all American League beat writers who come to mind. Otherwise, explain the situation, the call, and the rule if needed; answer their questions; and then hope that what is written or reported reflects your comments fairly.

But once I knew what Billy had said about me, I was interested in the back-and-forth between Richie Phillips and Dr. Brown and in what the Yankees were saying, so it was difficult to resist reading the news. Even though I played a part in all of this, it had started a few weeks earlier with Billy kicking dirt on Tim Welke. If Dr. Brown had backed up his umpires then and suspended Billy, maybe my incident wouldn't have happened.

There's also a bigger picture with all of this. As an umpire, when you see Don Denkinger miss that play in the 1985 World Series or Jimmy Joyce miss the twenty-seventh out in a perfect game in 2010, you say to yourself, *That could have been me. That can happen to anybody.* I just happened to be the guy on the hot seat as all of this was playing out.

It's the nature of the job. The next day, week, month, maybe even the next inning, somebody else could have a shithouse, and the attention would be diverted there. As an umpire, you understand that every time you walk onto the field, some fucked-up thing might happen. You might make a mistake; you might be right. But either way, it's a mess, and your name's getting dragged through the mud. You hope it doesn't happen in a huge game or the postseason, when everything is magnified to the nth degree, but you understand that it's part of the job. And when it does, you do the best you can to wade through and get out on the other side.

It got to the point where MLB commissioner Peter Ueberroth finally stepped in, announcing, "We're in a game of second-guessing. Second-guessing managers, general managers, umpires, league presidents. It's part of the game, and I encourage it to continue. But now there's talk of lawsuits being brought and names being called—'liar,' 'jerk,' things like that. I talked to both sides and told them it's got to stop and it's got to stop now."

Which it did. Billy apologized and promised that he would never kick dirt on umpires again. Richie announced that Billy could again come on the field without getting (automatically) ejected.

Publicly, Billy could not have seemed more contrite. Privately, though? Maybe not so much.

A few weeks after the Oakland series, we had the Yankees in Detroit, our first series with them since the ejection and suspension. What we couldn't know was that Billy was about to get fired.

This was the year when we were emphasizing no-stop balks. We'd started in spring training, making sure pitchers came to a full stop in their delivery, because Whitey Herzog screamed about it during the '87 World Series. He kept bitching that Twins pitchers weren't stopping and his base stealers were getting screwed. So that turned into a thing.

We were calling balks out of our asses, especially in spring training, trying to let everyone know, *Hey, this is what we're doing now, and it's going to happen all season.* Even though it actually didn't. But the first couple months of the 1988 season was a balk shit show.

So I'm at first base in what turns out to be Billy's last game ever. John Candeleria was pitching for the Yankees, and I called two balks on him that night.

The way it worked out, this was my honeymoon series: no plate game. I couldn't help but wonder how Billy was going to act, if he would bring baggage from the events in Oakland into Detroit. Not that it mattered, as I certainly didn't have any control over it. What I did have control over was myself, just going out and doing what I gotta do.

So I was right in front of the Yankees' dugout—at Tiger Stadium the dugouts were closer to first and third than home—and calling multiple balks on their starting pitcher. Both balks moved runners to second and third, and the second one also cost them an out. I was waiting for Billy to snap on that one, but I didn't hear him say anything. Let alone come out and argue.

The next day, he was gone, fired. George Steinbrenner had finally had enough. Again. This was the fifth time George fired Billy.

When I ejected Billy in Oakland that Memorial Day in 1988, I was the last one. Later I became the answer to a Trivial Pursuit question: "Name the last umpire to eject Billy Martin."

Our first series in New York after Billy's ejection (and firing) was scheduled to begin on the eighth of July. A few days before, though, Marty called and had me switch crews with Rocky Roe and report instead to Toronto. He didn't say why, and I didn't ask, as switches happen from time to time for a host of reasons.

I soon rejoined Richie's crew, and later in July we all went back to New York. It wasn't until later in the season that Marty told me the league had received a fairly specific threat: *If Dale Scott ever comes to New York again, he's leaving in a body bag.*

Which I thought was rather rude.

Fast-forward to 1994. Peter Golenbock's biography of Billy Martin came out, and I heard about a strange story that involved me. I found a Barnes & Noble and tracked down the book, in which this passage appears:

> Behind the scenes, Billy Martin wanted revenge on the umpires. In front of Mike Klepfer, Billy made a call to one of his friends and ordered him to find a mob triggerman to whack umpire Dale Scott. According to Klepfer, whoever was on the other end of the phone refused to be involved in any such thing. Some days later Billy was in Mike Klepfer's office in Binghamton, railing over the phone at his friend for not carrying out the hit on Scott. "You had every opportunity and you could have done it, and you didn't. You're supposed to be a friend of mine." In disgust, Billy hung up on him.

I don't know if that's been embellished or if anything like that happened at all.

As I'm reading this, though, I'm recalling what Marty told me about the death threat the league received. I did think, reading this, that an actual mob hit seemed a bit of a stretch. I mean, could it happen? Sure, I guess. I would have liked a second source. And this is well after Billy was gone, so he couldn't defend himself.

I'd be lying if I said this story wasn't a little unnerving, just as it was in '88 when Marty told me about the letter. Reading that passage and thinking about the letter . . . maybe someone out there actually wanted me dead? Yes, it rattled me. But at the same time, when in New York, I wasn't walking around looking over my shoulder every time I left the hotel.

Richie Garcia used to tell me that if you saw Billy off the field, at a restaurant or something, he was very cordial. Especially if it was early in the evening and he wasn't juiced up. He also told me there were times when an umpire's wife was injured in an automobile accident or when his kid needed an operation, and if Billy got wind of it, he would donate money or send a card.

Billy did have a heart.

I heard the same about Steinbrenner. As gruff as he was, as much as he yelled and screamed, Steinbrenner was also known to help umpires when something tragic happened to a family member.

So does that mean Billy Martin would never put a hit on somebody? No, it doesn't. It's just another layer of nuance. I don't *think* he would do that. But I can't prove it, one way or the other.

After getting fired in '88, Billy never managed again. He did remain under contract with the Yankees, and there were rumors that he might return to the dugout in 1990. But on Christmas Day in 1989, he and longtime friend Bill Reedy (who was probably driving Billy's pickup) left a Binghamton bar. Moments later, the truck skidded off an icy road, crashing into a culvert at the foot of the long driveway to Martin's home. An hour later Billy was pronounced dead.

12

"I Can Put Two and Two Together"

How did my parents find out I was gay? Well, that's an interesting story.

My mother . . . well, she actually told me.

In January '83 I was living with my parents and would continue to do so for three more years. I had a good friend Doug, whom I hung out with a lot, for a couple of really good reasons: he had his own place and he was gay. We weren't in a relationship, although considering the amount of time we spent together, someone might have thought that. I was just happy it wasn't my parents' house.

I had a great relationship with my parents and still do. My brother, Tim, who's four years younger, and I would tease my mother a lot; there was always a lot of banter, a lot of fun with her. At least, we thought it was fun. Both of my parents have a great sense of humor, which Tim and I inherited.

One afternoon, Mom and I were hanging out, talking about whatever, when she said, "Well, I know all about you. And what I don't know, I've got a pretty good imagination."

"Oh really, Mom?" I said. "Why don't you tell me something about me." I thought she was going to say something like, "I know you smoke pot."

"Well," she said, "I know your sexual preference is men."

Didn't see that coming! I paused. "What makes you say that?"

"I can put two and two together."

With that, I had a choice . . . deny the accusation and say she was crazy, or stop fighting the inevitable. I stopped fighting.

"Well then, you probably have a lot of questions."

And she did. We talked for the next hour. She had good questions, showing me that this was something that had been on her mind for a while, along with a few stupid questions, like "Who's on top?"

Tim knew; we'd already talked about it. And now my mom knew. So I asked her, "Does Dad know?" No, he didn't.

My dad, at the time, wasn't exactly enjoying his job and was counting down the days until he could retire. So Mom advised, "Let's not tell him, at least right now."

"That's fine," I said. "I wasn't going to tell you, either, at least not yet."

For seven years, Mom kept that juicy tidbit to herself.

Between her telling me and my coming out to my dad, I moved to Portland in '86 and met Mike. He was a roommate, which seemed legitimate to people. We rented a townhouse for about a year, and then he remained my "roommate" when I bought a house. I always had a built-in baseball excuse: "I'm on the road so much—it's just nice to have somebody there all the time who can take care of the mail," blah, blah, blah. This was a three-bedroom house. When my parents visited, Mike had a room, I had a room, and they were in the guest room.

The baseball excuse also worked with my cousin Sherri, who's a couple of years older than I am. She cut hair, and when doing mine, she was *always* trying to set me up with one of her girlfriends. I always came back with some version of, "When March comes along, I'll be gone for seven months. It's so tough to start a relationship—it's just better if I don't get involved." A semiviable excuse, at least for a while.

But the whole thing came tumbling down in 1990. Tim was living with Mike and me, so he had the guest room. My parents had come up for Thanksgiving, just for the day, along with my dad's mother, Helen. My grandmother and Mike were the only two who smoked, so they'd go out to the garage every once in a while to burn one. Mike came in after one of those cigarette breaks, called me over, and said, "You have got to tell your dad."

"Why?"

"Because sitting with your seventy-five-year-old grandmother, she said to me, 'Mike, I'm really glad that you and Dale have found each other. If you get my drift?' Your *grandmother* knows, Dale! My family, your family, everyone except your dad. You have got to tell your dad!"

A month later my parents were coming for Christmas, this time for a few nights. If we continued with this charade, they or Tim would have to get a hotel room. *Or* I could put a stop to all of this and tell my dad what's going on.

But how? When my dad retired, they moved to Sunriver, three hours away in central Oregon, on the other side of the Cascade Mountains. So I couldn't just drop by their house. I could always tell him over the phone, but instead, I thought, *I'm going to write him a letter*.

Part of me thought this was really copping out, but in hindsight it might actually have been perfect for this situation. You can absorb a letter, reread all or parts of it, contemplate what is being said without any expectation of an immediate response.

I composed my coming-out letter and then shared it with Mike and Tim, who both made suggestions. My brother did say, "He's gotta know already. There's no way he doesn't know." I felt the same way, but there had never been any hint of that from Dad. Mike and I had been together for four years now. He had attended family holidays with me, just as I had with his family. We traveled together near and far—we'd been to Australia and New Zealand earlier that year. I mean, come on. Do "just roommates" do that, for crying out loud? Yet my dad never hinted that he thought I was gay or that Mike and I were in a relationship. He never mentioned anything to my mom either.

Mike and Tim took a look at my final draft and gave me the thumbs up, so I drove to the post office. What a strange feeling of anxiety and apprehension when I dropped that sucker in the mailbox: *It's gone. There's no going back now.*

I called Mom. "I mailed it today."

But now there's this buildup as the letter takes a few days to arrive in Sunriver.

"Okay," she said, "I'll be on the lookout for it."

One thing I didn't think about when mailing the letter was the wait. It was out of my hands now, but it was not in his . . . yet. Those few days were flooded with anticipation and writer remorse; I felt like I'd set a bomb that was going to explode. I couldn't stop it, and I was totally responsible. I knew it was going to happen, yet I was not sure exactly *when*.

Then came the call from Mom. "Dale, the letter came today."

"Okay."

"Your dad, well, he's a little upset. But you'll be hearing from him." Click.

Oh God, what's going on.

I didn't hear anything else. He didn't call me; I didn't call him. For four days, crickets. Then in the mail, a brief note: "I got your letter. You're my son, and I love you. I just need a little time."

Which was fair.

As much as you think somebody must know, that doesn't mean they *do* know. Or even if they do know, or suspect, they might still need to think about what just happened, wrestle with what acknowledgment means.

My mom had two sons before she married my father, but I was my dad's first child. Growing up, you naturally dream of your kid going to college, your kid getting married, your kid having kids, and you having grandkids. All of a sudden, *those things are not happening.* Now everything's going in a completely different direction. It takes time for someone to deal with this new reality.

Of course, some never do. Whether it's religion or their own native homophobia, whatever. But that wasn't the case with my dad. There was about a two-and-a-half-week stretch that was uncomfortable for me, when that short letter was literally all I heard from him.

My parents were coming to the house on Christmas Eve, which would be the first time I talked to my father since I dropped that letter on him. Again, the anticipation. Mike, Tim, myself . . . none of us were sure of what would happen when they arrived.

Finally the doorbell rang. I opened the front door, gave Mom a big hug, and then stepped aside so she could come in. Then I turned to my father, who, without hesitation, gave me a huge bear hug. Nothing was said, and there were more hugs all around, including Mike. Just like that, we were now a family of five.

To this day, it's nothing my dad and I really discuss. Not that he doesn't understand. It's just never seemed like something that needed explaining. Like my mom's sister Dorothy said a few years later, when Mike and I visited her and her husband, James, in Potter Valley, "It's just the way it is."

For me, those few weeks were tough. I thought he'd call shortly after receiving my letter. But as my mom told me later, my dad just needed some time to process the end of those dreams and goals he'd had for me since I was born, thirty years earlier. But ever since that Christmas Eve bear hug, everything's been great with both my parents, and Mike's just as much family as Tim and I.

I don't know if coming out in general is as difficult now. When I talk with a younger generation of men, some of them came out when they were fourteen or fifteen, some even earlier, and don't understand how someone might think negatively about two guys getting married. But gay marriage blew people's minds twenty, thirty years ago.

You also have to put into context what was going on just a couple of years after I came out to myself in 1979. On June 5, 1981, a few days before I first took the field as a professional umpire, AIDS was reported for the first time, with five cases in the United States.

Soon more and more cases were being diagnosed, with a common thread: gay men. So began the stigma, as gay men became modern-day pariahs. Already shunned, now we were also feared. Initially, scientists and researchers didn't know how the virus spread, and misinformation reigned. People were afraid of catching "the gay disease" simply by using a hand towel, a bar of soap, or a hairbrush that had been touched by a gay person.

This was the backdrop as I started my professional career. The fear of being outed just added a deadly layer. Not only would that information likely impede my chance of advancing through the Minors, let alone reaching the big leagues, but now I might well be completely ostracized, as nobody would work with a partner who not only was gay but now might kill you just by being in the same locker room. My obsession to protect my secret was magnified many times over.

More than a few times, I would be hanging with other umpires in spring training or other settings and hear a crude "fag" or "AIDS" comment (or "joke"). As I'd been doing by then for many years, I did not show any emotion on the outside, but inside I was sad and hurt.

Being gay in the eighties and early nineties was fraught with fear, anxiety, grief, depression, and anger. Having finally come out to myself and, away from baseball, being true to who I was and the freedom that brought, I was still like every gay man, in the closet or out, in facing the reality that having sex could literally kill me.

In the summer of 1979, I discovered not only who I was but also a new community and lifestyle. I finally knew and hung out with people with whom

I didn't need to play the game or hide my true self. I also experienced a new sexual freedom that was both liberating and exciting. But as we got deeper into the new decade, that sexual freedom turned from exciting to a game of Russian roulette.

During those years, I lost several friends and acquaintances. When I read or saw a story about the devastation this horrific disease was inflicting on gay men—men who'd been young and healthy and with so much life in front of them and who were now suddenly dead or given just weeks or months to live—I recognized that there, but for the grace of God, went I.

13

TK

I always used to say that if every manager was Tom Kelly, it would make our lives a hell of a lot easier. All those years that he managed the Twins, he was only run five times. Naturally, I got him once. But he was great with umpires.

First of all, he didn't allow his players to be cheap-shot artists or bitch all the time.

Jack Morris was a prick with us, and he was a prick with his teammates. I mean, if a guy made an error or overthrew a cutoff guy or whatever, he would show the guy up with a gesture or some other obvious body language. Of course, he also had no problem letting umpires know about their strike zone when he wasn't happy. The guy could pitch, no doubt, but was not a fun guy to work. When Morris pitched for the Twins, though? He was actually a pretty good citizen. Because of Tom Kelly.

I remember one time when I ran Chuck Knoblauch in the Metrodome. The Twins were losing, 5–2, when he led off the bottom of the ninth, and I called him out on a close play at first. So he yelled and screamed a little bit on his way back to the dugout, on the third-base side. I'm standing by first base minding my own business, when all of a sudden I heard someone yell from the Twins' dugout. I looked over and clearly heard Knoblauch yell, "YOU SUCK." As I wrote that night in my report, "Knoblauch threw a wad of gum toward the field, and then with his right arm and right hand made an obscene gesture with his middle finger toward me. I ejected him. He yelled 'you guys suck' and then left."

It happened quickly, and Kelly didn't come out to complain. So the official scorer apparently didn't even notice the ejection, because it doesn't show up in my ejection log on the website Retrosheet.org (which lists virtually every other detail of my MLB career). I have a copy of the umpire report I submitted to the league.

After the game finished, we were barely back in our locker room before the phone started ringing. It was Tom Kelly asking for me. "Dale," he said, "I just want to apologize. That was absolutely uncalled for, and it's not something I believe in."

Another time, we were in Cleveland, and Minnesota's LaTroy Hawkins came in from the bullpen late in the game, with the Twins ahead by a run. I had the plate, and Hawkins walked a couple of guys and gave up the lead. At the end of the inning, Hawkins, while walking off the field, looked at me and yelled, "*You're a fucking piece of shit.*" You know, like I've never heard that before. I ejected him.

Again, I had just barely gotten in the locker room after the game when Kelly called to apologize, saying that what Hawkins did was uncalled for, et cetera.

The next night, we were sitting around before the game, and there was a knock on the door.

It was LaTroy Hawkins.

He came in, apologized for his actions the night before, saying he was truly sorry, and left. When we walked onto the field for the game, Kelly came out with the lineups and asked me, "Did LaTroy come by the locker room?"

"Yeah, he did."

"That was bullshit what he did to you last night," Kelly said. "I told him to go and apologize."

"I appreciate that," I said.

"It was kind of funny," Kelly said. "He comes back and says, 'You know, I went over there, and they're all sitting around in their underwear, playing cards and watching TV. They're really just regular guys.'"

But that's the kind of guy Tom Kelly was.

Oh, here's one more. We were at SkyDome (now Rogers Centre) in Toronto, and Kelly's pitcher threw one down near the dirt. The batter started to swing, and I ruled he checked it. But there was a question about whether maybe the bat just nicked the baseball, and I hear Tom yelling, "Dale! Dale!" and he's slapping his hands together. "Foul tip?"

I looked over and said, "No tip. I didn't hear anything, Tom."

Kelly fired back, "Ah, doesn't matter. It was a horseshit pitch anyway."

He was a guy you enjoyed working, because he was fair.

Now, Tom *would* argue. In September, because they shared the Metrodome with the Minnesota Gophers and it took four hours to convert from baseball to football, the Twins would play some Saturday games at eleven in the morning. Durwood Merrill told me a story about one of those morning games, when he had second base. In the top of the first, there was a close play at first: *Safe!* Kelly came out and argued mildly and then ran back to his dugout.

Right after that, the runner who was called safe tried to steal second. Durwood called him safe. Well, here came Kelly again. It was five pitches into the game, and this is his second trip out. Then, between the mound and second base, he looked at Durwood and the first-base umpire and said, "Jesus Christ, guys, did we start this game too early for you? Did you just get your wake-up calls?"

But one of the funnier arguments I ever had was one of those where the manager comes out and acts like he's pissed off (even though he's not, really) because he's trying to either protect his player or just fire up the team. It was a Monday night in Oakland, when Oakland and Minnesota were both in the American League West, and both teams were really good. With no score in the third, the Twins had Roy Smalley at second when Steve Lombardozzi, Minnesota's second baseman, laid down a sacrifice bunt.

It was a perfect bunt, and the only place A's catcher Terry Steinbach could go was first base. So he picked the ball up and threw it. But Lombardozzi was not in the running lane, and the ball hit him between the shoulders. I called interference. So Lombardozzi was out, and Smalley had to return to second.

Lombardozzi started screaming, jumping up and down. Out came Tom, and I was thinking that this was going to be a good argument since, with interference calls, players and managers usually go batshit crazy, because they don't know the rule.

Kelly got Lombardozzi off the field, so now it was just me and him, about forty-five feet up the first-base line. And if you were watching us, with him gesturing and yelling, it looked like he was chewing my ass. Meanwhile, he's saying, "Jesus Christ, Dale! I can't believe it! I got a guy, puts down a perfect fucking bunt, and what does he do? He can't run in the running lane! And what do you do? You do your fucking job, and you call him out! So now instead of a runner at third and one out, what do I have? I have nothing, because you made a great fucking call!"

Now I start to laugh, so he waves his finger in my face and says, "You can't laugh! You can't laugh! The camera's on us! You *cannot* laugh!" I suppress my smile while he says, "So now I gotta come out here like a raving maniac, because my guy doesn't know the difference between running right here"—now he's pointing down at the lines showing the running lane—"to right here," like he's showing *me* how I blew the call.

Tom finished by saying, "So now I gotta run back to the dugout and look like a freaking idiot," and off he goes.

After the game, Denkinger said, "Jesus Christ, I've never seen Tom like that. Why didn't you run him?"

"You have no idea," I replied. Then I told Don and the other guys what Tom had said, and we laughed our asses off.

You enjoyed working games when Kelly managed. When he thought you were wrong, he would argue, but he did it in a professional way. He was fair and funny and rarely got ejected. Plus, he wouldn't let his team, including guys like Jack Morris, beat up on umpires. He reined them in, made them play baseball, and did his own arguing when he had to.

Again, that was Tom Kelly.

Kelly's first full season as a manager was 1987, my second season. That season, he got ejected once, by Rocky Roe. He didn't get run again until 1990, by Jimmy Joyce. Then he went *eight years and three months* until his next ejection . . . by yours truly.

September 15, 1998. Seattle at Minnesota, and it was an ugly game.

Heading into the seventh, the Mariners were leading, 6–4. With one out, the Mariners had scored once and had a couple of runners on base. Kelly brought in "Everyday Eddie" Guardado from the bullpen. A few years later, Guardado became an All-Star closer. This was not an All-Star season. Or game.

There was a sac fly and then a couple of singles. Guardado wasn't overjoyed by my plate work, and he looked in after a couple of pitches I balled.

Then came Ken Griffey Jr., with two runners on. Guardado threw a 2-2 pitch to Griffey that was outside—really wasn't all that close. But catcher Javier Valentin had set up outside, so he barely moved his glove. I called a ball, and Valentin made a loud *Ooohh* sound, as if he couldn't believe the call.

I'll never forget it. Griffey smiled, looked at Valentin, and said, "That's outside, man. C'mon."

The Twins really wanted that pitch.

Griffey then turned Guardado's next pitch into his fifty-second home run of the season. It wasn't one of Griffey's usual blasts, instead just scraping the top of the fence in right field. But it was enough to get Guardado upset. He started screaming at me well before Junior got to second base, and I ran him before Junior scored.

Then Kelly came flying out. And of course, he was arguing balls and strikes. He was pissed, and he thought I missed that 2-2 pitch. I ejected him too.

That's what we might call a "situational ejection." They don't like that 2-2 pitch, but if Junior strikes out on the next pitch, they're grumbling but still in the game. Suddenly, Griffey jacks one, and the score's 12–4? Guess what—someone's gonna go. Situational.

Hell, if I missed it, I'd admit it. I looked at the pitch after the game, and it was clearly outside. This was just one of those things; they really wanted it badly and didn't get it.

So that's my Tom Kelly ejection. He went eight-plus years without one. Then I got him in 1998, Durwood got him in 1999, and Mike Everitt got him in 2000, before he went through all of 2001 without getting number six before retiring.

Manager arguments usually fall into one of these categories: (a) they were really pissed off at you, either throughout the entire game or because of a particular call; (b) they're just out there to protect their player, because they don't want their player ejected since the player's usually more important than the manager; or (c) they're trying to fire up their team or the crowd, because they're on a losing streak or they've been playing like shit or they just gave up six runs to nearly blow a seven-run lead or whatever.

Yeah, they're pissed off but a lot of times not necessarily at you. They're just using you as a vehicle to do something else. Once, I had an argument with Terry Collins when he was managing the Angels; he came out and put on a hell of a show and wanted me to eject him. But he wasn't arguing the play at all. He was actually telling me how horseshit his team was.

Those are fun, but you don't have a lot of those, where they just flat-out tell you they want to get run. A lot of times, a manager comes out and argues just to protect a player or to show the team he's got their back. I was involved in some epic arguments with managers, though. As we'll see a bit later.

14

Hardly the First

This isn't new news, but I was not the first gay umpire in the big leagues.

One of my instructors at umpire school was Nick Bremigan, who'd been on the American League staff since 1974. Sort of the league's rules guru, Nick was hilarious, and everybody on the staff loved him. Everybody on the staff also knew he was gay, and Nick lived with his partner in Dallas.

Early in my career, I was fortunate to work forty-seven games with Nick. When I first came up in '86 and was bouncing around, if someone asked me who I'd be working with next and I mentioned Bremigan, they'd say something like, "He's quite a character. You know he likes the guys a little better than the gals." But nobody ever said that negatively, more just like it was common knowledge.

I think his gaydar must have gone off with me. Talking to him one night, I told Nick about my spring-training trip to Key West, and he asked why I went there.

"Well," I said, "I've never been there before. I'm from the West Coast, and I've heard all about it. Just wanted to check it out."

"Ah, so you've got all of Florida, and you want to go to Key West?"

At that time, of course, Key West was considered a sort of gay mecca.

Some nights, he would go out with the crew. But he had his own places to go—not necessarily gay places, but his own holes in the wall—where he would have a few beers and a bite to eat. I think sometimes that was because his partner was in town with him. Of course he didn't advertise that.

One night between innings in Baltimore, Nick asked, "Hey, you going to Sabatino's tonight?"

"I don't know."

"Well, I've got this place next to Little Italy. You want to join me?"

Yeah, sure.

Later on, I found out he didn't invite many guys when he'd go off on his own. But he did invite me a few times. And once, when his partner was in town visiting, Nick invited me out, and he introduced us. Nick never said exactly who he *was*; he just said this guy was his housemate or something. Obviously, he had me figured out for sure, and we both knew what was going on. But we never talked about it. In 1989 Nick was in Palm Springs for spring training, when the California Angels still trained there. His last game was scheduled for March 28, but without informing the league, he had Mark Johnson take his place. After working on the twenty-seventh, he flew home to Dallas, where, in the early morning hours of March 28, he suffered a massive heart attack and died. He was six days short of his forty-fourth birthday.

Marty Springstead, alerted by a reporter about Nick's death in Dallas, said that was impossible because Nick was in Palm Springs. Marty called Mark Johnson to find out what was going on and learned that, indeed, it was possible.

Here's a funny story. Nick was bald and had this pathetic rug he would wear. In Seattle, Matt Walcott has been the umpires' clubhouse manager for nearly forty years now; he's the one who's stuck with rubbing up all the baseballs before every game.

When Nick went into the shower, he would just lift up his mop, clean his head, and then put it back. Well, when Matt was in his first or second year, only fourteen or fifteen years old, he didn't know anything about hairpieces. He just thought Nick had really ugly hair. So one day, he was walking by the showers, restocking towels, when he saw Nick pulling his mop up for a cleaning. Matt just about shit himself.

But Nick was a great guy, and everybody both liked him *and* knew he was gay.

That didn't make me more comfortable about *my* situation. Guys liked Nick, but he had been around for a while, whereas I was still extremely early in my career. I was a rookie in '86, of course, and then in '87 I had that disastrous season. Quite frankly, I was still trying to get established in the league and didn't want to throw up a rainbow flag for anybody who might be looking for one.

That meant that keeping my secret had become a constant thing. Night after night, I was going out with the guys and not exchanging numbers or getting a date. I was getting hit on, and I could flirt with the best of them. I just never closed the deal. Guys would get suspicious, so I had to come up with believable excuses.

I can't tell you how many "cousins" I had around the country or how many "friends from Oregon" who just happened to move to (fill in the city) whom I would supposedly meet up with after the game. These admittedly weak excuses covered me for a while. But let's be honest—it doesn't take a rocket scientist to figure out that something wasn't quite right. I needed a better, more convincing cover, one that would last awhile.

Then, during spring training in 1987, it hit me. My future husband Mike's sister Mary was a flight attendant for America West Airlines in Phoenix. She was beautiful and a year younger than me. They knew I had a roommate in Portland named Mike, so I could just say that I'd met his sister and we would get together at times to, you know, do what comes naturally—or should I say, naturally if I weren't gay.

A fun, sexy flight attendant? What a perfect beard!

First, I asked Mike what he thought of my idea. He loved it! The next step was to call Mary and see if she would play the lead role in this charade.

Mary was more than game; she thought the whole thing was hilarious. We came up with a backstory about how Mike and I became roommates, along with how, when, and where Mary and I would get together without Mike and his family finding out. After we concocted our fake history, Mary agreed to meet me at Frank's Friendly Tavern in Tempe, where umpires would hang out practically every night.

It couldn't have worked out better. Like I said, Mary is a beautiful woman. Long dark hair, brown eyes, sexy smile. When she walked in, everything stopped, with an audible wow from a couple of the guys. Then when I kissed her on the cheek and guided her to her seat, the guys' jaws dropped! *Who in the hell is this gorgeous woman, and more importantly, how in the hell does Dale know her?*

I introduced her to everyone and ordered beers. Billy Joe Speck, one of my favorites since we'd met at Bradenton after umpire school, took me aside and asked, "Who is this again?"

"My roommate's sister, Mary," I said.

"And, um . . . so how well do you know her?"

"Very well, Billy Joe. *Very well.*"

"Wow! Good for you, Scotty!"

Meanwhile, Mary was having a blast, flirting with and getting the attention of five or six amped up (and jealous) umpires, all the while knowing she didn't have to play defense, so to speak, since she was with me.

From then on, when the guys and I would get back from a night out, or when I would leave the group early, I had a ready-made excuse: Mary. Or better yet, there were nights when I wouldn't go out with the guys at all, because I was "going to Mary's." That meant I could hit a few of the boy bars and, if I got lucky, get back in the morning, having "stayed the night at her place."

I met Dave Pallone way back in 1983, when I was in the Texas League with Terry Mann. Terry and I had an off day, and Pallone was working on Paul Runge's crew in the Astrodome. We had no idea which crew was there; we just knew there was a game. Typically, you'd go to the box office and ask somebody to call the umpires' room, and usually they'd say, "Oh yeah, come on down."

So when I found out that Pallone was on the crew, I was like, "Oh, shit," because he was considered a scab. He had come up from the Minors in '79 and worked during the umpires' strike. When I was in the Cal League the year before, Tschida and I had gone to a Giants game, and Fred Brocklander, another scab, was on the crew with Lee Weier, Eddie Montague, and Randy Marsh. Those guys treated Brocklander like dog shit in the locker room after the game.

That was very uncomfortable for Tim and me. Especially for me, because the year before, when I was in Yuma working spring training, Fred had taken a couple of us Minor League guys out for drinks. So I knew him and liked him, and now I had to see this.

So when I saw Pallone was on the crew, I started thinking, *Oh fuck, the locker room's gonna be shit.* Because I'd seen it before.

We got to the locker room, and Runge—one of the biggest hard-liners in the union, union president on and off for years, and one of the biggest pricks when it came to the strike stuff—was treating Pallone like one of the guys. They were all laughing and joking, which blew my mind.

Back in Yuma, the four of us working the Padres Minor League camp went out with Dick Nelson, our supervisor, to the immortal Hensley's Beef, Beans, and Beer. During the '79 strike, Nelson had worked games; as management, he had to. Runge came in with his wife and another couple, and they sat across the room. I'd met him recently, but since Hensley's was packed and I didn't want to interrupt his meal, we just nodded hello.

Well, the next day, I saw him at the ballpark and said, "Hey, Paul. How are you doing?"

"Don't fucking talk to me," he growled. "If you can't get up and say hello to us while you're sitting with that scab, I don't need to talk to you now."

Whoa.

First of all, Dick Nelson technically wasn't a scab. Second, he was my boss.

That was the first time it was really in my face, all the '79 union crap that was going on. And this was only two years removed from that. But then in '83, Pallone was with Runge, and they acted like everything was fine.

That was the first time I met Dave. I had no idea he was gay.

Later, in 1986, I worked one or two spring-training games with him. Still no idea.

Then came 1988. First, Pallone was involved in a shithouse with Pete Rose (who got suspended for a month). Then in September, he was implicated in an upstate New York sex ring involving teenage boys. He was cleared in that, but that was the impetus for the National League to get rid of him, which they did.

Pallone's book came out in 1990, and I was very interested to read it. Great title: *Behind the Mask: My Double Life in Baseball*. I remember one part where he wrote about having sex with a player, and I thought, *Ah, I don't buy that*. Could it happen? Sure. But I just didn't see it.

Mike and I were in Los Angeles, and a friend who lived there asked me, "Hey, do you know Dave Pallone? He's in town for a book signing."

"Yeah, I know him."

"So do I. I'll see if he can stop by for a drink."

Mike and I went to the Mother Lode, a favorite bar for the boys of West Hollywood since 1979. After we'd been there for about thirty minutes, in strolled Pallone. If he didn't already know I was gay, he certainly did now. We talked for a couple of hours, having a few drinks while sharing war stories. Dave had a lot of sour grapes about getting fired and how that whole thing came about.

It really wasn't until the late 1990s or early 2000s that my defense mechanisms were coming down because (a) guys were approaching *me* and telling *me* they were fine with it and (b) it became more and more apparent that guys had figured me out earlier than I thought they had. You know, it's not brain surgery when your "roommate" goes with you on a trip to Australia.

A lot of people have told me—not necessarily umpires, but people like my cousin Sherri, for example—"You know, there were times when I thought you might be gay, but with your personality, it just didn't make sense."

And I would say, "Well, you haven't seen me late at night after a few Crown Royals."

Even Mike laughs, though: "You think you had all these people buffaloed until then? C'mon."

I mean, no. Not all of them.

But some, definitely.

I worked with Dave Phillips in '96, '97, '98, and before that, in '93 and '94. Later I heard that Davey and his wife, Sharon, were having dinner with Ron Kulpa and his wife one time when Ron said something about me being gay. Davey was surprised. "Is he gay, really?"

Sharon then scolded her husband, "David, I told you that ten years ago, and you wouldn't believe me."

But there were guys on the staff like that. It didn't really matter what they saw or heard; unless I told them, they just couldn't or wouldn't believe it. Partly because I didn't fit their stereotype and partly because they didn't *want* to believe it.

When I came out in 2014, some media people contacted Dave Pallone for a statement. At some point he called me, and reading between the lines, I thought he seemed bitter about the positive reaction I was receiving, which was quite different from what he had experienced roughly twenty-five years earlier.

Of course, 1988 was a very different time than 2014.

I've read various statements from him since I came out, and a few years ago he called about a project he was doing. When Mike and I met him in 1990, he sounded cocky and bitter about seemingly everything, but since 2014 he's always been complimentary about me. I don't have any reason not to like Dave, but he's got the sort of personality I'm usually not very cohesive with.

15

"What Do You Mean, Colorful?"

After Mike and I found each other in 1986, my first AL off-season flew by (granted, off-seasons always did). I kept trying to prepare Mike for *our* first season together (i.e., the reality that once I left for spring training in March, I would be gone for weeks at a time). Since the night we met, it had been nothing but fun and games. We made trips to the Oregon coast and spent weekends in Seattle and San Francisco. I really wanted him to understand just how different things would be in the spring.

Even knowing what was ahead, once the season started, the reality seemed harsh (it always did). I flew home on off days when it made sense, but living in the Pacific Northwest limited those opportunities.

For example, I might have a Sunday day game in Toronto, Monday off, and a Tuesday night game in Baltimore. Sure, I could rush to the Toronto airport, fly to Chicago, connect there for a Portland flight, and if everything went well—quick game with no weather delays or extra innings; getting through ballpark and regular traffic to the airport in time; getting through U.S. Customs relatively quickly; my Chicago flight not getting delayed by weather or a mechanical issue; the inbound connecting aircraft to Chicago also not getting delayed, so that my flight to Portland would leave on time, without *it* having a weather or mechanical delay in Chicago—land at PDX at 11:00 or 11:30 local time. Of course, my body would think it was two in the morning.

Then, to reach Baltimore for my Tuesday night game, I would have to take a red-eye from Portland twenty-four hours later, leaving Monday night at 11:30, connecting in Chicago and arriving in Baltimore Tuesday morning around 10:00—of course, hoping to avoid all those possible delays. Then I'd still have to check into my hotel, assuming the room was ready, and sleep a few hours before going to the ballpark. Oh, and guess what. You might also have the plate that night, and you damn well better not miss a single pitch.

That's why it wouldn't make sense.

A couple of times during the season, Mike met me on the road for a few days. Seattle, San Francisco, and Chicago were all fun destinations, reached easily from Portland. But I was so in the closet when living my baseball life that I would take what now seem like ridiculous and (frankly) demeaning precautions when Mike joined me during the season.

Staying at the crew hotel in Chicago, Mike and I would take separate elevators and walk through different sides of the lobby, just in case one of my partners was around. I didn't want any of them to see me with Mike; I didn't want to introduce him, explain who he was.

We would order room service, and when the food arrived, Mike would hide in the 'bathroom so the server wouldn't know it was two guys sharing a room with one bed. Most of the American League umpires stayed at the same hotels, and so a lot of the hotel staff knew us. One time when Mike and I were playing this stupid hide-the-boyfriend game—as we had done too many times before—we'd just started eating when there was a knock at the door.

"Room service. I forgot to deliver your rolls."

"Just a moment," I yelled, as Mike jumped up and shut himself in the bathroom again while I let the server back in. It was obvious we had begun eating, with poured wine and several bites off the plate, yet once again the bathroom was occupied. He delivered the dinner rolls and gave me a some-what puzzled look on his way out. Mike came back out, and we both started laughing at the absurdity of the situation. What the hell were we doing?

Mike understood why I insisted on this ridiculous charade and said he didn't mind. But it bothered me a lot. I was treating him, both of us, as a second-class citizen. It felt wrong because it *was* wrong. That is how terri-fying I found the thought of having my crew, or anyone else in the baseball world, finding out I was gay.

I vowed to Mike and myself that I would never do that to us again. I was taking a stand!

Except I didn't. For several years, Mike simply didn't join me on the road during the baseball season.

In 1993 I was assigned my first special event, the All-Star Game in Baltimore. I had the left-field line, working with crew chief Jim McKean and Mike Reilly from the American League and Bob Davidson, Mark Hirschbeck, and Gary Darling from the National League.

It would also be the coming-out party for Mike and me . . . sort of.

Gary Darling actually knew my personal situation already, because he had stayed at our house. I'd known Gary since the summer of 1980, a few months before I went to umpire school. He was working in the Northwest League, and I was living in Eugene. His partner Bill Spooner was sick and couldn't work, so Gary's partner for the game in Eugene was Ken Larson, the head of our local association. A bunch of us came to the game just to watch Larson work the bases (and he had an ejection, which was awesome).

After the game, we all went to the locker room, where I met Gary. I told him I was going to umpire school in December, and we talked about what I should expect. Later we taught together at umpire school in '84, in San Bernardino. After that, we used to have umpire camps during the off-season, up and down the West Coast, including in Portland, when Gary would stay with Mike and me. We never actually talked about it, but it would have been obvious. You know, since Mike and I were in the same bedroom.

But I didn't assume that Gary had told anyone on the staff.

I never considered not bringing Mike to the All-Star Game. But I was trying to figure out, *Okay, what's my best scenario here?* I was still very much trying to guard that part of my life, and with the exception of Gary, I don't think anyone on the All-Star crew had figured it out. I don't think they even thought about it. Yet in the back of my mind, I was thinking, *Well, if this whole thing implodes, at least I'll be out of the closet.* But I wasn't ready for that.

So while I never thought, *Well, I just can't bring Mike to this event*, I did think, *Okay, what's my story here?* Because this was the first time I would actually be in the position of introducing Mike to my colleagues. I was very cognizant about having a story, no matter how outlandish that story might seem.

I arranged and paid for all the flights and hotel rooms for Mike and both of our parents, and because I was working the game, I was given tickets for everyone to the many events. I didn't go into details with my crew and others;

I just told everyone my roommate was coming, along with our parents. I figured they could decide for themselves what that meant, while knowing it was risky . . . since it wouldn't exactly take a brain surgeon to figure things out.

But I wasn't going to work my first special event and *not* share the experience with Mike and our parents.

The All-Star Game essentially serves as Major League Baseball's annual celebration. Unlike the World Series, where you don't know where it's going to be played until shortly before it starts, the All-Star Game is awarded years in advance. So MLB has plenty of time to plan the huge party where league and team officials, participants, sponsors, and the families and friends of all those groups can celebrate baseball.

And what a party it was, held that year at the Maryland Science Center in Baltimore's Inner Harbor. The attractions included several open bars with top-shelf liquor and food for days—including one station where Mike's dad, Dick, hung out for half the party, eating oysters the moment they were shucked—all while the Naval Academy Band from nearby Annapolis entertained the guests.

As the festivities wound down, the umpiring crew, along with all our family and guests, took a leisurely fifteen-minute walk to Sabatino's Restaurant in Little Italy. They set up a private room for our group, which numbered around twenty-five.

Along the way, Mike and I separated a little from everyone else. I wanted to privately mention something to him, and this seemed like a good time. Or maybe an *opportune* time, since the topic I was about to broach didn't really have a "good" time.

Not wanting us outed, I felt I should remind him to not get too . . . umm . . . colorful.

"What do you mean, colorful?"

"Well, you've had a few drinks," I said, "and when you're loosened up, you sometimes can get, you know, colorful. Flamboyant."

I braced for his response, already questioning my judgement in bringing this up.

"Why would you say that? You think I'm going to embarrass you? I can't believe you would say that!" With that, Mike quickened his pace to walk ahead of me. End of discussion.

We arrived at Sabby's, with our private dining room well stocked with beer, wine, and a buffet of their mouthwatering food. It wasn't long before the guys naturally drifted to one side of the room, conversing about golf, sports, the game the next day—you know, exactly what you'd expect—while the ladies were chatting away on the other side of the room.

I glanced around to find Mike, hoping he'd calmed down by now.

Surrounded by the ladies, Mike was holding court. He was sharing catering tips, and rather . . . *colorfully*. "I learned that from Martha Stewart . . ." he was explaining when, in midsentence, he caught my expression and suddenly said, a whole octave lower, ". . . if you're into that kind of thing." He then excused himself and sheepishly wandered over to me. "Okay, you were right. Maybe a bit too colorful." To this day, we love sharing that moment.

Mike has always been there for me. He doesn't follow baseball or sports in general. He does have an uncanny ability to read and understand people. During my career, there were times when I was dealing with some kind of adversity—with the league office, someone I was working with, the union, or just the usual ups and downs of umpiring at the highest level in the unforgiving media fishbowl—especially early in my career, when nobody seemed to believe in me. Including, at times, myself.

I would vent whatever was worrying me, and it felt good to talk to somebody. Early on, I didn't expect Mike to have much insight into whatever I was ranting about. I figured this would be like him, as an artist, asking me for advice about the nuance of watercolors versus oil or what local gallery would best highlight his strengths as a painter. *Um, I know the infield fly rule . . . Does that help at all? No?*

But time after time, Mike surprised or amazed me with his almost zen-like understanding of people, no matter who they were or what they did.

He was, and remains, my rock. When I worked the plate for a big game, regular or postseason, I needed to hear his voice before leaving my hotel room to meet the crew and head to the ballpark. So I would always call to say hello and get a quick (but much-needed) confidence-building pep talk from him. I'm not superstitious, but I didn't feel right if I didn't get ahold of Mike before every one of those big games.

Okay, so maybe I'm a *little* superstitious.

My experience in baseball, my career, my life, would have been much different, and certainly not for the better, if Mike had not walked into a nearly empty bar on that Monday night in October.

Since right after we met, Mike and I have had an adage we say to each other. It's short and it's simple and it's not something most people would find intense or insightful.

But to Mike and me, it is profound.

"We're a team. The best."

And we still are. Thirty-five years and counting.

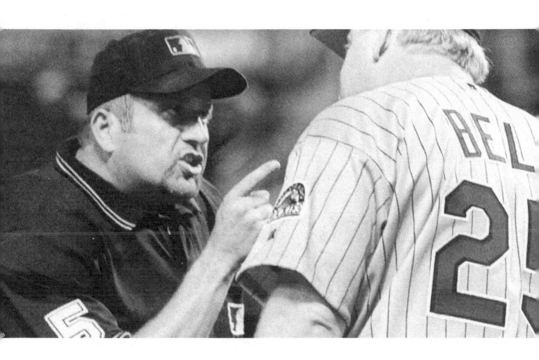

1. Colorado manager Buddy Bell getting ejected arguing balls and strikes with me, July 12, 2001, Arlington, Texas. Courtesy of Dale Scott.

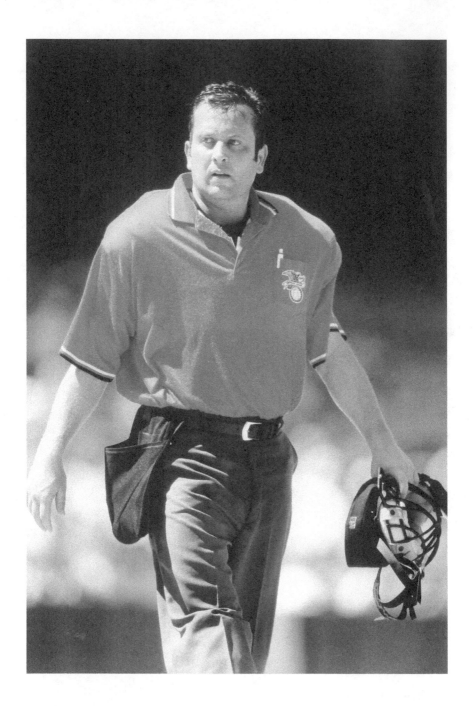

2. Me working a game behind the plate in July 1996, wearing a red shirt that was part of the AL uniform until 2000. Courtesy of Dale Scott.

3. My dad and a three-year-old me, circa 1962, Eugene, Oregon. Courtesy of Jess Scott.

4. Climbing the Harbor Bridge, March 19, 2014, Sydney, Australia. Courtesy of Dale Scott.

5. Playing the hits on KBDF, circa 1978, Eugene, Oregon. Courtesy of Jess Scott.

6. The Sheldon High School prom with Leslea, June 4, 1977, Eugene, Oregon. Courtesy of Jess Scott.

7. Flying with Mike to Australia, March 15, 2014, LAX. Courtesy of Dale Scott.

8. Sharing midinning laughs with Ken Kaiser and Ken Griffey Jr., July 11, 1990, at the Seattle Kingdome. *The News Tribune* (Tacoma WA).

9. Billy Martin's final ejection, May 30, 1988, Oakland, California. Courtesy of Dale Scott.

10. My parents, Jess and Betty Scott, 2019, Fairfield, California. Courtesy of Jess Scott.

11. Me ejecting Northwest League Medford manager Brad Fischer, August 14, 1981, Eugene, Oregon. Courtesy of Jess Scott.

12. Making the Oregon "O" with Dan Iassogna, June 4, 2014, Kansas City, Missouri. Denny Medley / Random Photography.

13. Working Lou Piniella's last game, with Dan Iassogna, Mark Wegner, Jerry Meals, and Bobby Cox, August 22, 2010, Chicago, Illinois. Courtesy of Dale Scott.

14. Game Three of the 2001 World Series with President Bush, October 30, 2001, New York. Photo by Eric Draper. Courtesy of Dale Scott.

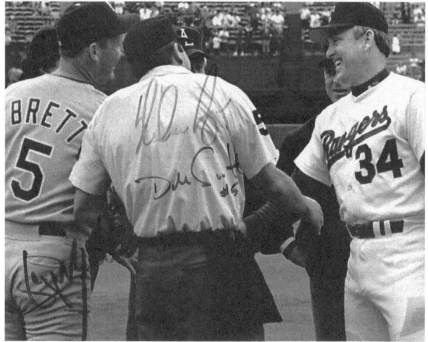

15. Opposite top: Nolan Ryan and George Brett's twenty-year postretirement reunion, June 2, 2013, Arlington, Texas. Courtesy of Dale Scott.

16. Opposite bottom: Nolan Ryan and George Brett's last game, October 3, 1993, Arlington, Texas. Courtesy of Dale Scott.

17. Above: A safe play at second, Astros at Diamondbacks, August 29, 2009, Phoenix, Arizona. Courtesy of Dale Scott.

18. With Sal Fernandez, June 25, 2019, Anaheim, California. Courtesy of Dale Scott.

19. Shilo, Tim, Dale, and Jess Scott, September 29, 2018, Berkeley, California. Courtesy of Dale Scott.

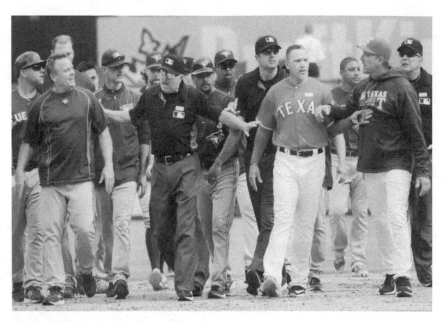

20. A José Bautista–Rougned Odor brawl led to several ejections of Blue Jays and Rangers, May 15, 2016, Arlington, Texas. Courtesy of Dale Scott.

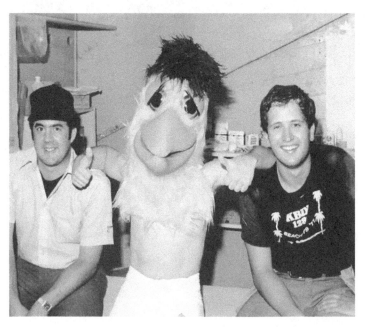

21. Tim Tschida, the San Diego Chicken, and me, August 28, 1982, San Jose, California. Courtesy of Dale Scott.

22. Tim Tschida, the Moose, and me, August 5, 2005, Seattle, Washington. Photo by Matt Wolcott. Courtesy of Dale Scott.

23. At umpire school. *Pictured left to right*: Mike Winters, Danny Toal, J. B. Hance, and me, January 1981, San Bernardino, California. Courtesy of Dale Scott.

24. Mike and I on our wedding day, November 2, 2013, Palm Springs, California. Courtesy of Dale Scott.

25. Wedding day selfie, November 2, 2013, Palm Springs, California. Courtesy of Dale Scott.

16

Nolan and George

Among the surreal things about becoming a big league umpire is suddenly finding yourself among players you'd followed, admired, and maybe even idolized when you were growing up.

One great example is Nolan Ryan, whom I actually worked quite a bit: eight plate games in the five years he pitched for the Rangers. Texas played at the Old Erector Set (as we used to call Arlington Stadium, which is now two stadiums ago). From June through August, instead of day games on Sunday, they would schedule first pitch for 6:05 p.m., because of the brutal Texas heat. And every time they could, the Rangers would start Ryan on Sundays, not only because he would be throwing out of the shadows, but because when he pitched, they sold a lot more tickets, with a big walk-up crowd.

The Rangers would also sell those dead center-field seats that were normally covered. So you have the setting sun and the tough shadows, plus the hitter's background is filled with people who are wearing white shirts and moving around. The first couple of innings were brutal, trying to pick up the ball. For both me and the hitters.

In '92 I drew Nolan on the Fourth of July. He pitched a complete game against the Yankees, had thirteen strikeouts, and beat them, 4–1. He would start twenty-seven more games in his career—thirteen more that season and fourteen the next, including two plate games for me—but that July 4 game was the last complete game, the last truly dominant game, that he would ever pitch.

Obviously, Nolan's fastball was great even then, in his early forties. But when he *pitched* great, it was because everything else was working too. In a game in Baltimore in '91, Ryan pitched into the eighth inning, with ten strikeouts, shutting down the Orioles. His fastball was working, and so was everything else, which means he got a bunch of those strikeouts with his slider and his changeup. A few Orioles walked away after striking out, muttering to themselves. They couldn't pounce on anything, because everything was working. It didn't seem fair.

Ryan started 773 games in his career, and I had the plate in numbers 769 and 770. In the former, he pitched seven innings and beat Cleveland. In the latter, six days later, he walked four Orioles in three innings and had to leave the game with an injury. One month later, after a really good start against the Angels, he literally couldn't get anybody out in the first inning against Seattle. The last pitch of his career was a ninety-eight-mile-per-hour fastball, and then he walked off the mound for the last time, with a torn elbow ligament.

I was actually supposed to have Nolan's last game; George Brett's too.

By September of the 1993 season, both Ryan and Brett had announced their retirements. And they were scheduled to face each other in Texas on the last day of the regular season: Sunday, October 3.

Brett had always been great with the umpires. Back in '85 he'd been the first player to welcome me to the American League. And George would always say, when he first saw me in the infield or when he came up to bat, "Hey, Dale, how's my favorite umpire today?" Not just to me, he'd say that to everybody. Sometimes he'd also visit our locker room. Once, working first base, with George there as a base runner, I had a check swing and said the batter went around. George whipped around, "Jesus, Dale, that's terrible. That's the worst call I've ever seen."

"Oh no, George," I said, "I've had much worse than that." He laughed. George was a funny guy, with a good disposition. After he retired as a player, but still working for the Royals, I saw him at the stadium from time to time, always very friendly with a smile.

As the '93 season was winding down, I saw that our crew was scheduled to work the last game of their careers, so I said to Rocky Roe, "Hey, I did the gazintas on our rotation, and I've got the plate for the last game of the season, with those two guys. What the hell am I supposed to do? Two Hall of Famers. Should I just tell 'em, 'Hey, listen. George, you get a hit your first and third at bats; Nolan, you get a strikeout his second and fourth. Will that work? Is everybody happy then?'"

Of course, it didn't work out that way, as Nolan was hurt and didn't pitch. But he did come out before the game with the lineup card, as did Brett.

Fast-forward twenty years. In 2013 George was briefly the Royals' hitting coach, and in uniform, when they visited Arlington to play the Rangers. And it just happened that my crew was there as well.

The Rangers had planned a celebration for this anniversary, with both George and Nolan bringing out the lineup cards again. The night before, the Rangers' public relations director came to our locker room and said to me, "We just realized that when those guys finished their careers in '93, you were the plate umpire. Even though you don't have the plate tomorrow"—this was a honeymoon series for me—"will you do the lineup exchange again?"

Absolutely.

So before the game, they made a big announcement over the stadium's PA system: "George Brett and Nolan Ryan are here, nearly twenty years after their last game." This was followed by, "THE HOME PLATE UMPIRE THAT DAY WAS DALE SCOTT. DALE IS ALSO UMPIRING TODAY'S GAME, AT FIRST BASE. LADIES AND GENTLEMAN, WE DIRECT YOUR ATTENTION TO HOME PLATE. JUST AS THEY DID TWENTY YEARS AGO, DELIVERING TODAY'S LINEUP CARDS TO DALE SCOTT, PLEASE WELCOME NATIONAL BASEBALL HALL OF FAMERS, GEORGE BRETT, OF THE KANSAS CITY ROYALS, AND NOLAN RYAN, OF THE TEXAS RANGERS."

Big standing ovation from the crowd, which I assumed was mostly for me.

George and Nolan walked out, and I shook their hands.

Naturally, George had something to say.

"What's the deal here, Dale? Nolan and I look older, and you look exactly the same."

"George," I said, "are you planning on playing today?"

I've actually got two framed photos, one black-and-white from 1993 and one from 2013 in color, both of which are autographed by those guys, with me standing between them.

Two years earlier, in 2011, I had (shall we say) an awkward moment with

Nolan. He was an executive with the Rangers, who played Tampa Bay in their 2011 Division Series. After the last game—Texas won the series, taking three straight after losing the first game—I was in our locker room at Tropicana Field, one of the smallest in the Majors. Four of the guys on the crew had flights to catch and rushed out right after the game. But two of us were going to the West Coast and not flying until the next day, so we took our time.

I'm in the small, two-person shower, just me all soaped up, and because there was so much media and chaos in the (also) cramped Rangers clubhouse, Nolan slipped over to our locker room to use the restroom.

I'm standing in the shower, no curtains or anything, unaware he has entered our room.

I turn around, and there he is.

"Oh, hey, Nolan."

"Hey, Scotty. You guys did a great job."

He's using the urinal and, as one does when using a urinal next to a soapy naked man, starts making small talk.

"So do you know who's working the World Series yet?"

Well, here's a new one. I'm stark naked in the shower while having a conversation with Hall of Famer Nolan Ryan. He's finishing his business and washing his hands, and we're casually chatting about World Series assignments. Is this normal?

On the mound, Nolan Ryan was very intense, very much the competitor you would expect. The same with George Brett. They were both good guys, and the random times our paths would cross after they retired, both were extremely courteous.

17

Hello Again, Boss

My first postseason plate game, in 1995, was one hell of a way to break in. I knew I had the second game of a Division Series at Yankee Stadium, but I didn't know who the visiting team would be. The day before the Division Series started, Jimmy Joyce and I were in New York, watching the one-game tiebreaker between the Angels and Mariners to find out.

I had butterflies for my first playoff series, and I'd had them for a few weeks. Until it was changed five years later, both the American and National Leagues contractually had to give us our postseason assignments by September 10. On that date, I was informed I had an American League Division Series.

Then I had three weeks to think about it.

One of the teams in my series wound up being the Yankees, who hadn't reached the playoffs since 1981, fourteen years earlier. It reminded me of when Mike and I went to Bill Clinton's first inauguration, in 1993, which was the Democrats' first celebration in sixteen years. The Democrats were abuzz and fired up then; Yankees fans, really the whole city, were abuzz and fired up now.

The 1995 season had started late. First, the players had to come back from their strike, which had started in August the year before and didn't end until April 2. Once they settled, the actual season didn't start until April 25 . . . but with replacement umpires. Our contract had expired on the last day of 1994, so we were locked out while MLB focused on settlement talks with the players. Once that was taken care of, MLB then began negotiating with our union. Finally, we reached an agreement, and on May 3 we returned to the field.

My last series of the regular season was in Texas. I was on Jim McKean's crew with Vic Voltaggio and Jimmy Joyce. But Voltaggio was hurt, so Triple-A (and future MLB) umpire Brian O'Nora was filling in.

The last day of August, Seattle had been seven and a half games behind first-place California. But when the Mariners arrived in Arlington for the last four games of the season, they *led* the Angels by two games. Because of a scheduling quirk, we were working the last three games of the series, not all four. Meanwhile, the Angels were hosting Oakland for their final four games.

Both the Angels and the Mariners won the first two games of their respective series—two games left and still two games apart in the standings. Going into my plate game Saturday night, if the Mariners won *or* the Angels lost, the M's would clinch the West. Easy, right?

Not so fast. Texas pounded the M's, and California beat the A's. So just one game separated the two clubs as we entered the last (scheduled) day of the season.

This was a honeymoon series for McKean, with O'Nora scheduled to work the plate Sunday. Jimmy and I, and frankly Brian, were sure that if the final game meant something, Jim would bump up and strap it on. Jim was a practical joker; he was making the Triple-A guy sweat a little, that's all. Nothing was said Saturday night after the game, but all three of us assumed that Jim would tell Brian Sunday morning, on the way to the park. Except he didn't.

So with the American League West title on the line, Brian strapped it on. Fortunately for him, the game was a blowout early, with Texas scoring three in the first and leading, 9–3, going into the seventh. Seattle's loss, coupled with the Angels blowing out Oakland, set up a one-game tiebreaker in Seattle the next day.

Jimmy Joyce and I flew to New York Sunday night, and Monday we watched the playoff in the Sheraton bar. Randy Johnson shut the Angels out for eight innings, and the Mariners took the West with a 9–1 victory.

The Division Series started Tuesday. In the first game, I had first base, working with Mike Reilly, Jim McKean, Larry McCoy, Rich Garcia as crew chief, and Jimmy. I had heard from senior umpires that you can't understand the atmosphere, the couple extra notches of intensity, until you walk onto the field for a playoff game.

There's an electricity for every postseason game, with a distinctly different feel from a regular-season game. And even more so for the first game of a city's first postseason series in fourteen years. *Plus*, Yankee Stadium is always a bear to work. The league office is in New York, so you never know who's going to show up during the season—league president Gene Budig, Marty Springstead, or who knows who else. Oh, and a sidebar for this series? O. J. Simpson had just been acquitted, so that weird energy was floating around everywhere.

A playoff locker room isn't typical either. Sure, it's the same one you've always used, but suddenly there's more security in the stadium and in your room, with a supervisor or two hanging around and a few other people from the league office you don't recognize and probably won't see again until the *next* time you're working in October.

They always seemed to congregate in our room, because there wasn't anywhere else for them to hang out before and after games. All season long it's been our office, and now it's suddenly theirs too, which, for us, was frustrating and distracting. I always thought, *This must be a lot of fun for you guys. You get to hang out and watch a playoff game. But we gotta work this son of a bitch. It would be nice if you gave us some time before the game, got the hell out of our room, and let us focus.*

The second-base umpire keeps a stopwatch for timing on the field, so you have the network TV production coordinator and a couple of assistants coming in to go over it: what time we walk on the field (8:14); how much time between innings or midinning pitching changes (2:35, as opposed to the usual 2:05 in regular-season games); when to start the watch when a relief pitcher comes in (when he enters the outfield, not when signaled to come in); the three extra-long between-inning breaks (3:05, in the middle of the third, bottom of the fifth, and top of the eighth); when to start the watch during the seventh-inning stretch (*after* "God Bless America" is finished); and the official first-pitch time, along with when, and from where, the plate umpire will be cued (8:20, plate end of the Yankees' dugout). The audio technician also makes an appearance, to find out when the plate man wants to be miked up, which coincides with him donning his uniform and equipment a few minutes before we walk.

Then there's the meeting with the managers and GMs (done before the first game in each city) maybe a half hour or forty-five minutes before first pitch, to talk about ground rules, anything we need to know about rosters, inform them of the longer-than-normal times between innings and pitching changes. Then comes the annual speech from the crew chief or some higher authority: *These are big games. We're not there to throw anybody out, but you know there are certain things we're not going to brush off because it's a playoff game. Please do your best to keep your guys in the game, and we'll do the same.*

As a young guy working one of these for the first time, it's a bit of a whirlwind.

Finally, you walk onto the field. It's loud, it's rowdy, and everyone there is ready to burst. These games usually start later than normal, so everyone's had all day and half the evening to get amped up. When I worked a Division Series on days with multiple games, I loved having the first or second game of the day, a one o'clock or four o'clock eastern time start. You get it over with and then have the evening for a nice dinner.

But if the Yankees or Red Sox are playing, you're guaranteed a late start. For TV ratings.

The first game in New York—again, I'm at first base—moved along rather smoothly until the sixth inning. The Yankees were ahead, 2–1, but Seattle had loaded the bases, with catcher Dan Wilson hitting. Wilson fouled off the first two pitches. With one more strike, David Cone would be out of the inning, and the Yankees would keep their lead. Wilson took a pitch for ball one and then another foul.

On Cone's next pitch, Wilson got fooled and checked his swing. Maybe.

On a checked swing, the plate umpire is doing a real disservice to his base umpire if he hard sells the no swing: *No, he didn't go! He didn't go! No, no, no, no, no!*

I worked with Mike Reilly for three seasons, '88 through '90, and Mike had a tendency to do that. By rule the plate umpire is supposed to check with the first- or third-base umpire on a called no swing if the catcher or manager asks. But selling it like crazy and *then* asking for help really handcuffs the base umpires.

In my mind Wilson had swung. But Mike delayed pointing to me, while screaming and selling his call with, "*NO, NO, NO, HE DIDN'T GO . . . NO, NO, NO!!!*" Then he casually points. I said no swing.

Does that make it right? No. I mean, obviously, I should call what I see, no matter how much time has passed or how much he sells the call. But Mike flat-out sold the shit out of it. We were both wrong, and the moment I said no swing, I regretted it. Still do.

The Yankees were upset. George Steinbrenner was so upset that he went off in his private box, screaming about the "rookie umpire" at first base. That was odd since (a) this was my tenth season in the league and (b) in 1988 I'd been his and Billy Martin's least favorite umpire for a few weeks.

Wilson wound up drawing a walk to force home the tying run, but the Yankees wound up winning, 9–6.

The game ended in three hours and thirty-eight minutes, not that far off from a typical American League game. And once that last out was recorded, I had around twenty hours to think about my first postseason plate job.

Everybody handles the pressure of big events differently. Some guys are more quiet than normal. Some guys just never shut up, all nervous talk to still the nerves a little bit. My routine for all the plate games I did in the postseason, and for really big games during the season, was doing hardly anything. I rarely went out the night before; if I did go out, I didn't stay out late. The day of the game, I didn't do much. Lunch, sure, but mostly I'd just hang around my room, pretty much shut down, and stay within myself. Everyone had a different routine, but that's how I prepped for a plate game.

By the time you get back to your hotel after one of these postseason games, it's one or two in the morning. I slept okay after that first game, but I couldn't stop thinking how big of a step this was going to be and hoping like hell that everything would go okay. The next day, I went to lunch and tried to nap in the afternoon but failed. I kept running all the possible scenarios and situations through my head. As much as I tried, I couldn't stop.

One thing that calmed me down when I would get too worked up was this thought: *You know what? It's baseball. It's what you've been doing for years. They still need to pitch, hit, and throw the ball. It's just another game, and I've been doing this since I was fifteen.*

I also needed to remember that I was in this position because people had confidence in me; I had proven I can do this job.

Something struck me that night in Yankee Stadium. You walk onto the field with your crew, your five partners. The place is loud; it's buzzing. The managers come out and exchange the lineups; the meeting finishes; and then the six of you stand together for the national anthem, followed by the ritual of crewmates tapping my chest protector, wishing me a good game.

Then your crew turns around and runs away.

So then it was just me, standing alone at home plate in the middle of Yankee Stadium. The place was rocking, the music was blasting, and I thought to myself, *Well, Dale, you are now officially on your own.*

Of course, you're not *really* on your own. You have your partners there to help you with whatever situations, but you *feel* like you're on your own. It was time. After all the buildup since getting the assignment in September, it was now showtime. *So let's go, big boy.*

Any time you work the plate, you want to get that first called strike. Sometimes it's the first pitch of the game; sometimes it's not until a few batters in or, worse, not until the bottom of the first. It feels like the game doesn't flow until that first called strike.

I got that first one and many more as this game just kept going and going and going. Looking back now, twenty-six years ago as I write this, the game is kind of a blur. You're so focused on every pitch, and all you're thinking about is *that pitch*—the mechanics, the timing. One pitch at a time, and don't let one pitch screw up the next two.

I had double Andys starting this game: Pettitte, for the Yankees, and Benes, for the Mariners. I had worked the plate several games with Pettitte on the mound and would rather call balls and strikes than have him while working first. The left-hander had such a great pick-off move, always on the fine line between a balk or legal, that you really had to be on your toes.

Benes had joined Seattle from San Diego at the end of July. I had been behind the plate for two of his starts, including his second with the Mariners at home against the White Sox, August 8, when he gave up five runs in three and two-thirds innings, with six walks, in a no decision. My only other time behind the plate with him had been his last start, four days earlier in Texas. And if Seattle had won that one, they would have clinched the division title. That night, he didn't survive the second inning.

Andy ended up doing better on this night . . . until the first two hitters in the sixth, when a 2–1 lead turned into a 3–2 deficit and a trip to the showers as Ruben Sierra and Don Mattingly stroked back-to-back home runs. That sent the crowd into hysteria, and we had to stop the game as the grounds crew picked up all the debris thrown onto the field. Lou Piniella, Seattle's manager, pulled his team back to the dugout while fans launched whatever they could throw from the stands.

Both teams had issues with my ball and strike calls—some with merit, many more without. McKean had a couple of wackers at first base, in the top of the fifth and seventh, that brought manager Buck Showalter out onto the field and set off the Yankees and, once again, their fans.

The bottom of the fourth was a lot of fun after I called Yankee Dion James out on strikes. He went apeshit crazy, planting his face against my mask—I literally had no room to take it off—all while screaming incoherently. I'd called strike three and was barely done with my mechanic, and *boom*, there he was, going from zero to insane in about half a second. I have a picture in my office that shows me leaning back, trying to clear at least a little space between him and me. He didn't bump me, but he was *leaning* on me while not saying anything personal or automatic. I didn't eject him, although if this were a regular-season game, I probably would have.

Because it was the Mariners, there was plenty of coverage back home in Portland. Dwight Jaynes was in the press box from the *Portland Oregonian* and witnessed a rare, unethical, impromptu press conference in the middle of the game from Steinbrenner, who was a bit pissed when a few calls didn't go his way.

After the game, Jaynes wrote of Steinbrenner,

One of the world's biggest crybabies, he was almost irrational in his complaints about a few things that went on during the game that took more time to decide than the Simpson jury did.

This man's mind ought to be on the disabled list. He questioned the integrity of the umpires and said the Mariners should have been made to forfeit the game because their manager, Lou Piniella, pulled them off the field in the sixth inning, when fans littered the field after a couple of home runs.

On top of that, he questioned the impartiality of plate umpire Dale Scott—*because he's from Oregon!*

Steinbrenner was fuming over a couple of called strikes by Scott, including one he called Dion James out on in the fourth.

"Look and see where Scott's from," Steinbrenner said. "He's from Oregon. By my geography, that's close to Washington."

Remember, this was twenty-four hours after he'd complained about the "rookie umpire" at first base who wouldn't reverse the plate umpire's checked-swing call and should have spent the whole series working one of the outfield spots.

For the offense of questioning my integrity all because of geography, Steinbrenner was later fined $50,000 by American League president Gene Budig. Granted, according to Bill Madden (one of Steinbrenner's many biographers), his lawyer got the fine rescinded because Budig didn't have the authority to discipline Steinbrenner. One of Steinbrenner's lawyers told Madden that his fees were more than $50,000, "but with him it was all about the winning."

Of course, I didn't know that any of this was going on. I had my hands full with this unbelievable game that went from 1–0 to 1–1 to 2–1 to 3–2 to 4–3 and finally tied, 4–4, in the seventh inning. Neither team scored in the eighth or ninth. As an umpire, you don't care who wins. You just hope somebody does in nine, but that didn't happen.

You have fifty-seven thousand people in the stands who were living and breathing on every pitch, even more so as the game went into extra innings. Umpires love the finality of walk-offs for obvious reasons . . . you literally walk off! It's over. In extras, if the visiting team scores, there's still the possibility the game's not going to end anytime soon, since the home team can still tie it.

And that's exactly what happened in the twelfth. Seattle's first two hitters were retired. I'm thinking about another scoreless half inning. But hold on. Ken Griffey Jr. was coming up.

Before the series, he'd reportedly said to his teammates, "You can get on my back and ride me through the playoffs." In the first game, he'd homered twice off David Cone.

Now Junior did it again, driving a 3-1 fastball from John Wetteland over the 385 sign in right-center field and giving the Mariners a one-run lead. Then Edgar Martinez got a hit, and Buck Showalter brought in some kid named Mariano Rivera, a name that would have meant nothing to me at the time. Rivera did get the third out, but I'm thinking, *Well, at least something happened. Maybe it'll be enough to end this marathon.*

It wasn't. In the bottom of the twelfth, with one out and a runner at first, Tim Belcher came in to pitch for the Mariners. Belcher could be tough. When he thought you missed a pitch, he would let you know with his body language at least, maybe a comment. He walked the first hitter he faced, Bernie Williams, putting runners at first and second. He then got Paul O'Neill to fly out, and the Mariners were just one out away from tying the best-of-five series at one apiece. But clutch-hitting Ruben Sierra doubled to left, scoring pinch runner Jorge Posada with the tying run while Williams was waved around third to score the winner.

Left fielder Alex Diaz hit the cutoff man, shortstop Luis Sojo, who threw a perfect strike to Seattle catcher Chris Widger. Williams had good speed, but not quite good enough, as Widger caught the textbook relay and tagged him out to end the twelfth and extend the game.

Unlike officiating basketball or football, where rarely do you have time to set up and develop the best angle and highest probability to see a play and call it correctly, in baseball you often do. As the Yankee runners are rounding the bases while the Mariners are setting up their relay throws home, I had plenty of time to see everything unfolding and set up for the perfect look at a tag play. What we call the *wedge*.

The what? What the hell is the wedge, besides a salad?

Think of a wedge or the shape of a triangle. The path of the runner and the flight of the ball represent two sides of the wedge. Using the wedge puts me between those two lines and in position to have a clear view of the *point* of the triangle, where the tag will be applied.

You don't get to a spot and then just plant yourself. You have to read the throw and adjust, depending on the path of the ball. If Sojo's relay is off-line and Widger moves right or left, I move with him, staying on his glove-side hip and maintaining my view to the point of the wedge. Like I said, this relay was perfect—no adjustment needed.

It was the potential winning run in extra innings of my first playoff plate game. But none of that was on my mind when the ball was hit or when I was reading the ball and setting up for a play. My only concern was getting the best look—not being too quick, with deliberate timing—and calling the play.

The next two innings were quiet for Seattle, while the Yankees did get runners on base but failed to score (and win). As we entered the fifteenth inning, nearly five hours since the first pitch, it began raining. Not hard, at first, just a few drops here and there. But I couldn't help thinking what a disaster a rain delay would be at this point, as we approached 1:00 a.m.

The Mariners got runners on first and second with one out but didn't score against Rivera, still in the game—again, not that I knew anything about him, let alone that I'd spend the next almost twenty years watching him become a Hall of Famer. As the Yankees came up, it started raining harder. I knew that we were going to play as long as possible and that if we were forced to take the teams off the field, there was a good chance we wouldn't get back on.

At this point, we hit the five-hour mark, and I had seen close to 450 pitches. Or looking at it another way, I had done about 450 deep knee bends, and my legs were basically numb. I was on autopilot and adrenaline. As long as this game had been—as much as it seemed like it would never end—the end did come, and suddenly.

With one out and a runner on first, Jim Leyritz, at precisely 1:22 in the morning, hit the 466th pitch of the night over the fence.

Sudden victory. Or for the Mariners, sudden defeat. Finally, after five hours and thirteen minutes, my first strap-it-on postseason game was in the books.

What's it like to spend five-plus hours on your feet with fifty-seven thousand people screaming at you, not to mention Dion James leaning on you? Physically, you're drained. Mentally, you're drained. But you're so tired you can't sleep. You've just run a mental marathon—not to mention not taking a piss for those five-plus hours—but you're so full of adrenaline that it takes time to finally relax enough to sleep.

A couple of hours after leaving the stadium, after working in the middle of that madhouse, with millions more watching at home, Jimmy Joyce, his brother Tim, and I were sitting in a nearly empty hole-in-the-wall deli. It was after 3:00 a.m., but I was still a couple of hours away from falling asleep.

Two tables away, two guys were raving about the game, with no idea the plate umpire was sitting fifteen feet away.

It's one of the strange and unique aspects of this job. When you're out of uniform in bars, restaurants, hotels, and airports or walking around town or sitting in a deserted deli at four in the morning, after millions of people watched, yelled at, commented about, or sometimes even applauded you a few hours earlier, they have absolutely no idea you're sitting right next to them.

The Yankees and Mariners traveled to Seattle for the third game of the series, with the Mariners shocking everybody by winning three straight, including the dramatic fifth-game clincher in eleven innings. Not only did they eliminate the Yankees, but that game might have been the spark that kept the Mariners in Seattle, with a new stadium.

We weren't in Seattle, though. After the second game in New York, our crew got on a plane for Boston, to work (after a day off) the rest of the Red Sox–Indian series in Fenway Park. We ended up working just one game, as Cleveland completed their series sweep. When I boarded that flight to Boston, it was still raining in New York. The storm that arrived in the fifteenth inning stayed for a day and a half. If Leyritz hadn't hit that home run, we might not have started the sixteenth until two days later.

I remember Larry McCoy after the game that night. Larry was from Piggott, Arkansas. I don't think you can get there from . . . well, from anywhere. For an off day, he would fly into Memphis and then drive two hours just to get home.

Larry did not have an indoor voice. He had one child, April Dawn McCoy. And the umpires had a joke about the McCoys: April and Larry are out deer hunting in Arkansas, and Larry goes, "I DON'T KNOW WHY WE DON'T SEE ANY DEER, APRIL DAWN," as every deer in the county hears him.

I'll never forget when we came in after that five-hour game and Larry says to me and Richie, "ISN'T THAT A DAMN SHAME? IT'S JUST A DAMN SHAME. THIS POOR KID WHO'S NEVER HAD A PLATE GAME IN THE POSTSEASON, HE'S GOTTA GO FIFTEEN FUCKING INNINGS." The way, and decibel, he said it, we all just started laughing. What else could you do?

18

Jeffrey Who?

I got my first League Championship Series in 1996, and it was a rough one.

I would have the plate in the second game, at Yankee Stadium. It was already a tough series going in, because in addition to the Yankees, we had the Orioles, which meant we had Roberto Alomar.

A couple of weeks earlier, just before the end of the regular season, Alomar led off a game against the Blue Jays and got rung up by John Hirschbeck on a pitch that didn't look close from the overhead camera (this was in SkyDome). Alomar beefed some on his way back to the dugout, and John ejected him. When Alomar came back to argue—with Davey Johnson between the two, trying to get Alomar away—he spit directly into John's face.

This was Friday night, the last weekend of the season, with the Orioles close to clinching a wild card playoff spot. I wasn't there, but my buddy Jimmy Joyce saw everything from his spot at first base.

The next morning, as Jimmy recalls, the crew met in the Sheraton lobby before heading to the ballpark. Crew chief Jim McKean told Joyce and Ted Hendry that Hirschbeck had already left and was doing a press conference. When those three got to their locker room at the stadium, they walked in on John's press conference. A reporter asked Hirschbeck if he was aware of Alomar's comment that John hadn't been the same since the death of his son a few years earlier.

"With that," Joyce recently told me, "McKean stepped in and said, 'Okay, that's it, boys. Everybody out of here.' But John started fuming right away and said, 'You want a story? I'll give you a story.' He stormed into the Orioles' clubhouse, yelling, 'Where's Alomar? Where's Alomar?' I'd been two steps behind him, and then I caught him, pinned both his arms to his side, picked him up, and literally carried him out of the locker room."

Alomar had been ten feet away, sitting in a chair. "John was so mad," Joyce said, "that he didn't even see him."

McKean wound up sending Hirschbeck back to the hotel, and they worked with a three-man crew. In the tenth inning, Alomar hit a home run to clinch the Orioles' playoff spot.

Alomar had actually been suspended that morning, for five games. But he appealed, which made him eligible that afternoon, and eventually it was decided that Alomar wouldn't serve his suspension until the next season.

Our union went crazy. We really felt that such a grievous offense should have been met with a very stiff penalty (shades of Billy Martin back in 1988). And if Alomar had been suspended for a couple of games in the playoffs, that would have been a huge penalty. But so be it. We were neither happy with the decision nor surprised by it.

The problem going into this League Championship Series—and this was after the Orioles beat Cleveland in their Division Series—was this perception that now the umpires were going to screw Alomar; since the league didn't sit him down, we were supposedly going to take the bat out of his hand.

When that's repeated enough times—and leading up to the first game, it was repeated constantly—the perception is that whenever a close pitch doesn't go Alomar's way, it's because we're screwing him. Yes, as a union, we were upset with the American League and their refusal to deal with a player who (by the way) wasn't an angel and had had his share of ejections. He committed one of the vilest things you can do to another human. Revenge, though? It wasn't happening. We never discussed it.

So going into the series, we had all that hanging over us. Again, this was my first LCS. It was different from the year before, when I had a couple of days off at season's end and then was right back at it, working the first round. When you're assigned an LCS, you finish the season, go home, and wait to see who survives the Division Series. You have about a week before hitting the road again, to wherever you may be going. That meant I had a week to think about it, knowing I had the plate in the second game. Too much time to think.

The night before I flew to New York, I was walking Leo, our two-year-old black Lab. The only thing on my mind at this point was the series and, more specifically, my plate job three nights later. It was around ten o'clock, and as Leo was doing what black Labs do, I remember thinking, *Whatever happens in the next ten days, Leo, I know that when I come home at least you'll still love me.*

The constant drumbeat from the media was Robbie Alomar and what the umpires were going to do to him. I was also thinking about the pitching and who I'd have starting for both teams. It's nice to have an elite pitcher, because there's a good shot he's around the zone, forcing guys to swing the bat, with a better chance of calling strikes and having a nice pace. The downside with elite pitchers is that with any close pitch, you're screwed, *whatever you call.* A strike? You're giving it to him. A ball? You're squeezing a Hall of Famer.

Finally, the series started, and as if we didn't already have enough to deal with, real or imagined, the first game turned into . . . *the Jeffrey Maier game.*

I could feel the intense atmosphere the moment I walked onto the field. Yankee Stadium, filled beyond capacity for a playoff game, has a feeling all its own, and this was the second year in a row that I was right in the middle of it.

The game was progressing at a snail's pace as we entered the Yankees' eighth, with the O's up, 4–3. There was a feeling that at any time, something would happen, detonating what felt like a ticking time bomb. In other words, that monkey was looking for someone to jump on.

Jim Leyritz led off and struck out, leaving the Yankees with five outs to get at least a tying run.

It didn't take long.

Derek Jeter hit a fly ball to deep right field. As Baltimore's Tony Tarasco settled under it, his back against the wall, the ball suddenly disappeared. It had been touched by a fan, who we later found out was a twelve-year-old named Jeffrey Maier. The Question of the Year was: Did Maier reach over the wall and interfere with Tarasco catching the ball, or was the ball going to leave the field regardless of Maier?

From my position at first base, it looked like someone might have reached over and interfered, but I was far away and without a great angle. I didn't think, *Oh, yes, absolutely he reached over.* But yeah, he *probably* did. Then I saw right-field umpire Richie Garcia giving the home run signal, emphatically.

Right or wrong—and not having them is wrong—crew consultations weren't really a thing in 1996. That didn't happen until 2000, when Sandy Alderson joined the Commissioner's Office and became the vice president of baseball operations, which included overseeing the umpires.

This wasn't a question of fair or foul, which was something we *would* consult on, even then. But we didn't consult for much else, nor did we have any set protocols as to when we should. Also Richie never looked for help, which was another sign that he felt he saw it clearly.

The thing about that particular play? To really see it, with the best angle, you would need to be at the wall. That would give you the context of where the fan was, relative to the wall and the playing field, and where the ball was when touched. If the ball was not going to leave the park by itself, then you would have interference, and you would need to determine what would have happened *without* the interference. If you think the trajectory had the ball leaving the park regardless of the fan touching it, it would be a home run, which is what Richie ruled.

Richie busted his ass to get out there and, in trying to get closer to the play, gave up some of his angle. There is no way to get the perfect angle at the wall; the play happens too fast. Richie got as much distance as the play allowed and made his ruling: no interference, home run.

There was no replay and further review, although this was a *perfect* play for it. Looking at it now, there's no question the ball would not have left the park without interference. Would it have been caught, as Tarasco and the Orioles claimed? Or stayed in play but not caught? If I were working replay now and given this play, I would rule spectator interference *and* a catch, even with just the camera angles they had in '96.

When the ball is hit, you're taught to pause, read, and react. Pause and read the ball: Where is it going? Is it in my area of coverage or my partner's? Once that's determined, then react to where you're supposed to go: take the ball, rotate, or cover a base. Obviously, all of this happens quickly. Very quickly.

In theory, you want to make every call when you're stationary. Your eyes are a camera, and you know what happens when you take a picture as you're moving a camera: blurry.

Here, it's a little different, because you're the right-field umpire and that's the only thing you have. When the ball is hit and you don't have a fair or foul situation, you don't have to worry about the line. The perfect angle would be at the wall, but you're not going to get there. So you try to get some distance closer to the play while not sacrificing your angle.

The umpire's credo is *angle over distance*. You'd rather be farther away with a good angle than closer with a bad one. This time, it was spectator interference, but next time, it might have nothing to do with a spectator and everything to do with the attempted catch: Did he catch it against the wall? Did the ball hit the wall before it was caught? There are all kinds of things that can happen.

No right-field umpire, unless starting ten feet from the wall, would have seen this from the perfect angle. Outfield umpires set up closer to first or third base than they used to, since we now have replay to help on spectator interference at the wall. Line umpires used to get too deep, which causes polebenders to explode on you; you turn around and the foul pole is in your face, with no perspective on fair versus foul.

Bottom line, if you start too deep, you're in a better position for a possible spectator interference but in a horrible position for a catch or no catch or fair or foul home run.

Jeter's disputed home run tied the game, and the Orioles went batshit crazy. Tarasco was vehemently arguing with Richie as center fielder Brady Anderson and pitcher Armando Benitez, all the way from the mound, joined the fray. Mike Reilly, working second base, arrived around the same time as O's manager Davey Johnson and myself. Mike and I tried to peel off players, letting Richie and Johnson go one on one.

The screaming and chaos went on for about five minutes. I didn't see Richie eject Johnson, although he did. The Yankees crowd was delirious, and fans in right field had knighted the twelve-year-old Maier, with someone putting him on their shoulders and prancing him around as a hero. Before the game, in our locker room, we'd met with stadium operations and security, and we had been assured there would be additional security in the outfield stands where fans could interfere with batted balls or fielders. Obviously, that wasn't effective.

In the middle of the ninth, Richie, Reilly, and I were talking in shallow right field. The American League box seats were not far away, just past the Yankees' dugout, a camera well, and the tunnel where we entered and would exit the field. It's where AL president Gene Budig spent the game, along with Marty Springstead and others from the office.

Richie said to both of us, "See the front office, where they're sitting?" I looked over, and every seat was empty.

"There's nobody there," I said.

"Exactly, and I know where they're at," Richie said. "They're in our locker room, watching the replay, formulating what we're going to say. I have a pretty good idea I kicked the shit out of this. If I got it right, they'd still be sitting there." Chalk one up for Richie. He'd been around a long time and knew how these things work.

The Yankees won the game in the eleventh, on Bernie Williams's walk-off homer. We walked into our locker room, and they were all in there: Budig, Springstead, the head of PR, and a couple of others.

Barely through the door, Richie asks, "I missed that play, didn't—"

Marty cut him off, "Okay, this is what we're going to say . . ."

In the postseason, reporters don't come to you; you go to the press room. There wasn't much anyone could say. Richie admitted the ball was interfered with, but in his judgment, from where he was, it looked like the ball would have left the park regardless. That hardly satisfied anyone.

For me, that first game was the appetizer for my entrée the next day. From the beginning, the Orioles thought we were going to screw Alomar, and now they figured they were all getting screwed because of Jeffrey Maier and Richie Garcia.

The only game the Orioles ended up winning was my plate game, as David Wells outpitched David Cone. Wells could be a bitch to work. It's not like he's throwing a thousand miles an hour, but he's got movement on the ball, changes speed, and spots it well. Oh, and he's a pain in the ass on the mound. The pitch left his hand? Then it must be a strike.

The game was long, ridiculous really—four hours and thirteen minutes to play nine innings, two innings fewer than the first game but only ten minutes shorter.

I don't remember any issues with Alomar. I'd ejected him once as a Blue Jay, a few years earlier. He was no virgin when it came to getting ejected, different from his brother. Sandy, a catcher, had a personality. Robbie did not.

There was a lot of outside pressure, with the Alomar thing and then what happened the night before, and the Orioles were on the edge of their seats. As an umpire, there are those days when you walk on the field and one or both teams make you warn your partners, *All right, boys, let's strap it on. A couple may go today. They're just waiting for someone to light the fuse.* You can feel it.

Oftentimes, if that team happens to score a few runs early, it takes a little air out of the balloon. Instead, sure as shit, the Yankees scored two in the first. But the Orioles went ahead with a few runs late and then held on. Personally, I was thrilled to get off the field. Only nine innings *and* without another shithouse.

Then off to Baltimore we went.

Richie, Reilly, Rocky Roe, and I hired a car service. Instead of taking the train or flying the next day, after the game, we got into the limo and rode to Baltimore. It took some time to get out of the stadium area and New York traffic. The ride to Baltimore took four hours, and naturally we all had the beverages of our choice, not to mention that I had just—as we say after a big plate job like that one—*gotten out of jail.*

With a bottle of Crown Royal and a few bottled waters, I was set. By the time we rolled into Baltimore, that bottle of Crown had been deeply impacted. Meanwhile, only one of the waters was open, and it was maybe two-thirds full. You're in the car for a few hours, it's warm, you're talking and laughing. As we pull up to the Hyatt in Baltimore and open the door, the air is *crisp*. As I stepped out of the limo and hit that upper-forties temperature, I suddenly realized how much Crown I had consumed.

Rocky doesn't drink, so as we were exiting, he was laughing his ass off. "Oh, Dale?" he said. "Look at your Crown Royal. It's over half empty. Now look at all those full waters."

I was *so* happy to get off the field after my plate job, without any real issues. Richie, on the other hand, was now in Baltimore, where folks were *not* happy, especially with him. He actually registered at the Hyatt under a different name, and MLB beefed up security. Richie had been around a long time, and with his white hair, he was very noticeable. In the four seasons I worked with him, he was constantly being recognized in airports, restaurants, hotels. When he walked on the field for that third game, the fans were all over him.

With the Orioles splitting the two games in New York, we all thought, *This bitch is going seven.* Or at least we were for sure going back to New York for a sixth game. But New York won the next two, so now we were thinking that maybe we could get the hell out of this series without a return to New York.

Before the fifth game, the last game in Baltimore, Gene Budig was in the locker room. Gene was a nice man but seemed so ill cast as a league president. Prior to this job, he'd been chancellor at the University of Kansas and president at Illinois State and at West Virginia University. He definitely seemed like an academic, and definitely not a baseball guy.

Our room in Camden Yards was L-shaped and not big. In the long part of the L were our lockers, trunks, and equipment, and in the other part of the L were a table, refrigerator, and food. There was not a lot of room to begin with, and then you add two extra umpires, a clubhouse attendant, Springstead, Budig, and security.

Crew chief Larry Barnett was an outstanding umpire and a great human being, but he had a tendency, in general, to be a bit nervous. With a six-man crew and a best-of-seven series, Larry, the plate umpire in the first game, would also have the plate in the seventh game. Of course, the entire crew was hoping that we wouldn't have to go back to New York, but both Richie and Larry were *really* hoping this thing would end. Richie wanted to avoid the controversy lingering after the first game and his prospective plate job in the sixth, and Larry didn't want to have to work a second game behind the plate.

Offhandedly, Budig says to Larry, "It seemed like this series was destined for six or seven games, and now the Yankees could take it tonight. For TV ratings, it would be great if Baltimore can pull one out and get the series back to New York."

Barnett's head exploded. Larry has kind of a high voice, and he said, "*What* did you say? Don't you *ever* come into an umpires' locker room and tell them that they need to extend a series for your goddamn ratings. I'll be on the first *fucking* plane to Marion, Ohio, tomorrow. You don't *ever* come in here and say that. Now get the hell outta here!"

Budig is not a big guy. Larry is. And like I said, there's not a lot of space here. Gene was up against a table that was against a wall with bubble gum, sunflower seeds, and candy on it. Larry was leaning into him, with seeds and gum falling all around him, reading him the riot act.

This is why I say Budig was a fish out of water. I don't think he had a clue of what he was saying. I'm sure they would have loved a seven-game series; you just don't say that in the umpires' room. It's like a couple of pilots dead-heading in coach and talking about emergency flight procedures. Sure, you discuss it *somewhere*. Just. Not. Here.

Budig's eyes were . . . I mean, he's wearing glasses, but they were wide open, as seeds were falling off the shelf and gum was flying everywhere. Meanwhile, I'm in the corner, thinking, *This is hilarious.*

I worked with Richie a lot. Trust me, he was not afraid of working the plate. Sometimes it's just the way things work out; you have a shit show. But guess what. You still have to strap it on and go do it. So he would have worked the sixth game, with flying colors. But the baseball gods were nice to us. The Yankees won that fifth game, we all got to go home, and Richie didn't have to strap it on in New York.

That night after the game, the crew went to Sabatino's, our traditional Baltimore hangout. Umpires have been going there since the sixties. Supposedly, in the early seventies, American League umpires were told that certain restaurants, including Sabby's, were on a no-visit list because of criminal gambling activity that might have been going on there. Of course, umpires went anyway.

Rocky and Larry aren't drinkers. Usually after a night game, Larry showered and grabbed a quick bite, and then he was heading back to the hotel, stat! But after this one, we were so happy to be done with this series, all of us went out.

There was a woman in front of the restaurant, selling roses from a basket. It was late, but she still had about fifteen left. Larry bellows, "I'll take all of 'em! I'll take everything you got." With that, we go inside, and he's handing out roses to the staff.

Rocky proclaimed that he was going to have a drink.

"Well, Rocky," I asked him, "what are you going to have?"

"The only drink I know is a Bloody Mary."

Okay, Rocky.

It's midnight and he orders a Bloody Mary. Drinks arrive, and a couple of minutes later, I look over and see that his glass is empty.

"Rocky?"

"What? It's like tomato juice."

He wound up getting three bloodies, downing them like he was in the desert and drinking water for the first time in a month.

We were a happy group. So happy that the next morning, I slept through my alarm and woke up just as my flight home was taking off. I rebooked and then went back to sleep. Finally, when I was in the lobby to check out a few hours later, Mike Reilly, who had a later flight, said, "I thought you were leaving at seven?"

"Yeah, I was supposed to. Didn't quite make it."

He started laughing, "You don't look good. You gotta connect somewhere and fly all day, clear across the country? Yeah, you're gonna have a lot of fun with that."

I remember a lot of things from that series, and two of them involve drinking. For my first LCS, it was quite an introduction.

19

A Long Way from Bradenton

The night of September 5, 1998, I was in Toronto when Marty Springstead called.

"Scotty, just letting you know you've got the World Series. You'll start at second, with Game Three behind the plate. Congratulations, Scotty!"

I'm not sure how to describe the emotions that flow when hearing that. You dream of working a World Series; hell, I used to fantasize about it before I ever thought of going to umpire school. When it became reality, it felt surreal.

So the following day, working the plate, I went out and got the hat trick, ejecting both managers and a relief pitcher.

Marty called again. "Scotty, did you hear me? I said you *got* the World Series! Jeez!"

The 1998 World Series crew chief was Rich Garcia, who was joined by Tim Tschida and me from the American League, along with Jerry Crawford, Dana DeMuth, and Mark Hirschbeck, from the National League. I was thrilled to work my first World Series with Richie, who had helped bring me out of my 1987 ditch, and, of course, Tim, uniting again as we'd done so many times since 1981.

In the opener, as the Yankees were warming up before the game, Tim and I were standing behind the shortstop in shallow left field. Both of us were looking around, taking it all in, when Tim said, "Man, it's a long way from Bradenton and the Cal League to here." Isn't that the truth! *How did this happen?*

The game went well until the seventh inning, when, with the game tied,

5-5, there was a controversial pitch. The Padres thought Mark Langston struck out Tino Martinez, but Richie called the 2-2 pitch a ball. With Langston's next delivery, Martinez hit a grand slam, and the Yankees went on to win, 9-6.

That was typical umpire luck, just good clean living right there. I've missed a pitch, or had one that could go either way, and then thought, *Just an out here . . . It's horseshit, but at least it'll be over with.* Instead, the hitter smashes it off the wall, while the team that thinks you missed a call are going apeshit crazy. The gift that keeps on giving. That is a textbook definition of umpire luck. Once, I had a manager in the Texas League yell from the dugout, "That's your run!" I couldn't help myself: "Yeah, but I still have a better ERA." Professional? No, but it felt good.

Harold Reynolds on ESPN, talking about the pitch Richie balled on Martinez, said if you looked at pitches around that location during the game, Richie was consistent. Because of the grand slam, it turned into a controversy. It's an occupational hazard, situational calls. A pitch or play early in a game when nothing happens practically goes unnoticed. That exact same pitch or play in a tie game in the ninth with runners on? Well, that's the worst call known to man.

From where I was standing, it was a nutcutter pitch. But it's been more than twenty years, and Padres fans still complain about that one.

The Yankees won Games One and Two in New York. Then it was off to San Diego, where I would have the plate in Game Three, something I had known since September 5, and since September 5, I'd been a nervous wreck about it.

Even though I knew better. Because early in my career, Marty tried to tell me.

"Scotty," he said. "I used to do the gazintas and figure out two, three weeks in advance that for my upcoming plate job in Minnesota, I was going to have Denny McLain or somebody else I hated working. I worried about it for weeks. Then in Minnesota, after stressing out for a couple of weeks, the game started, and after two pitches, he threw his arm out. I had two weeks of knots in my stomach for two pitches.

"So don't fucking worry about it," Marty continued. "There's going to be two guys on the hill, one for each team, every time you walk out there. So you've just got to work 'em."

But I still had a tendency, early in my career, to do that. *Shit, I've got Randy*

Johnson. Or Clemens. God, what a dick he was. I'd figure out I was drawing him and go, *Oh, man.*

When I got the assignment for the World Series, Marty told me I'd start the Series at second, so I knew I'd work the plate in a National League stadium. But that was all I knew. We didn't know which teams, so I had no idea who'd be pitching.

At the time, San Diego, Houston, and Atlanta were all doing well in the National League (this was years before the Astros switched leagues). So instead of taking Marty's advice, I started thinking about it: *If the Padres are in the Series, we'll probably have a five-something start, and that means shadows, unless it's a cloudy day.*

I had a month to think about all this stupid shit.

Marty gave me great advice on a lot of stuff. He was the one who said, "This is a marathon. Don't get too high when things are going well, and don't get too low when things aren't. Try to keep an even keel. Because the second you nail a plate game and you're flying high, the next day at third base you could have the biggest shithouse you ever had."

"It's never as bad as you think it is," he said, "and it's never as good. Keep an even keel. Don't be that roller-coaster guy."

For the most part, I did that pretty well throughout my career. I knew when things weren't going well, and I knew when I'd knocked one out of the park. *Great. You did a good job. Now move on.*

Walking off the field in San Diego, I felt I had a solid game. In the bottom of the ninth, though, I called a strike on Steve Finley. Why? I don't know, because I hadn't called that pitch a strike all night, which was a good thing, since it was inside. He looked at me like, WTF? Even as I was in my motion to call the strike, I was thinking in that split second, *What am I doing?*

I'm not saying I only missed one pitch, but that's the only *glaring* miss I remember.

David Cone started for the Yankees. He was great to work, usually around the plate and a decent disposition. In the sixth inning, when he was due to lead off, there was a delay—where was Cone? I looked at the Yankees' dugout, and they were saying, "Yeah, we know. Hold on, hold on."

He finally comes up with this smirk on his face, telling me and Padre catcher Jim Leyritz, "I forgot I have to bat now. I was in there taking a dump." He then proceeded to knock a base hit to left field.

Sterling Hitchcock started for the Padres and could be a pain in the ass, but he threw well that game. Might have glared at me a couple of times, but that was below his "glare per game" (GPG) average.

In Game Four—the final game as it turned out—I was on the right-field line. Tschida had a bunch of close plays at first, right in front of me. Kevin Brown, pitching for San Diego, was consistently a *dick* (nothing unusual there). One play where Brown had to cover first, Tim called the runner safe, and Brown screamed and really got in Tim's face. Later Tim told me, "Regular season, I woulda run that son of a bitch."

One more thing about that game. At one point between innings, I retrieved a baseball after seeing actor Wayne Knight sitting in the front row nearby. Walking over, I handed him the ball and said, "*Hello, Newman.*"

You know, like he's never heard *that* before. I got a kick out of it, even though it was probably annoying for him. He laughed anyway and thanked me for the ball.

20

"What Flavor Was the Kool-Aid?"

I have always had an interest in politics. I announced, to anyone who would listen, that I was going to be president of the United States when I grew up. I was riveted by the election in 1968, one of the most tumultuous years in American history, with the assassinations of Martin Luther King Jr. and Robert F. Kennedy, not to mention the bloody and dysfunctional Democratic National Convention in Chicago.

I was nine.

My parents were (and remain) Republicans. They supported Richard Nixon that November, so I did too. They were Oregon Republicans, which, at the time, meant moderate and, dare I say, even progressive. The state had GOP mavericks like Governor Tom McCall and Senators Mark Hatfield and Bob Packwood. All these political moderates would today be labeled as radical liberals and finish fourth in a three-person Republican primary.

I was nine months too young to vote in 1976, so when 1980 rolled around, I was eager and enthusiastic. Following my parents, I was a registered Republican, but at twenty-one, I thought Ronald Reagan was too old. I wasn't happy with President Jimmy Carter, either, so after waiting in anticipation to finally cast my first ballot for president, I voted for . . . *wait for it* . . . John Anderson. A U.S. representative from Illinois's Sixteenth Congressional District, the Republican ran as an independent and received 6.6 percent of the vote.

During the Reagan years, my ideology evolved, as did the Republican Party in the opposite direction, and in 1990 I changed parties. I voted for Barbara Roberts in her winning election for Oregon governor—the first time I voted for a Democrat. Two years later, Mike and I enthusiastically supported Bill Clinton and attended his inauguration.

So, yeah, I enjoy watching and following politics. However, I do not enjoy participating at ground zero or finding myself in the middle of a political shitstorm. But that is exactly where I and every umpire in both the American and National Leagues, not to mention many working in Triple-A, ended up in 1999.

The world prepared for Y2K and disaster when the clock struck midnight on December 31, 1999. Fortunately, nothing happened. The Major League Umpires Association prepared for our Y2K and disaster six months earlier. Unfortunately, something happened.

Long before I was in professional baseball, there had always been competitive and philosophical differences between American and National League umpires. Sure, they were in the same union, but the NL arbiters held an attitude of superiority over those working in the Junior Circuit.

Working my way up in professional baseball, I became close friends with several fellow Minor League umpires, with everyone pulling for each other as equals in our quest to make the Show. Then, when I went to the AL and they to the NL, suddenly you felt an edge, an attitude that, because of that NL patch on their shirt, they were in the superior league: better umpires, better cities, better clubhouse attendants . . . better everything.

In spring training in 2000, the year staffs were combined and working games in both leagues, I asked a former NL umpire, "Which are your least favorite National League cities and clubhouse attendants?"

His answer? None.

It seemed that every National League city and clubhouse attendant was outstanding, which I would learn that season was simply not the case. Like the American League, there were a few less-than-desirable destinations and subpar umpire rooms in the National League. But this was the mindset that had been handed down the line from senior NL umpires for decades.

In 1979 the Major League Umpires Association (MLUA) staged a labor action from mid-March until a settlement was reached on May 15 (and signed three days later). It was technically not a strike; but in effect, that's what it was, as MLUA members—on the advice of union head Richie Phillips— simply refused to sign their contracts, which created the work stoppage.

MLB used replacement umpires for the rest of spring training and well into the regular season, with instructions to managers and players: *Hey, take it easy on these guys. This won't be forever, but you gotta be patient.*

That didn't last long, as missed calls, botched rule interpretations, poorly handled rain situations, and bungled, mismanaged ejections quickly became too much for everyone involved.

The 1979 stoppage was not without sacrifice for umpires and their families. But they never wavered in their commitment and solidarity, and it paid off, with substantial gains in salary and working conditions. It was a major victory for the MLUA and for Phillips's twenty-two-year reign as its leader.

Twenty years later, the situation and attitudes had evolved within the union. Operational changes involving all of MLB were coming as well. The final year of our collective bargaining agreement came in 1999, and although not yet official, it was apparent that there was a major transformation coming, with the elimination of the two league presidents, combining umpire staffs, and everything operating under the umbrella of the Commissioner's Office.

Most everyone on the National League staff were against working both leagues, while most of the AL staff were ambivalent, at worst. Many of us looked forward to working in NL ballparks with NL rules and to the additional strategy that came with the pitchers hitting (no DH).

At our annual union meeting, before the '99 season, I ran for a position on the MLUA board and was elected. Per our bylaws, the president and vice president alternated between AL and NL, with the VP in the opposite league as the president. The rest of the board included the secretary treasurer and three representatives from each league.

In June we were notified of an emergency meeting for all union members, in Philadelphia the day after the All-Star Game. It was billed as a strategy meeting for the upcoming negotiations, which were scheduled to start shortly after the World Series.

I was on vacation, at home in Portland, during the two weeks before the break. The night of the All-Star Game, Jimmy Joyce and I flew a red-eye from PDX to Philadelphia, arriving at 7:30 a.m. for the 9:00 a.m. meeting.

Once we got started, it quickly became obvious that this was *not* the strategy session everyone expected. This was, instead, the unveiling of a resignation scheme, designed to force MLB to the table ahead of schedule *and* prevent consolidation of the two umpire staffs.

Our current CBA paid every umpire a severance when they retired or resigned, with the amount depending on years of service. Now Richie Phillips said that if the membership signed letters of resignation, effective September 2, then upon their submission, the immediate effects would be (1) severance compensation for all sixty-eight umpires, something in the neighborhood of $15 million in toto, and (2) crisis mode for MLB, with pennant-race games looming in September and then the postseason in October. Obviously, MLB didn't want replacement umpires working any of those.

Phillips said he would keep these letters, once signed, in his proverbial back pocket, as leverage if MLB declined to open negotiations early. The letters *would not be disclosed to management* until we got closer to September. If then.

Okay, a couple of things here.

As a union, you hire an attorney to advise the membership of your options, the legalities and possible outcomes of those options, and to counsel membership about any ideas that may come from the members. You need sound legal advice that can include shutting down ideas or strategies that open the union and its members to legal exposure or (worse!) the possibility of losing their jobs. As head of the MLUA, Richie had done a few unorthodox things. Some succeeded, and some failed, with the '79 strike the undisputed highlight.

As suspect as Richie's resignation scheme sounded, I was not an attorney, nor did I sleep at a Holiday Inn Express. The attorney for our organization said that this was legally sound and a winnable plan. I believed him, as did most everyone else in attendance.

But there was something else happening in the Airport Marriott meeting room that day: groupthink.

group·think
/ˈɡro͞opˌTHiNGk/
noun: *group-think*
Groupthink is a psychological phenomenon that occurs within a group of people in which the desire for harmony or conformity in the group results in an irrational or dysfunctional decision-making outcome.

Although questions were raised throughout the meeting, the answers all seemed to make sense. So again, even though it seemed off, nobody could pinpoint how or where, and our attorney sounded as confident as ever. So the personalized resignation letters were distributed, signed, and collected. Meeting adjourned.

Jimmy and I were back in the air, scheduled to arrive home in Portland twenty-four hours after leaving. We were both exhausted and quiet, contemplating what the last nine hours really meant. About an hour into the flight, I looked at Jim and finally verbalized what I was thinking.

"What did we just do?"

Jim's wife, Kay, was meeting us in Portland and dropping me off on their way home. This was pre-9/11, so she was at the gate. The moment we walked up to her, she said, "What the hell did you guys do today, resign?"

"How did you know that?" Jimmy asked.

"ESPN has been talking about it for a few hours. Richie Phillips was interviewed and said the entire staff was going to resign in September unless MLB comes to the table. What's going on?"

Jimmy and I looked at each other. Keep them in your back pocket, Richie? Only use them for leverage, Richie? Will not disclose them until September? Really, Richie? Sounds like you dropped the mic before we boarded our flight!

Still, I wasn't sure of what to make of everything.

Sandy Alderson, the ex-A's GM who'd been hired ten months earlier as executive vice president of baseball operations, was point man for the commissioner's plan to consolidate operations and umpire staffs. When asked about Richie Phillips's mass-resignation scheme, Alderson famously called that "either a threat to be ignored or an offer to be accepted."

He was literally doing high fives in his Park Avenue office. MLB accepted the offer.

Less than twelve hours after arriving from Philadelphia, I was in the air again, flying to Orange County for four Angels games with Joe Brinkman, Derryl Cousins, and Doug Eddings (who was filling in for John Shulock). Doug wasn't full time yet, so he was not a member of the MLUA. Cousins, as one of the umpires who crossed the picket line in '79, was not in the union either.

Joe, who'd had a falling out with Richie Phillips and a few others within the union during our yearly meeting in February, missed the Philadelphia meeting. All three guys had heard the news on ESPN and other outlets the day before. They were shocked about the resignations, had a ton of questions, and were anxious to hear exactly what went on from someone who was actually in the room.

Once all four of us were in the locker room, I started my meeting recap. I actually sounded enthusiastic! *This is really going to work, you guys!*

However, as I described the idea, the reasoning, and Richie's optimistic endgame, the looks I was getting, especially from Joe and Derryl, were not the ones you see when someone's buying what you're selling. In fact, as the words left my mouth, I realized I wouldn't buy either.

When I finished, all three of them stared at me. Then Joe, in his dry, poignant, and borderline mocking tone, piped up: "So what flavor was the Kool-Aid?"

I went through that weekend with little but the union and the resignations on my mind. Our next series was in Seattle, so I flew back to Portland for a few hours at home before driving up to work the second series ever in the Mariners' new stadium.

After the Sunday game in Anaheim, I showered quickly and hit the road for the thirty-five-mile trip to the LAX Marriott, where I was spending the night before my early flight home the next morning. Davey Phillips had called me during the game, and I called him back from the car.

"Dale," he said, "you need to rescind your resignation. Tonight. I've been in contact with my personal attorney. He said this proposal to resign is insane, that Richie Phillips is dead wrong. If you resign, you're done. You lose all labor laws and protections you have as a union member. Plus, it's a direct violation of the CBA if we participate in a 'concerted work stoppage.' I have already talked to Rocky and Durwood. Call Jimmy Joyce and tell him to do the same thing."

Of course! It makes perfect sense! When you quit, you quit . . . and whatever protections you had, they vanish. This now seemed so obvious! Yet on Wednesday in Philadelphia, with our optimistic salesman and the sales job he pulled on us, and a full dose of Grade A groupthink, it was not registering.

"Yeah, I'll call Jimmy. So what do I need to do?"

"I'm emailing you the letter I sent. Just fill in your information instead of mine. You need to fax this *tonight* to the American League office, so they have it first thing tomorrow. Drop the original in the mail. Dale, this resignation bullshit is suicide. My attorney was dumbfounded when I explained what was going on."

I got to the Marriott, called Jimmy, and then went straight to the business center to put my rescind letter together and fax it to New York. And I had another resignation letter to send that night.

RICHIE PHILLIPS
1735 MARKET ST.
PHILADELPHIA, PA 19103

July 19, 1999

Dear Richie,
This letter is to inform you of my resignation, effective immediately, from the Major League Umpires Association Board of Directors.

Dale A. Scott

I had been semipissed since the meeting. It was ludicrous that something this monumental was never presented to the board, never discussed, never briefed. Since I'd been elected to the board five months earlier, I'd been on multiple conference calls. Somehow this was too minor to make the agenda?

Now, after talking to Davey, I was really angry. This was purposely done, to go around the members elected by the body to represent them. If we had been informed and able to discuss it as a board, we could have avoided the mess we were now all in.

I barely slept before my early flight home. Just before boarding at 5:40 a.m. (8:40 in Philadelphia), I got a call from Pat Campbell, Richie Phillips's second in command.

"Hi, Pat," I answered, curtly.

"Dale, what's going on? I got your fax; what are you doing?"

"How could you propose such a significant, risky strategy of resigning our jobs without discussing it with the board? Why the hell are any of us on there if you and Richie are going to do whatever you want anyway?"

"We didn't want any leaks. Shit gets back to the league before we finish our meetings. We wanted everyone at once to hear our plan," Pat explained.

"Pat, this isn't going to work. Davey talked to his lawyer in St. Louis, and this takes away any power we might have. I rescinded my resignation this morning. So did Davey and several others."

There was a pause before he replied. "I'm disappointed to hear that, Dale. This will work, if we stick together. We know what we're doing. Why didn't you talk to me if you had doubts?"

"Why the fuck didn't you talk to *me*? To all of us on the board before dropping this out of nowhere? I gotta go; they're about to close the door to my flight. I'm disappointed, too, Pat. You guys are the lawyers. You're supposed to protect us, not put us in jeopardy." With that, I hung up and boarded my flight.

It soon became very apparent, and not surprising, where the split in the union was. The breakdown:

AMERICAN LEAGUE

Resigned (9): Drew Coble, Jim Evans, Dale Ford, Rich Garcia, Ed Hickox, Mark Johnson, Ken Kaiser, Greg Kosc, Larry McCoy

Rescinded (12): Larry Barnett, Gary Cederstrom, Al Clark, Jim Joyce, Chuck Meriwether, Dave Phillips, Rick Reed, Mike Reilly, Rocky Roe, Dale Scott, Tim Tschida, Larry Young

Never resigned* (11): Joe Brinkman, Derryl Cousins**, Terry Craft, Ted Hendry, John Hirschbeck, Tim McClelland, Jim McKean, Durwood Merrill, Dan Morrison, John Shulock**, Tim Welke

NATIONAL LEAGUE

Resigned (33): Greg Bonin, Jerry Crawford, Kerwin Danley, Gary Darling, Bob Davidson, Gerry Davis, Dana DeMuth, Bruce Dreck-man, Bruce Froemming, Brian Gorman, Eric Gregg, Tom Hallion, Angel Hernandez, Bill Hohn, Sam Holbrook, Jeff Kellogg, Jerry Layne, Randy Marsh, Jerry Meals, Ed Montague, Paul Nauert, Larry Poncino, Frank Pulli, Ed Rapuano, Charles Relaford, Rich Rieker, Steve Rippley, Paul Schreiber, Terry Tata, Larry Vanover, Joe West, Charlie Williams, Mike Winters

Rescinded (2): Wally Bell, Jeff Nelson

Never resigned* (1): Mark Hirschbeck

Either didn't attend the meeting or kept the letter when collected after the meeting.

**Not a union member.*

Once we started rescinding resignations, things moved quickly. The week of July 19 was a chaotic mess full of debate, accusations, misinformation, innuendo, intimidation, stress . . . and unfortunately, threats relayed via email or phone.

I had long, intense conversations with two close friends, Gary Darling and Mike Winters, who both insisted that the union strategy would work if we all stuck together. Anyone who withdrew their resignation, they said, was no better than a scab crossing a picket line.

I countered that, no, this would not work even if everyone were together. Quitting and throwing away protections you've collectively bargained, even with every member on board, still leaves you with no legal protection. The mere fact that it was obviously a "concerted work stoppage," and thus a violation of the CBA, would legally relieve MLB from making severance payments.

Meanwhile, I received an anonymous threat via another umpire: if I didn't fall in line with the union, I would be publicly outed, my career ruined. I was not intimidated, but I was disgusted by how low some would stoop.

I had a much-needed conversation with Rocky Roe, who basically talked me off the proverbial cliff. Of my thirty-two years in Major League Baseball, these couple of weeks in July 1999 were my lowest and most depressing.

I believed in unions and was well aware of all the gains that were possible only because of a strong union. To openly defy and denounce the MLUA went against everything in my being. The conflict tore apart longtime relationships. To this day, some of them remain severed, while others are repaired but not what they were.

But within a few days, I *knew* this was a horrendous legal miscalculation by Richie Phillips. A suicide plan that would cost guys their jobs, and it did. The disastrous resignation plan has been taught at law schools as an example of one of the worst blunders in the history of labor negotiations.

That week, AL president Budig informed our staff that they had until the close of business on Friday, July 23, to withdraw their resignations; after that, all resignations would be accepted. The NL made no such cutoff date, which, as all this played out in the following months, proved to be to the league's advantage, as NL president Leonard Coleman Jr. could simply choose whom and whom not to rehire.

That season, I worked on Joe Brinkman's crew. I loved working with Joe anyway, but this season was special. With the MLUA imploding, Joe— along with John Hirschbeck, Tim Welke, and Dave Phillips—led the charge to form a new union, which meant I had a front-row seat for the reshaping of our future.

On July 26, just twelve days after the ill-fated Philadelphia meeting, Joe and I were in Baltimore on an off day. That evening, we had a meeting at Ron Shapiro's home in the Maryland countryside. Shapiro was (and is) a highly respected attorney and sports agent. His client list has included Cal Ripken, Kirby Puckett, Jim Palmer, Brooks Robinson, and Joe Mauer. To name just a few.

Joe had previously met Shapiro, and now he'd reached out for advice on creating a new union. A driver picked us up from the Hyatt for the drive to Shapiro's, where we were introduced to Baltimore attorneys Joel Smith and Larry Gibson.

Joel is a well-respected labor lawyer, the type of attorney you would want when forming a new labor union, and a real departure from Richie Phillips, who, believe it or not, didn't specialize in labor law. Larry was an attorney and law professor who, under President Jimmy Carter, served as associate deputy attorney general of the United States.

Joe and I were impressed by their knowledge and demeanor. Richie Phillips could be bombastic and overly aggressive, and he tended to suck the oxygen out of a room. He often used intimidation to push the agenda of the MLUA. This approach worked for years, but we were facing an entirely different animal with Sandy Alderson and his team: more corporate, less nonsense, and perhaps impossible to intimidate. Richie's tactics had worked in 1979 and later. But not now.

In late August, while working a series in New York, Joe and I had a clandestine meeting in a massive suite at the Waldorf Astoria Hotel. Why clandestine? It was with Donald Fehr, the longtime executive director of the Major League Baseball Players Association. Fehr, in his position as the players' union leader, could not be viewed as taking sides in the MLUA upheaval. Privately, though, he welcomed a change at the top of our union, having had issues with Richie Phillips in the past.

The meeting, facilitated by Ron Shapiro, was to answer whatever questions we had concerning the umpires' road ahead.

On the field, players and umpires can look like mortal enemies. But when it comes to negotiations with MLB (i.e., the owners), we usually support each other. What's the old proverb? The enemy of my enemy is my friend?

The resignations, as stipulated in the letters sent to both league presidents, went into effect on September 2, 1999. On July 26, three days after the American League cutoff for withdrawing a resignation, the MLUA filed a lawsuit seeking to allow all umpires to withdraw. On July 27 the union request for a temporary restraining order was rejected. Later the same day, the forty-two umpires whose resignations were still active rescinded as a group.

The two leagues hired twenty-five replacement umpires from Triple-A. While the AL brought back all the umpires who rescinded by the cutoff date, the NL received all those rescinding letters in one big batch. The NL opted to hire back on "performance standard," picking and choosing who would return. When the dust cleared, twenty-two umpires—thirteen from the National League and nine from the American—who'd started the season as full-time staff would work their final games on or before September 2.

Major League Baseball had simply called Richie Phillips's bluff and welcomed the resignations as an opportunity to discard members of the staff they'd wanted off the field for some time. And all without getting dirty, as the umpires themselves had quit.

Joel Smith and Larry Gibson were eventually hired and led us through the process of planning, gaining support, and participating in a National Labor Relations Board (NLRB)-sanctioned vote in November. With ninety-three umpires considered in the bargaining unit, the result of the vote was 57–35 in favor of the new union. The MLUA appealed, with the final ruling coming February 24, 2000, when the World Umpires Association became the official union and bargaining unit for Major League umpires.

Negotiations to replace the now-expired CBA finally began and proceeded for the majority of the 2000 season. In the meantime, both sides agreed to work under the old CBA . . . except for one *major* change: umpires now worked both leagues, with the title of Major League Baseball umpire.

In September we signed a new CBA, one radically different from previous CBAs. With a new union and attorneys and with a completely reorganized MLB under the Commissioner's Office and Sandy Alderson leading a new team of executives, the new CBA basically started from scratch. It took months to create and reflected a much more corporate looking contract. Salaries and benefits improved substantially, as did umpire accountability. The days of the inmates (i.e., us) running the asylum were over.

Meanwhile, arbitration and negotiation for the twenty-two umpires who'd lost their jobs continued for many months. In 2002 eight umpires were rehired and returned to the field. Rich Garcia was hired as a supervisor and remained in that capacity until he was let go in 2010 (more about that later). Also in 2002 nine umpires retired, with five being paid a severance and four receiving back pay. Incredibly, three others—Bob Davidson, Tom Hallion, and Ed Hickox—were rehired in 2005, but only after returning to the low Minors and working their way back up.

After the turmoil of 1999, there were several years of animosity, mistrust, bitterness, and resentment. A few hard-liners didn't conceal their anger with those like me, who didn't "stay together." They insisted that if we had remained united, the resignation plan would have worked. They were openly hostile to Joel and Larry and, even though they were members, openly mocked the WUA. It made for some awkward crew situations, both during the season and in the postseason.

The retirement of a few of those hard-liners and new battles with the Commissioner's Office—over the computerized pitch-tracking system, for example, used for evaluation—brought the membership closer. Eventually, the 1999 disaster was far enough in the rearview mirror that we coalesced as a group. But the upheaval and the MLUA's implosion will never be forgotten by those who were there.

21

W.

On the morning of September 11, 2001, I was home in bed.

It was the Tuesday of my week off. My dad called, waking me up, and immediately said, "Do you have the TV on? We're being attacked."

I turned on the TV and watched in horror—with Mike and the rest of the country—what was happening in real time. When the second plane, United 175, flew into 2 World Trade Center, Mike and I both had tears in our eyes. So much emotion: sad, angry, scared, confused, enraged.

Our house has a spectacular view of downtown Portland, Mt. St. Helens, and Mt. Hood. We can also see, from a distance, commercial jets as they depart or approach PDX. For the next week, with all air travel suspended, the only jets we saw from our place were Oregon Air National Guard F-15s patrolling the skies above Portland, a surreal and frightening image that remains seared in my mind.

I was grateful to be home. A lot of guys were stuck in various cities and couldn't get rental cars, and of course, all flights were canceled. At first, MLB wasn't sure what came next, but eventually they restarted the season on the seventeenth. Crew assignments were scrambled, as they tried to make travel easier for everybody.

I was back on the field on the eighteenth, in Seattle, where I worked second base and saw Freddy Garcia shut out the Angels. After two more games, I was back home for a few days, followed by a series in Los Angeles and another in Phoenix. I had the last week of the regular season off, before going back to Phoenix for the first two games of the Diamondbacks' Division

Series against the Cardinals. They were still splitting up Division Series then, so after the second game, I went to Atlanta, where the Braves immediately closed out their sweep of the Astros.

This was the second year of our new CBA, according to which we didn't get our postseason assignments until ten days before the end of the regular season. Then, after evaluating the twenty-four umpires who worked the four Division Series—any problems? any controversies?—they released the World Series assignments for umpires who had worked that first round.

Because the Braves-Astros series ended in three games, I had to wait three days before learning that I'd been assigned my second World Series. I didn't know *where* I'd be working; all I could do was watch from home the two League Championship Series—Yankees-Mariners and Diamondbacks-Braves—and consider the four possibilities for my World Series matchup. And yes, I was hoping for Mariners-Diamondbacks, because my travel would be so easy.

I got half of that. Both championships lasted only five games, resulting in a Diamondbacks-Yankees matchup . . . and four days for me to think about it.

Aside from me, the 2001 World Series crew was chief Steve Rippley, Mark Hirschbeck, Ed Rapuano, Jim Joyce, and Dana DeMuth.

Games One and Two were in Phoenix. I had second base and then first, watching Curt Schilling and Randy Johnson dominating the Yankees. Considering how those guys had pitched all year, this was hardly shocking. Also not shocking, Yankee hitters were doing a lot of bitching about pitches. Meanwhile, I've got the plate for Game Three in New York.

You can have big games during the season, especially in September during the homestretch, as teams are fighting for playoff spots. Every umpire gears up for a big game differently, with their own routine. But the postseason is a different animal.

Yeah, I was nervous and had a ton of butterflies and anxiety. The anticipation and hype was plastered everywhere. In my career, I had a ton of big games, but the one that left the biggest impression on my mind was Game Three in 2001.

The buildup was incredible.

There I was, with Roger Clemens on the mound for the first World Series game in New York, with dozens of Secret Service agents and massive security everywhere inside and outside Yankee Stadium. Oh, and by the way? *I've got the plate and need to stay focused on why I'm actually here.*

I'm not going to lie. That was a challenge.

Just seven weeks and fourteen miles from Ground Zero, with a nation and city still grieving, the president of the United States was in attendance, set to throw out the ceremonial first pitch.

Jimmy Joyce and I were the first from our crew at the stadium. We got there really early, knowing that security would be insane. When we walked into our locker room, there was a gentleman we didn't know sitting across the way. He immediately identified himself as a Secret Service agent and said, "I'm going to be on the field with you guys when the president is on the mound."

He put on an umpire's uniform, but underneath were a bulletproof vest, two guns, and handcuffs. He was loaded. He was wearing an earpiece and giving us updates on the president: *He's leaving the White House on* Marine One. *He's on* Air Force One. *He's five minutes away.*

First pitch was scheduled for 8:25 p.m. Suddenly, our Secret Service agent umpire announced, "The president will be here at 7:56."

Okay! That is specific!

I happened to be at the urinal when I heard a commotion; obviously, somebody was coming in. When President Bush arrived, of course he'd have his own contingent of security. And a few seconds later, one of them came up behind me and said, "You have a visitor."

"I'll be right there—just finishing up!" Awkward? A little!

The president had already gone around the room and introduced himself. As I walked out of the bathroom area and into the locker room, still drying my hands with a towel, I said, "Hello, Mr. President. Dale Scott."

"Yeah, Dale, I remember you. You're the one who was always sweaty when you came over to get baseballs."

Before he was governor of Texas, he co-owned the Rangers and would sit in the front row next to the dugout, on the other side of the screen from where the batboy would sit. Sometimes between innings, if the batboy was busy, instead of me waiting for him to bring me baseballs, I would walk over and get them myself. Bush, sitting there, would give me a look and say, "It looks like you're sweatin' out there." *You do realize that it's Texas in June, right?*

"Yes, sir, that's me," I said, noticing several additional agents in our room.

Looking at my Ducks hat, which I wore before every game, he said, "You're from Oregon?"

"Yes, sir. Portland."

"I didn't know you're an Oregon fan. How are the Ducks gonna do?"

"Actually, they were doing well until last week. Stanford beat 'em."

He said, "Aw, don't worry about it. The Ducks will have a good year." (As it turned out, the president was spot on, as the Ducks won the Fiesta Bowl and finished number two in the country.)

He then added, "The only thing I know about Portland is every time my dad or I went there, there was a riot."

"Yes sir, that's kind of what we do."

Everybody laughed. He was spot on about that too.

It was 8:00 and we were walking at 8:20. The president was asked to sign a couple of dozen baseballs for the crew, which he did. Jimmy Joyce had a video camera and asked if he could record while he was signing baseballs and chatting with the crew. Sure. Jimmy then told the president it was for his son, who couldn't make the New York trip because, as a senior, he was playing in his final high school football game.

President Bush asked his name, and when told it was also Jimmy, he looked directly into the camera and said, "Jimmy, this is President Bush with advice I received from my father: Always listen to your mother!"

Meanwhile, I'm putting on my gear, because I've still got this pesky little *Game Three of the World Series* in a few minutes. I'm trying to appreciate what's happening, appreciate the moment with the president in our room at Yankee Stadium—I mean, *pinch me*—but I'm also trying to get ready for the game, mentally. There's a lot of stuff going on.

Finally, it's time to say our goodbyes, shake hands, and head down the tunnel to the field. As a crew, we're standing for the national anthem, except for Mark Hirschbeck, who stays in the tunnel and is replaced by the Secret Service agent, so everyone would see only the requisite six umpires. Also on the field were two more Secret Service agents, dressed in Yankees grounds-crew uniforms. The president was introduced, walked out of the Yankees' dugout wearing a flak jacket underneath his coat, and then threw a strike to Derek Jeter behind the plate. Everything felt both surreal and patriotic. The ceremony ended, and then . . . I had an actual game to call.

Again, it was Clemens pitching for the Yankees, and lefty Brian Anderson for Arizona.

In the bottom of the fourth, I had a nutcutter call. The Yankees' Shane Spencer was at second with two outs, running on Alfonso Soriano's pop-up right in front of the plate. It was a chilly late-October evening, with the wind swirling everywhere; just a moment earlier, catcher Damian Miller had misplayed a catchable foul pop next to the screen. Now Miller ripped off his mask while looking up for the ball, with Mark Grace running in from first base.

Again, Miller's got trouble with the wind, and the ball dropped to the ground right next to him. Did he touch it? This matters, because even though the ball landed four feet fair, it was spinning so much that when it hit the ground, it took a sharp right turn and crossed the first-base foul line into foul territory. If he touched it, the ball would be fair, and the runners would all be safe. If not, it would be just a routine foul ball on your scorecard.

Jimmy Joyce was at second and had the same angle I had, although from farther away. Our eyes met for just a split second, but I knew we saw the same thing. The ball, although as close as you could get, never touched the mitt. Miller picked up the ball after it crossed the line, and I yelled, "Foul ball!"

Damian looked at me like I had four heads. His expression seemed to say, "Dale, I feel so sorry for you. Foul? Dude, you're going to get ripped. I like the call, but you're going to get killed for this." He truly thought I was out of my mind.

Mark Grace, who had charged in, had a confused expression. "Foul ball?"

"Foul ball!" I repeated, a bit louder, while they both looked at me with that we're-sorry-about-what's-going-to-happen-to-you look.

"Damian, your glove didn't touch the ball, right?"

"Right."

"The first time you touched the ball, it was in foul ground."

"Yeah?"

I said, "That's a foul ball."

"Yeah! Yeah, you're right!"

In the meantime, Spencer had run home from second, presumably scoring what everyone thought was the go-ahead run, so of course the home crowd was ecstatic.

Yankees manager Joe Torre trots out, hands in his jacket pockets.

"Dale, whaddaya got?"

"Joe, he never touched the ball until it was foul."

"Can you get help on that?"

I immediately looked at Jimmy, who'd walked in a couple of steps as if he knew how this was going to play out. I said to him, "Jimmy, the ball was never touched."

"Never touched," he said.

"Okay," Torre said and walked off.

Torre was calm and spoke in a conversational tone, not yelling or excited. I'd just returned a runner to second base who most thought had put the Yankees ahead, so I was surprised by Torre's low-key demeanor. Soriano went back to bat and flew out to center field, ending the inning.

Meanwhile, on the field, I was thinking, *Oh my God. We've got a thousand cameras here. I hope there's one angle that proves I'm right.* Because if there was not an angle that showed that it *didn't* hit Miller's glove, it'd be the grassy knoll and we'd debate this forever. I knew what I saw, but that didn't mean the cameras or millions of viewers saw the same thing.

When I finally saw the video, Joe Buck and Tim McCarver, doing TV for Fox, didn't know what the hell had happened. Not at first, anyway. *Miller drops it, and the go-ahead run will score! Now they're saying what? Foul ball? Foul ball! Nobody touched it!* Fox showed an angle where it was tough to tell if Miller touched it or not. *Did it hit his glove?*

So Soriano flies out, the inning's over, and when they come back from commercial, Joe Buck says, "You really have to give Dale Scott, the home plate umpire, a lot of credit. Because in my opinion, he was the only guy standing in that group who knew that ball was foul. And he was right on top of that."

That remains, to this day, one of the few times when Joe Buck has ever praised an umpire. Or me.

After the game—which the Yankees wound up winning, 2–1—I had a ton of texts from friends, all with a similar message: *Unbelievable call! That's awesome! You nailed it!* That's always nice to hear and definitely beats the alternative: *Hang in there. Hey, that was a tough call. I can see where you might call it that way.* Ouch!

Of my three World Series plate games, that was the most intense.

In Games Four and Five, I was on the outfield lines. Game Four, in right, all I could think about was fricking Jeffrey Maier. I didn't want to live that nightmare again, except with me in the jackpot this time. Both games went extra innings, with the Diamondbacks blowing saves and the Yankees hitting dramatic home runs. Back in Phoenix for Game Six, I had third base, but we had no drama that night, as the Diamondbacks won a blowout to force one last game.

In Game Seven, I was at second base, just like in the Series opener. This one had plenty of drama.

Clemens started for the Yankees, Schilling for the Diamondbacks, and the score was 1–1 after seven innings. Alfonso Soriano led off the eighth with a homer off Schilling. In the bottom of the inning, Mariano Rivera took over for the Yankees, giving up just a two-out single while striking out the side. Randy Johnson, who'd entered with two outs in the eighth in a rare relief appearance, came back for the ninth and set down the Yankees in order.

Mariano Rivera returned for the bottom of the ninth. He gave up a single to Mark Grace and then committed an error on Damian Miller's sacrifice bunt, putting runners at first and second with no outs. Jay Bell pinch hit and attempted another sacrifice bunt, but this time, Rivera threw out the lead runner at third.

That brought up Tony Womack, who doubled to right field; that scored the tying run and left runners on second and third. Rivera, making his second wild throw of the inning, then hit Craig Counsell with a pitch. That loaded the bases, with Luis Gonzalez coming up and the winning run on third base.

In the booth, Tim McCarver told viewers, "The one problem is, Rivera throws inside to left-handers, and left-handers get a lot of broken-bat hits to . . . the shallow part of the outfield. That's the danger of bringing the infield in with a guy like Rivera on the mound."

McCarver got that one right. With the infield in, Rivera's next pitch was inside but not quite inside enough, and Gonzalez hit a little humpback fly toward short center, landing in the grass just two feet beyond the infield dirt.

The ball went over my head as I turned and watched it drop. Derek Jeter raised his glove, even though he had no chance at the ball. If the infield hadn't been in, I would have called infield fly, and Gonzalez would have been automatically out. But with the winning run on third base and fewer than two outs, you have to play the infield in.

I still had responsibility for the runner from first, Counsell. Technically, all runners are forced and have to touch their next base before the game is officially over. Once I saw Counsell touch second, I started running toward our locker room.

The crowd was going crazy, and the D'backs were streaming out of their dugout onto the field, jumping up and down. Arizona manager Bob Brenly was running across the diamond, arms in the air, screaming. We came near each other while heading in opposite directions. In the split second we made eye contact, he sort of nodded to me and gave a smile as if to say, *Good job*. It was just a blip, a quick and random moment in time, but I'll never forget it.

I'll never forget those nine days in the fall of 2001 either. A country reeling from the events of 9/11. A seven-game World Series in which the home team won every game, filled with comebacks, blown saves, strange plays, and a Series walk-off.

One of the most dramatic World Series in baseball history, and I'd been right in the middle of it all.

22

Like a Human Blood Clot

Crew dynamics can be a tricky thing. But they certainly exist and can change a great deal with the addition or subtraction of any individual umpire, and those dynamics go a long way toward determining just how much of your sanity is retained over the long, *long* baseball season. And these days, that season is filled with long, *long* games. And yeah, all those games add up.

Umpires always joke, *We do not get paid by the hour.* Which is to say, *We hate long games. We couldn't care less who wins, but why does it take so @#&%$ long to find out?*

It wasn't always this way.

In 1946 the nine-inning average for both leagues was one hour and fifty-six minutes; that was the last year it came in under two hours. Five years later in 1951? Two hours and nineteen minutes, a whopping twenty-three minutes longer. It took thirty-five years to increase another twenty-three minutes, reaching two hours and forty-four minutes in 1986 . . . which just happened to be my rookie season. In my last year of service, 2017, the average nine-inning game in Major League Baseball lasted *three hours and five minutes.*

In the early 2000s, Major League Baseball made a concerted push to lower game times with its pace-of-game initiative. Initially, there were positive results, as the average game time fell eleven minutes in six seasons, from two hours and fifty-seven minutes in 2000 to two hours and forty-six minutes in 2005. But since then, the average game has steadily lengthened, topping out (so far) at three hours and seven minutes in 2020, despite the addition of even more (theoretically) time-saving rules.

With all those long games and (let's be honest) all the dead time *during* games, having good partners—or at the very least, partners you can tolerate—has probably become more important than ever. And every happy crew winds up figuring out their own ways of getting along.

For example, when I worked in 1992 with Rich Garcia, Dan Morrison, and Tim Welke, Richie mentioned, after one particularly long game, a traditional National League crew game called pig. None of us knew exactly how it was played, but all of us had heard of it. Guys on the crew would put money in the "pig," with the amount of money tied to total runs scored, something like that. When the pig had grown enough, they'd use the money for a crew dinner.

That got us thinking about designing our own version of pig centered on game times. We brainstormed and pieced together a few rules, and before you knew it, we had our own game: BlueBucks. I got the name one night while working in Kansas City. Between innings, they ran a promotion with fans earning "Blue Bucks" that could be spent on Royals merchandise. We were all trying to think of a name for our new game, and suddenly there it was on the big screen. BlueBucks! Perfect!

BlueBucks was based on the game time of your plate job and if it was longer or shorter than the previous game's time. If, for example, Tim's plate job was three hours and six minutes and the next game was mine and came in under that, Tim owed $5. If mine was over three hours and six minutes, I paid $5. The other two crewmates paid regardless, so every game, you add at least $15.

It was at least $15, because there were several other ways to add to our BlueBucks total. The plate man had to announce his projected game time before first pitch, and if you got within five minutes either way of your projected time, the rest of the crew paid an extra $5 apiece. If you hit it exactly, they paid $10. If you forget to announce your projected game time, you owed an extra $5. A few years later when working with Durwood Merrill, I think he spent more on forgetting to announce his plate time than for anything else. Right after the first pitch, the three of us on the bases would all point to our wrist, and Durwood would stand there, hands on knees behind the catcher, shaking his head. Forgot another one.

But wait, there's more! If the previous game time was three hours and fifteen minutes or less, you could "press," meaning you were guaranteeing you'd beat it; if you did, everyone else had to pay double. If you didn't, *you* paid double. There were penalties for games going four hours or longer, for going an hour or longer from the previous game time, for the longest game of the series, and several more that we adopted.

In fact, we had so many rules that I typed everything up, had it printed and bound, and presented each member their own official BlueBucks Rulebook. For my efforts, I was voted commissioner, which meant I convened BlueBucks court when protests were lodged and made my final judgements after hearing pleas to the court. The days we had BlueBucks court, I was booed both on the field *and* in our locker room . . . lucky me!

All these rules and opportunities to "contribute" to the BlueBucks account paid off. The lowest season total was $2,600, while the highest was $3,200, and we split the money four ways. I kept a running total of how much everyone paid over the course of the season, so even though we may have each received $800, usually a couple of us made money while the other two lost. Obviously, whoever made the most was declared BlueBucks champion.

Yes, it was just a silly little game. But it also helped bond the crew during the season, which feels like a marathon. When you spend so much time together and are coping, as the third team on the field, with high-pressure, stressful situations, you need some kind of outlet to keep guys loose. We played BlueBucks not just in 1992, its inaugural season, but also when I joined Dave Phillips's crew in 1993 and eventually in all five seasons I worked with him.

A lot of crews, getting to the locker room about an hour and a half before the game, will play cards. It's a ritual. All four play, and they play for cash. I've never been a cards guy, though, so my crew never played.

I remember a story—I believe it was Bruce Froemming's crew, where cards seemed bigger than the game—about how a supervisor came into the locker room before the game and the guys barely looked up, just continuing playing cards. The supervisor didn't send out a league memo or anything, but he did say, "Hey, give us a little courtesy, guys. When we walk in the room, give us fifteen, twenty minutes and tear yourselves away from the fricking game."

That just wasn't my thing, though. I would read *USA Today*, but what I really enjoyed was watching NBC *Nightly News*. When I was with Davey,

Rocky, and Durwood, if it was on, we would rate Tom Brokaw's tie. That was *our* ritual.

I just loved watching that half hour of news in the locker room. I would either do that or read something. Jim Folk is the stadium operations manager in Cleveland. After Jacobs Field opened in 1994, he made sure to be in our room at the start of *Nightly News*, when we were in town, so that he could also rate Brokaw's tie.

Here's my philosophy about the locker room.

My first few years, when I was a young umpire and struggling after the '87 season, I was placed with Rich Garcia and rightfully so. Richie was a great motivator, great with young guys; and starting in '88, I worked with him three out of four years.

Richie was a little more serious in the locker room. About a half hour before the game, he liked to turn off the TV, I think more because that's what *he* needed to do, kind of get in his own head space a little bit, think about what we were going to be doing that night.

He wasn't strict. You could talk and laugh about things. But that was Richie's MO in the room, as crew chief.

Davey had a loose locker room. He hated when guys would talk union politics, which some did constantly. There were some on staff who were always negative: every glass was half empty, the union screwed this up, next time we gotta do this, or we gotta do that. When I was a rover early in my career, I couldn't wait for the game to start, on some crews, just to get out of the locker room. It was so negative.

Davey didn't want Debbie Downers as partners. He loved laughing and had three great guys to do that with in Durwood, Rocky, and myself. There were times when we consciously had to stop laughing as we left the locker room, since it wouldn't look good having the crew laughing hysterically while walking onto the field.

From 1995 through 1999, the American League uniform included a red shirt, but it was rarely worn, except by Derryl Cousins . . . and me. Some guys wore it occasionally; others, literally never. Basically, the plate umpire could choose what color the entire crew wore. At first, if the plate man wore the red, the entire crew also had to, unless the base umpires chose windbreakers. It got to the point where base umpires wore the pullovers even when it was warm, and in domes, just so they wouldn't have to wear the red shirt. Meanwhile, wearing my red shirt behind the plate, I would just laugh, watching them sweat their asses off with their faces a deeper red than the shirt they refused to wear. But in 1997 that policy was relaxed, allowing base umpires to be different from the plate man, as long as they all wore the same top.

Dave, Durwood, Rocky, and I worked three consecutive seasons (1996–98). Durwood was fine with the red, but Davey and Rocky hated it. I loved tormenting Davey and especially Rocky, who usually worked third base when I strapped it on. He would always complain, "I hate the red. Every time I run across the infield to second, I look like a human blood clot." After hearing that, I insisted on wearing the red shirt for practically every plate game until they were discontinued after the 1999 season.

As a crew chief, my locker room was similar to Davey's. I didn't want to be surrounded by negative people. I wanted people who were optimistic and funny. We have enough shit on the field that we have to take seriously. I didn't want that during the hour and a half *before* we walked onto the field, so by the time we got on the field, we'd be ready to throw grenades just for someone asking for the count.

From my first year in 1986 until we combined leagues in 2000, I was the crew's fourth man—purely in terms of seniority—every year except one: 1995, when I worked with Jim McKean. That year, I was a three man, with seniority over Jimmy Joyce. In 2000 and 2001 I jumped to a two man, until the last month of '01, when I was promoted to crew chief. In two years, I went from the bottom of the crew food chain to the top.

Being named a crew chief is an honor. It's the Commissioner's Office putting faith in your people and management skills, not only with your crew and the office, but also with the players, managers, stadium operations personnel, and media.

The last day of August 2001, I was sent over to head Jim McKean's crew, as he'd gotten hurt just before the All-Star break. And in fact, he never made it back, retiring after the season. Marty Springstead asked Ralph Nelson, then our supervisor of umpires, whom he had in mind as his next crew chief in 2002.

"Scott," Ralph told him.

"Well then," Marty said, "put Scotty in there now; let him chief for the last month. If he's your next crew chief, then get him going."

So that's what Ralph did, telling me, "You're the new crew chief; take McKean's crew." It was semiawkward, since Jimmy was McKean's two man and had been chiefing that crew since McKean had gotten hurt two months earlier. Now, suddenly, I showed up, and if Jimmy and I hadn't been such good friends, it might have been a bit uncomfortable.

Naturally, I thought that in 2002 I would start fresh with my own crew, submitting the names of whom I wanted and picking my schedule. But in November, an email was sent to the entire staff, saying that there was one crew chief position open in 2002 and that anyone who wanted to apply should do so by a certain date.

Now I was confused. I knew that McKean was the only retirement, and Ralph had already told me I was a crew chief. He never said *interim* chief or that I would need to apply this winter. I emailed Ralph and, as diplomatically as possible, said, "If this concerns a chief opening besides McKean, please disregard this message. But if this is for McKean's position, I guess I'm throwing my hat in the ring." It felt like having to apply for a job I had already been given.

As it turned out, that's exactly what I did. According to our CBA, when a crew chief position officially becomes available—that is, when a crew chief retires, resigns as chief, or is demoted—the league must open the position to anyone on the staff who wants to apply. I wasn't aware of that, and apparently neither was Ralph.

I was flown to the winter meetings in Boston along with the other applicants: Derryl Cousins, Chuck Meriwether, and Tim Tschida. We all interviewed, and about a week later Ralph called to congratulate me on my promotion to crew chief. Again.

I did jump over a few guys with more experience, but crew chiefs aren't necessarily assigned by seniority. This was also only a couple of years after the leagues' umpiring staffs had been combined. The National League had tended to rely solely on seniority for crew chiefs, while the American League would often consider seniority along with other factors.

In the AL, for example, Larry McCoy was passed over by less senior umpires for a crew chief position, but I don't think Larry wanted to be one anyway. He was content as a two man, not dealing with the extra responsibility. Cousins was frequently passed over, and he did want to run his own crew. But for years he was punished for working during the '79 umpires strike. In 2011 he was finally named a crew chief (and then retired after the 2012 season, his thirty-fourth).

When filling chief openings for the newly combined MLB staff in 2000, Mark Hirschbeck from the NL was promoted with less seniority than I had. Ralph made a point to contact me, saying that with the blending of staffs, they needed to equalize the number of new chiefs from each league. That was why Mark got the nod over me, but I was now at the top of the list.

I took being a crew chief seriously, because it *was* serious. Being a member of a crew was easy. When there's rain, you just play until the chief tells you not to. Oftentimes in those tough rain situations I thought, *Man, am I glad I don't have to deal with this.*

Suddenly, I did have to deal with rain and everything else; now *you* have to make those decisions. Your crew is looking up to you. Having a strong two man is a huge help, someone you can lean on as your sounding board in various situations, be it weather or anything else.

In 2002 I opened in Tampa with the new Scott crew: Jim Joyce, Jeff Nelson, and Chris Guccione, who was filling in for Ron Kulpa. During the long flight to Tampa, I reviewed all the crew chief material once more. I had some butterflies in anticipation of the season and how it would all play out. But once I got a few games as a chief under my belt, I got comfortable with my responsibilities.

Being named a crew chief is definitely an honor, but you have to be ready. Because if the shit hits the fan, you're the one on the field who has to decide what's going on, what you're going to do, and what you think is right. You're also a conduit to the Commissioner's Office. If anyone on the crew screws up, they're coming to you. They want to know what happened, why it happened, why I did or didn't do this or that. You have to be prepared to deal with all of it.

There is a pay bump for being a crew chief. My last few years, it was an extra $100 per game. Before that, it was a lump sum for the season. Becoming a crew chief wasn't something you did to get rich. One of the biggest benefits was bidding on the schedule and choosing your crew. When I first got the job, you submitted three names, and they tried to set you up with at least one. Later it was changed to submitting five names, from which they'd get you at least one, but most every year, I would get two out of the five.

For several years, starting in 2010, I told our main supervisor, Randy Marsh, "If you give me Dan Iassogna, then I don't care who else you put on the crew." Danny and I became and still are great friends. In 2003 he was in Triple-A and filled in on my crew for a month. The first week, I was off, but then we were together three weeks in a row. That's when we got to know each other and bonded both on and off the field. When Danny left to join another crew, I told him that the moment he was hired, he should call me and I'd do my best to get him on my crew.

The next January, Danny got the call, and then I got his. But the crews had already been put together, so even though I tried, we didn't work together in 2004. However, starting the next year, he was on my crew for ten of the next thirteen seasons. In total, of the 3,897 regular-season games I worked, 1,097 were with Dan Iassogna on the field, which ranks (through the 2020 season) twenty-second on the all-time partners list (Joe Brinkman and Derryl Cousins are number one, at 2,123 games together).

Dan is an outstanding umpire and an even better person, and from day one, we just clicked. Together, Danny and I could deal with anything. He wasn't a yes man. If he thought I was making the wrong decision about something, he told me. I also was fortunate to work with Ron Kulpa for six consecutive years, and four of those (2005–8) were with Dan. The three of us had an absolute blast.

There are always a couple of guys on staff who aren't much fun to work with, either on or off the field (or both). There were also guys I didn't know well, and vice versa. But with Dan on the crew, I really did feel that Randy could put anybody with us, and we could deal with it.

In 2007 Paul Emmel joined us. After the 1999 resignation fiasco and the consolidation of the two league staffs, there was some animosity between former National League and American League guys. Most (not all) NL umpires believed in Richie Phillips and his strategy in '99, while most (not all) of us in the AL didn't. Paul and I didn't know each other very well. He was from the National League side, and I perceived him as someone more aligned with Phillips's thinking than mine.

When I found out he had been assigned to my crew, I was a little apprehensive. The labor events of '99 split our new union and for years strained a lot of relationships. My hope was that the ugliness of a few years ago wouldn't affect the crew. And once the season started, it took no time at all to get to know each other. We had a great season on the field and fun off it.

Jerry Meals and I didn't know each other at all. He was another guy from the NL who was perceived, at least by me, as very anti–American League. The most we had ever talked was the year before, at our January retreat in Phoenix. We both had an off-campus stress test, with a car service taking us back and forth, so for the thirty-minute drive each way, we made small talk . . . which was the extent of our relationship.

That first season with Jerry, in 2009, he was going to be my two man, along with Kulpa and Mike DiMuro. Your two man is extremely important. You need someone you can lean on, openly and honestly, while dealing with issues on and off the field. Jerry has a dry sense of humor and can come off as unapproachable. Like with Emmel a couple of years before, I went into opening day hoping there wouldn't be a conflict or personality issue.

The first few weeks of the season, Jerry and I would have a drink or two after the game, usually at the hotel bar. That broke the ice. And I soon realized that Jerry was not only approachable; he was hilarious. We finished that season in Milwaukee, and chatting between innings, he said, "I want to let you know, I've really enjoyed working with you and would love to come back." We ended up working together for three consecutive seasons.

I think I can work with anyone. Not that there weren't guys I didn't particularly want to work with, but if one of them was assigned to my crew, I could make it work. As it turned out, in my sixteen years as a crew chief, I had fantastic partners, and I'm grateful for every one of them.

23

"Hell Has Frozen Over"

When you work close to four thousand games, it's tough trying to remember all the personalities you deal with . . . let alone the nonpersonalities. But there are certainly a few who remain vivid, not because they were nice but, let's be honest, because they were usually a pain in the ass.

Great example? The Ripkens generally were a challenge. As a family, I mean. Maybe it was an organizational thing, as the Orioles were traditionally tough to work. I didn't have any of their farm teams in the Minors, but umpires who *had* worked their games all said it was just a tough organization. They had a tendency to rag on umpires, get in a lot of arguments, get ejected, all that fun stuff. As if Earl Weaver's mentality had somehow seeped down through the whole system and just stayed there.

Cal Ripken Jr. was obviously the star of that team, the catalyst, and he didn't necessarily have to say anything. You'd call a strike on him that he didn't like, and with just a slight slumping of his shoulders or some other negative body language, the dugout would start chirping. *How dare you call a strike! Cal didn't like it? Well then it can't be a strike.*

It was worse when Cal Sr. was the Orioles' third-base coach. He was a fiery guy who did not like umpires. At all. I've heard stories from older umpires who had him in the Minor Leagues as a manager. In the Majors, our tolerance level for coaches was pretty low, because you've got one spokesman and that's your manager. Let him deal with it.

If you're a first-base coach, you have three things worth saying:

"Freeze on a line drive."

"Back."

"Break up a double play."

Anything else and you're talking too much (and now with the new sliding rules, "break up a double play" is somewhat of a relic).

Third-base coach?

"Freeze on a line drive."

"Be ready for a passed ball."

"Tag on a fly."

When Old Man Ripken coached third—and listen, I'm sure he was a proud father—it was obvious not only that he didn't like us but that when his sons were involved, he *really* didn't like us.

Cal Jr. didn't have to say anything. Usually, Cal didn't say much anyway. But with looks and body language, he made it quite clear when he wasn't happy. His first at bat, every game, he always said, "Hey, Dale, how you doin'?" He always said hello, which was probably the last positive thing you'd hear from him that day.

But Cal Sr. was just tough, man. Rocky Roe ran Old Man Ripken in 1987, the one year he managed the Orioles (not including the O's 0-6 start in '88, at which point Sr. got fired). Now they were getting into it, and Rocky said, "You couldn't manage a Sunoco gas station." Ripken said something else, and Rocky went, "The only reason you're a manager is because you had two good nights with Mrs. Ripken."

That's when crew chief Larry Barnett stepped in and said, "Okay, that's it fellas. We're done here."

Billy Ripken was much more vocal than Cal. Billy didn't have Cal's stature, obviously, but he was much more verbal about pitches and plays, whether he was on the field or in the dugout. He reminded me more of his dad than Cal did. Billy could be surly, and you just didn't trust him, even if he was saying something nice, which was rare.

The vast majority of players are there to do their job, and they're focused on that rather than on us (or anything else). There are a few, like Harold Reynolds, who talk a little more and have a little more personality, and rarely would you see those guys go off. And then there were a few on the other end of the spectrum who *always* seemed to be arguing or saying something, usually nothing good. And with that rap sheet, you wouldn't give them as long a leash. Because you know that's how they are.

If a guy you get along with pretty well says, "Hey, you missed one," you're going to cut him a little more slack. Maybe the best example is Derek Jeter, who never got ejected in his entire career. I remember calling him out on strikes in Toronto, and as he started walking away, he just looked at me and said, "Dale, that ball's outside." I said, "I got it on the plate." And he said, "I'm telling you, it's outside." I took a couple of steps with him as he walked to the dugout, and I said, "Derek, I got it on the corner. But I'll take a look."

When somebody like Jeter questions a call, you pay attention. First of all, he was doing it the right way—he wasn't showing me up, wasn't screaming. Also, he didn't bitch much, so you think, "Whoa, maybe I did miss that one."

So I did look at it. Borderline. Really could have gone either way. This was before QuesTec and all that.

Another time with Jeter, he questioned a strike three in Yankee Stadium. I looked at it later, and I was wrong. The next day, I was at third base, and when he came out in the top of the first to warm up, I walked over to him and said, "I took a look at that pitch, and you might've had a gripe." He replied, "That's cool. It's all good." I think most players appreciate when you're willing to look at things and acknowledge that you might have been wrong.

Now, when it's a guy who *always* bitches about pitches, that's a whole different thing. Joe Carter never seemed to care much for anything I did. George Bell, Pete Incaviglia, and Tony Phillips were players I ejected multiple times: Bell and Incaviglia twice, Phillips three times.

George Bell was just a miserable guy. You couldn't call a strike on him. Always, either he'd say something, or there'd be the body language. Tony Phillips was another one, just a dick.

Phillips was actually my fourth *and* fifth ejections, within a few months during my rookie season. Then we took a little break before I got him one more time in '93. He was always pissed. Balls and strikes, steal attempts . . . it really didn't matter.

In 1992 we opened the season in Detroit; by then Phillips was a Tiger. I was on Rich Garcia's crew with Dan Morrison and Tim Welke. The second game of the season, I walked over to Welke in shallow right field during a pitching change. As we were talking, Phillips, who had walked and was standing on first base, caught our attention and said, "What's up fellas?"

Tim replied, half jokingly, "Tony, are you gonna behave this year?"

"I've turned over a new leaf," Phillips said. "I'm a different guy, not gonna argue."

We're thinking, *Yeah, and monkeys will fly out of my ass.*

The next afternoon, on getaway day, Tony had a few things to say in the fourth inning when Richie called him out on a steal attempt. In the bottom of the ninth, Welke rang Phillips up for the second out and then ran him when he went slightly goofy yelling and bitching about the pitch.

It had taken three whole games for that new leaf to hit autumn.

Phillips would snap, going from zero to out of control in a split second. Maybe there was a pitch he didn't like, followed by a snide remark. You'd respond with a benign, "It was on the plate, Tony," and BAM! The fuse hit the TNT, and off he'd go. Some guys think that if they don't swing, it's a ball. None of us umpires seem to have gotten that memo. Phillips was one of those guys.

Then there was Paul O'Neill. At least once every game (but usually more than that), he would question a pitch. Or just flat out tell you it was a ball. I got into an argument with him once in New York when he fouled off a pitch and asked me if it was a strike. I said yeah, and he barked, "No it wasn't!" *Seriously? He swung at the damn pitch!*

"Well, then why did you ask? If you don't want the answer, don't ask!"

He couldn't help himself.

Another time, I worked the plate in Cleveland for a Saturday afternoon game. Everything went smoothly. The next day, Paul was on third during a pitching change and said hello. He would always say hello, usually right before bitching about you missing a pitch. So I said hi back and then added, "By the way, Paul, hell has frozen over."

He gave me a puzzled look and said, "What are you talking about?"

"I had the plate yesterday, and you didn't question a single pitch. The way I figure, hell must have definitely frozen over."

He started laughing. "I think it must have." The planets must have been aligned or something.

Then there are certain guys with whom, for whatever reason, you can never relate. They wouldn't bitch at every umpire, but we just couldn't get on the same page. On Gorman Thomas Night at the old County Stadium in Milwaukee, I called Thomas out on strikes twice. After the second strikeout, while walking away, he yelled, "*GODDAMMIT! IT'S GORMAN THOMAS NIGHT, NOT DALE SCOTT NIGHT!*"

Great line. I had to laugh.

24

"Hey, Lou, You Missed a Spot"

It wasn't for long, but I did have the "pleasure" of working three of baseball's legendary hothead managers. Throwbacks, you might call them.

Billy Martin, you know about already.

I also got to experience Dick Williams, with Seattle. He wasn't as flamboyant as Billy and Earl Weaver (more about him in a minute). I didn't have Williams for long, basically two seasons and a couple of months, and I worked just a fraction of the Mariners' games before they fired him. He was actually the first big league manager who argued with me, on a play at first base in Seattle. He came out to tell me how wrong I was and how easy the call should have been and I still blew it. I told him this wasn't a day at the beach out here, a line that crew chief Davey Phillips thought was hilarious.

As I said, he wasn't terribly flamboyant. He was just a sarcastic son of a bitch who would talk down to you like you were a piece of shit. That was how he approached you. And I don't know if this was universal, but from what I've heard, a lot of his players didn't even like him much. He really could be a surly prick.

I did briefly have Weaver too. He had retired after the '82 season, when I was still in the Minors. But he came back in the middle of '85 and stuck around for all of '86 before quitting again. I worked nineteen Orioles games that year but never had the pleasure of ejecting Earl, which for a long time had been a rite of passage for American League umpires. In '86 he might have mellowed some with age . . . but he was still run six times. Just not by me.

We did have one quick "discussion." I was working the plate in old Memorial Stadium when he came out for a pitching change. After the change, instead of going straight to the dugout, he walked over to me and said, "Those are good pitches."

"Earl, those pitches are up."

"Well," he said, "they don't look up from the dugout."

"So you'll be perfectly fine if those are strikes when you're hitting?"

"I didn't say that."

"Okay, then I think I know what you're saying."

Earl was notorious for whistling from the dugout to get your attention when he didn't like a pitch. *Whistle, whistle,* until you finally look over, and then he'd gesture that a pitch was high, low, whatever. A real pain in the ass, but I didn't have any big run-ins with him.

Those three, especially Martin and Weaver, were kind of in a class of their own. At least in the American League, when I was first coming up.

Then there was Lou Piniella. My first three seasons were his first three as a manager with the Yankees. He got run more than his fair share, but not by me. He then went to the National League, and I didn't see him again until 1993, when he returned to the AL with the Mariners.

I liked Lou, and I liked working Lou. Because he wasn't a whiner. Some guys will spend a whole game whining about this pitch, whining about that pitch, making umpires insane. They don't do enough to get run, but they're always in your ear.

Jim Fregosi, when managing Louisville in the Association, was chirping off and on during one of my plate games. "That pitch isn't low." "He didn't miss by much!" "Why is that a ball?"

It was irritating, to say the least. Finally, when he asked, "Where was that pitch?" I responded, "It really doesn't matter, Jim, you're not going to like whatever I say."

There was a pause, and then he said, "Well that's a fine attitude now, isn't it?" I had to laugh. Another time in Triple-A, in a game I wasn't involved in, all four umpires were gathered around him as he was going off about some ruling. Getting more frustrated as the argument went on, he yelled, "You're all a bunch of cocksuckers!" Three of the four umpires simultaneously ejected him, each gesturing in a different direction. Fregosi immediately pointed his finger at the one umpire who didn't throw him out and screamed, "It must be you! You're the cocksucker!"

I later had Fregosi when he managed the White Sox and Toronto. He had a great sense of humor and often would say something funny, even during an argument.

Rarely will you eject a chirper for saying any magic words, because they usually don't; they just bitch constantly. Many times, fans or the media aren't aware anything is going on, making it look like you're the aggressor when you suddenly bark at the dugout. *"Man that umpire has a short fuse. Why the rabbit ears?"* Or the annoying *"Get your ears out of the dugout"* from a manager or player when you look their way. Really? You yell to get my attention, and then you get it and blast me for it? Here's a thought: *Get your voice off the field.*

Short of an ejection, you need to let chirpers know early: *We're not doing this for nine innings, or somebody is leaving early, and I'm here all day.* They've been warned, so now it's their decision. If the whining continues, they ran themselves.

Piniella wasn't one of those guys. He rarely sat in the dugout bitching and moaning.

However, when he had had enough, he would explode. I mean, just BOOM, and you'd have the full Lou Piniella Experience, with his hat launched, dirt kicked, maybe a flying base or two, whatever antics came to him that day. Without warning, you were suddenly at DEFCON 1.

I had that luxury once: Lou's first Kingdome ejection in 1994.

In the seventh inning, he yelled on a called ball on Royals first baseman Wally Joyner. This wasn't part of a game-long chirping session; in fact, it was his first audible reaction to a pitch since the first inning. Looking over, I told him to knock it off. And he didn't, so I ejected him.

Lou bolted out of the dugout with his hat off and veins sticking out everywhere. Then he spiked his hat and got in my face while crew chief Davey Phillips wandered in from first to observe the meltdown. Then Lou started kicking dirt all over the plate, yelling about *fucking pitches* and how I was *screwing him.*

Meanwhile, Davey and I just stood there. Davey was resting his chin in one hand, watching Lou, as I was holding my mask, with both hands on my hips. Frantically kicking dirt, Lou finally started to slow down, exhausted (after sixteen kicks). When it looked like he was done, I said, "Hey, Lou, you missed a spot."

"Oh, fuck you!" And with that, he scooped four handfuls of dirt to finish his artistic plate cover-up.

Usually, when a guy is going nuts, the umpire is yelling back at him. What makes the video of this one fun? Davey and I are just standing there, quietly watching Lou. Hilarious.

A few years later, in the Mariners' new stadium, with the Red Sox visiting, there was a play at the plate in which Lou wanted obstruction called on the catcher, for blocking the plate. This was before the current sliding rules. Back then, if the catcher had the ball *or* was about to immediately receive the ball, he could completely block the plate.

But what does *immediately receive* mean? Is the ball ten feet away? Twenty feet? This was a throw from the outfield that was cut off and then relayed by an infielder. As our rule of thumb, if a throw was on its way to the plate and had entered the infield, the catcher was about to *immediately receive* the ball. The catcher blocked the plate and made the tag, and I called the runner out. Lou ran out to argue.

He didn't go crazy, but he did argue. Then he went back to the dugout. When the inning ended, Lou came up to me between innings and said, "Dale, I watched the video on that play, and he was blocking my runner before he had the ball. That's obstruction."

So I started explaining the rule, and I got to the part about *immediately receiving the ball.*

"Wait. What the hell does that mean?"

"It means, in my judgment, he's about to receive the ball."

"Well," he said, "what if in my judgment he *wasn't* about to receive the ball?"

"Lou," I chuckled, "that's why I'm out here, getting paid big bucks to make that judgment."

He laughed. "I'd never heard that. I know he can block the plate when he's got the ball. I'd never heard that about receiving the ball."

"You've been around a long time, Lou. But school is always open."

"I never liked school," he laughed on his way back to the dugout.

Another Lou argument in the Kingdome had the entire crew laughing. I had the plate, with Davey Phillips at first, Rocky Roe at second, Durwood Merrill at third. With the Mariners hitting, Rocky went out on a long fly ball, ruling it a home run. It looked like a fan might have interfered, but from the plate, I didn't have a great angle and was the farthest away. Both Davey and Durwood had better angles but saw something different, so we got together as a crew. Durwood said, in his gravelly drawl, "Rocky, a fan definitely touched that. That was interference. Should be a double." Davey agreed, so Rocky turned to the Seattle dugout and signaled spectator interference while announcing, "Come back out here, two bases."

Lou flew out of the dugout, screaming, "Who changed it? Who changed it?"

Durwood said, "Lou, I changed it."

"What?! Durwood, you can't *see* that far!"

We tried not to, but we all started laughing. Classic line.

I actually had Lou's last game ever, on August 22, 2010, when he was managing the Cubs. The Braves were visiting Wrigley Field with manager Bobby Cox, the all-time leader in ejections (although I never ran him). Lou had announced a month earlier that he was going to retire at the end of the season; Bobby made the same announcement at the beginning of the season. However, the evening before, Lou said he was retiring after the game on the twenty-second, to be with his ailing ninety-year-old mother.

I had the plate that Sunday afternoon. Both managers brought their lineup cards to the plate meeting, something not seen very often now, but it used to be the norm. I shook hands with Bobby, knowing I would see him again a few weeks later in Atlanta. I then shook hands with Lou and said, "Lou, I'm honored to work your last game. Time's running out, so you better get your shots in."

He laughed. "I don't think it's a good look, to get run in my last game."

"Well, that's up to you."

Like I said, I liked Lou. We disagreed and had some pretty good arguments. But I would rather have a guy like him who pretty much leaves you alone until he doesn't, instead of a guy who whines and moans, inning after inning, always in your ear but rarely enough to get ejected.

One manager whom I absolutely did not get along with was Cito Gaston. This was when he had really good teams in Toronto, including back-to-back World Series champions in '92 and '93. With Cito, I could say it's Tuesday night, and he would say it's Wednesday afternoon. We simply could not agree. On anything.

When walking on the field with the crew—and this was long before I was a crew chief—I swear, in Cito's mind I was wearing a huge target, the go-to guy; I was the one he, and by extension his team, was going to pick on. I only ran him twice, but we always had some kind of disagreement. Once, with the A's in Toronto and Rickey Henderson leading off for Oakland, I called the first pitch of the game a ball. Cito piped up, "C'mon, let's go!" The first pitch!

In 1990 he actually challenged me to a fight during a game in Texas. Cito was bitching about pitches, as usual. In the bottom of the seventh, after a Rafael Palmeiro double, Texas was up 3–1. The Blue Jays walked Ruben Sierra to load the bases, and then Cito made his second trip to the mound that inning, which meant the pitcher had to be removed.

Gaston didn't signal for a relief pitcher as he crossed the foul line on his way to the mound, so I started out to find out who he wanted. He then signaled to the bullpen, and as I turned back toward the plate, Cito yelled my way.

"My guys are saying you are missing pitches."

"We're not going to talk about balls and strikes, Cito."

"Fuck you!" was his rather direct response. I ejected him.

After he called me several names, asked me to do things that are physically impossible, and once again informed me I'd been missing pitches, I told him he was "out to lunch." Not a particularly aggressive statement and certainly not offensive unless you have some weird compulsion about lunch, but it nonetheless set Cito off.

"I'm sick and tired of this shit. I'd like you to have the balls to say I'm out to lunch to my face outside the stadium. Why not meet me after the game?"

I told Gaston that he'd just threatened me, which would be in my report, and then I added, "Dr. Brown will love that you're threatening his umpires."

Cito's response: "Fuck Dr. Brown."

"Dr. Brown will love that too!"

Cito would yell, but he didn't throw theatrical tantrums. It was a personality thing; I just didn't get along with him.

Many years later, in 2008, Cito was in Toronto's front office when they fired manager John Gibbons. My crew was in Pittsburgh, where the Blue Jays were playing that night. About three hours before the game, I was watching

ESPN in my room when they reported that Cito Gaston would be managing the club for the rest of the season.

You gotta be shitting me. I hadn't seen this guy in years, and now here we go again.

Heading to PNC Park, I told the boys, "Be prepared to strap it on, guys. Cito Gaston's managing the Jays now, and he and I have never gotten along."

Walking onto the field, I didn't know what to expect. I'd last been on the field with Cito on August 31, 1997, nearly eleven years earlier. Now I was the only guy on the crew he even knew, and he came out of the dugout with a big smile. "Hey, Dale! Great to see you!"

After he introduced himself to the rest of the crew, I asked him, "How are you, Cito?"

"I'm just minding my own business," he said, "and suddenly here I am again, in uniform."

It was like we were best buddies and always had been. Meanwhile, I was thinking, *When we weren't getting along, I was always the youngest guy on the crew. He was always picking on me. Now I'm a chief and the only guy he knows. My, how things do change . . .*

We didn't have any problems the rest of that season, or the next two before he retired.

For my entire career, I'm credited with eighty-nine ejections by Retrosheet (which, as I mentioned earlier, shorts me by at least one). That might seem like a lot, but considering they came over the course of thirty-two seasons, it's really not. And some of those eighty-nine were part of mass ejections, where the crew had to eject multiple players because of a fight or bench clearing, not over a call or ruling I made.

In the world of umpires, I was probably more even-tempered than most. Got along with just about everybody and usually didn't take things personally. When I think back on my career, I have a hard time remembering moments when I was really *pissed*—you know, to the point of really losing my shit.

I remember just once, really. This was 2016, the last full season of my career (although I didn't know that then).

In 2015 the Rangers and Blue Jays had played an intense five-game AL Division Series. I know it was intense because I was there (for the details, you'll have to wait a few chapters) and well aware the Rangers would love to give the Blue Jays, and in particular José Bautista, a big Texas hello. Well, the next spring, we got our schedule, and my crew had the same two teams in Arlington in the middle of May.

A couple of weeks earlier, they were also scheduled to play in Toronto. I thought maybe they'd get it out of their system by kicking the shit out of each other there, and by the time we saw them in Arlington, hopefully they would just play baseball. Of course, in Toronto they were like church mice, quiet and subdued. *Move along, nothing to see here.*

Then came the series in Texas, the last time they were going to play each other all season. If something was going to happen, it was going to happen in those three games.

First game: nothing.

Second game: nothing.

Maybe they're over the emotion of last October? Calmer minds prevailed?

Yeah, right. Everything erupted in the eighth inning of the third game. But first there were a few housekeeping details.

In the top of the third, I ejected Tim Lieper, Toronto's first-base coach, for arguing with me about not calling a balk. Lieper was always kind of a whiny jerk. With Jays outfielder Kevin Pillar on first base, Cesar Ramos delivered a pitch to Josh Donaldson. Lieper, standing just a few feet to my left, started screaming, "That's a balk! He's not stopping!"

"It's not a balk."

"You're not looking; it's a balk!"

Ramos threw five pitches to Donaldson, and Lieper bitched about a (nonexistent) balk on every one.

On the sixth pitch, Donaldson hit a fly ball to left. Lieper, as soon as the pitch was delivered and while the ball was in play, was screaming.

"Goddammit, that's a balk!"

"No, Tim, it is not a balk!" I responded, trying to stay calm.

"You don't fucking know!" he screamed. "I watch tape every day. Do your fucking job!"

Remember what I said about first-base coaches and their duties?

You have a manager, and your manager does the arguing. That's not your job, okay, Tim?

Lieper has always been a whiner about this or that. You get *tired* of it, like fingernails on a chalkboard.

Now I was officially triggered.

First, I ejected him. Then I went off on him.

"You wouldn't know a fucking balk if it hit you in the face! I've told you a hundred times that's not a fucking balk!" Now in his grill, with my arms in the air, I was unloading on him. It was one of the few times in my career when I basically lost control.

It wasn't because he thought it was a balk (which it wasn't). It was how unprofessionally, disrespectfully, and aggressively he'd ambushed me. Having a difference of opinion is just another day at the office; what set me off was being attacked like I'm brain-dead.

So now we were all warmed up. In the bottom of the inning, John Gibbons—who'd been rehired to manage the Jays in 2013 and was now maybe a bit wired after watching Lieper and I go at it in the preliminary bout—started chirping about pitches. It didn't seem situational, as Toronto was ahead, 1–0, and it was still early in the game. For whatever reason, John kept harassing Dan Iassogna even after being warned, so Dan dismissed him for the day and he went to the clubhouse. But this wouldn't be the last time we saw Gibbons.

Leading off the eighth, with the Rangers up, 7–6, the number one villain in this story approached the plate.

José Bautista's thunderous home run and infamous bat flip in Toronto, seven months earlier, was the catalyst of the bad blood between these two clubs. Sure, there were other unwritten rules that may have been violated, but those were just minor subplots compared to Bautista and the flip.

Now, after five games this season and only two innings left in their sixth and final matchup, with Texas having failed to address the Bautista situation thus far, if the Rangers were going to "police" their grievance, it had to happen now.

Toronto knew it, Texas knew it, and we certainly knew it.

Matt Bush's first pitch hit Bautista. Immediately, Dan issued a warning to Bush and both managers. When José arrived at first base, he was angry but not surprised. Complaining to me and anyone else within earshot, he repeated several times how gutless Bush and the Rangers were. He was also glancing into the Texas dugout near us, while some Rangers in the dugout were throwing out their own pleasantries.

Toronto DH Edwin Encarnación flew out, which prompted Rangers manager Jeff Banister to bring in Jake Diekman from the bullpen to face Justin Smoak. During this time, and with Bautista having already been plunked, I hoped we had seen the worst, while knowing full well that emotions were still running high. If Bautista attempted to steal second or slid into another base on an extra-base hit or if there was a double play ball, the potential of José going in hard and being involved with some kind of collision was still very much a possibility. Three pitches later, it became a reality.

Smoak hit a ground ball that third baseman Adrián Beltré fielded and threw to second baseman Rougned Odor for an attempted double play. You can guess what happened next.

Bautista slid hard and late, his first contact being the middle of second base, taking out Odor's right leg and resulting in a wild throw toward first. Bautista continued sliding a couple of feet past the bag as Odor immediately squared up facing him. Odor pushed Bautista and then administered a clean right-handed punch to the jaw, a shot heard round the world . . . or certainly around Major League Baseball.

I didn't see Odor's famous right hook, because I was too busy avoiding his wild throw that almost hit me. Watching the ball all the way, it was just from the corner of my eye that I saw the Rangers' mass evacuation of their dugout, running toward second base.

And so the chaos began, with both teams engaging in a scrum in shallow right-center field. In these situations, you listen and observe, comparing notes with the rest of your crew when things settle down and you're able to get everyone back to their dugouts. Often but not always, managers try to reestablish peace.

Not today.

Toronto's Gibbons, ejected innings ago, came back on the field, which will just about automatically double your fine and be cause for a suspension, while the Rangers' Banister was worked up at least as much as his players. The two managers had to be separated, as I escorted John and Lance Barrett did the same with Jeff, walking them to their respective dugouts.

Once we cleared the field, which took nearly five minutes, the four of us got together to figure out who was getting run. With a melee like the one we'd just had, it's not unusual after the game to add names to our report after viewing the video, but on the field the crew came up with the following ejections: Toronto's Bautista and Donaldson and Texas's Odor and bench coach Steve Buechele. Of course, we'd also write up Gibbons a second time for entering the field after already being thrown out.

In the spirit of never letting a grudge fade away, once the game continued, Rangers DH Prince Fielder was hit by the first pitch in the bottom of the eighth. Warnings had already been issued, so Dan ejected Jays pitcher Jesse Chavez and acting manager and bench coach DeMarlo Hale, as per rule. Although the benches cleared once again, there were no more ejections, as nobody got overly aggressive.

Afterward, it took a while to watch the video and write the lengthy report, and of course, this was a getaway game, with all of us trying to fly home for an off day. But we got it done. This is a great example of me getting credit for five ejections (Bautista, Donaldson, Odor, Buechele, and Leiper), when only one of them (Leiper) was actually over a call (or in this case, a noncall).

Besides Cito, another manager I ran a few times was Tony La Russa. Off the field, Tony is a pretty chill, nice guy. He worked in the Commissioner's Office from 2012 through 2014 and was one of the main contributors to the expanded replay system at the beginning of the 2014 season. But once he put on the uniform, he was the most competitive son of a bitch you ever saw.

If Tony thought someone was throwing at one of his players, or if you actually *hit* one of his players, he didn't just retaliate once; he wanted to hit you twice, if not three times. Then he might consider being even. And he always thought his team was being thrown at.

With umpires, he could be an ornery prick.

I ran him four times: three when he managed Oakland and once when he was with St. Louis. The last one, in a game played in Atlanta, I got him and relief pitcher Alberto Reyes at the same time, and then later I wrote up his center fielder, Jim Edmonds, in a postgame ejection, since he gave me a couple of cheap shots as we were coming off the field next to the Cardinals' dugout.

Tony and I had an intense argument when I ran him over pitches. The next day, after the plate meeting, which Tony didn't attend, I ran to my position at third. Just before the first pitch, I heard, "Dale! Dale!"

I looked over at the Cardinals' dugout, and Tony was all the way at the third-base end, halfway up the steps, trying to get my attention. Once we made eye contact, he gave me a little salute, his way of saying, "Hey, new day. No grudges. Let's move on."

I worked the World Series in 2004, when the Red Sox swept La Russa's Cardinals. Game Four was in old Busch Stadium; I had left field. After Boston clinched, I was the last umpire getting off the field. Immediately behind home plate, there was a doorway. Going through that doorway and taking a left turn brought you into our locker room. Once all six of us had entered, we started high-fiving and congratulating each other; the Series was over with no controversy. We were going home, and so we were happy.

I sensed someone behind me, so I turned around. And there was Tony. Instead of going up the dugout runway to his team's clubhouse, he had followed us to our room. Immediately we stopped celebrating. Tony had tears in his eyes. One of the most competitive managers I have ever been around, who'd just gotten swept in the World Series, had followed us in and said, "I just wanted to come in and tell you guys, you had a hell of a Series and a hell of a year. Have a great off-season."

He shook all our hands, and off he went.

Tony was always this conundrum. He could be the most unwavering, pissed off, intense guy on the field when wearing that uniform. Then he'd do something like that after Game Four, and I'd think, *Gee, that was pretty classy*.

25

"I Am the Walrus"

Today's umpires, especially younger ones, are incredibly fit.

It hasn't always been this way.

Back in the late sixties and well into the seventies, both leagues preferred *big guys*. That's when you got Greg Kosc and Eric Gregg and John McSherry and Ken Kaiser. All of them were big boys, but that was by design. They wanted guys who looked intimidating.

Eventually, they realized the BIG look wasn't the *best* look, because it reinforced the perception (and sometimes the reality) that umpires were just old fat guys who couldn't move around the field much. There were also problems with injuries and medical issues.

Serious medical issues, on occasion.

John McSherry was an outstanding umpire, reaching the National League in 1971, when he was only twenty-six. By the 1990s he'd gotten big—his official weight was 328, but who really knows—and before '96 he'd exited a few games because of dizziness or dehydration.

On opening day in Cincinnati, April 1, 1996, John got through seven pitches, called time-out, and a few seconds later suffered a massive coronary and died. He'd been scheduled to see a heart specialist the next day. Like McSherry, Eric Gregg was probably pushing four hundred pounds by then; in fact, the two of them had talked about getting together for a weight-loss program. Shortly after John's death, Eric took an extended leave of absence. When he returned to the field in July, he wasn't exactly *thin*, but he was noticeably less big.

Meanwhile, in early May of that same year, my crewmate Rocky Roe did the same thing, going to an intensive inpatient weight-loss program, with everything paid for by the American League. When he came back a month later, he looked great and has been pretty successful keeping the weight off ever since.

But it really wasn't until 2001, when both leagues' umpiring staffs were combined and under new management, that MLB got serious about this stuff. Mackie Shilstone, an internationally known sports-performance specialist out of New Orleans, was hired to work with us. Every January at our umpire retreat in Scottsdale, Shilstone would administer different baseline tests and set up customized exercise and nutritional programs for each umpire. The bars we had to clear weren't exactly strenuous, but this was the first time *any* recommendations were set up for our fitness and well-being.

I was at my heaviest in the early nineties, and at that point—perhaps comparing me to a few others on the AL staff—the bosses didn't seem to care and never said anything to me.

When I broke into the Majors, I weighed around 195. I did beef up over the next few years. Right around then, three sets of umpire cards were produced for the retail market. If you look at those three cards, as each year went by, my neck was a little bigger. I would stick my head out a little, trying to disguise it. By 1992 I was at 225, the biggest I ever got. Within two or three years, with some dieting, I got back down to around 205, since I knew 225 wasn't where I wanted to be.

My fitness and my weight were one thing, and I felt okay about that after '94 or '95. On the other hand, my face . . .

It was weird. For whatever reason—there was no real medical reason, just kind of the way it was—starting around 2003, I was gaining weight under my chin, really my whole upper neck. All this fat was just deposited *there*. I looked way heavier than I was, because when I gained a little weight, it didn't show in my stomach or ass; it was mostly in my face.

This all came to a head (so to speak) in 2005, when I had a situation with Frank Robinson and Mike Scioscia.

We were in Anaheim, and Robinson was managing the Washington Nationals. He had a player, José Guillén, who'd been suspended by the Angels at the end of the previous season after an in-game run-in with Scioscia, his manager. Guillén was then traded to Washington in the off-season.

In the seventh inning of this 2005 game, Scioscia lifted his starting pitcher and called to the bullpen for Brendan Donnelly. Tim Tschida had the plate, and I was at third. When Donnelly got to the mound for his warm-up pitches, Robinson strolled out and asked Tschida to check Donnelly's glove for pine tar.

Since I was crew chief, Tim called me over. But unlike most cases when the manager has a suspicion, Frank told us *exactly* where to look. Later we found out that Guillén, Donnelly's ex-teammate, knew exactly where Donnelly loaded his glove with pine tar, and tipped off Frank. The pine tar was right where Robinson said it would be, and it was obvious.

Scioscia, who was standing with Tim and me when we received and inspected the glove from Donnelly, saw the same pine tar we saw. He grabbed the glove; said, "No problem, we'll just get another glove"; and started walking to the Angels' dugout.

"Whoa, Mike, that's not how it works," Tschida said, stopping him.

"Donnelly's ejected for having a foreign substance," I said while taking the glove back.

"He hasn't thrown a pitch! He didn't do anything! We'll just switch gloves! Pine tar doesn't affect the ball," he pleaded.

"Sorry, Mike. Donnelly's done. And we're keeping the glove for the league to look at."

I gave it to Dan Iassogna and told him to secure it in our locker room with our clubhouse attendant.

That was when things got really interesting. As we waited for Donnelly's replacement, Mike looked toward the Nationals' dugout and started yelling at Robinson: "That's fucking bush league, Frank! You're better than that!"

Robinson, who was a tough SOB and simply refused to be intimidated, came out of the dugout, calling Mike a gutless cheater. Scioscia said he'd have every one of Robinson's pitchers "undressed" when they reached the mound. Of course, as these guys started jawing at each other, the dugouts and bullpens emptied. Guillén was the only player who got pretty amped up, but he was held back so that he couldn't do any damage.

We finally got the managers away from each other and the field cleared. When we went to the bottom of the seventh, Gary Majewski came back out to pitch for the Nationals. And Scioscia left his dugout and motioned for me. "I want you to check his glove. His laces are too long."

Frank came storming out as Tim and I approached the mound. The laces on Majewski's glove *were* too long. In this case, however, it wasn't a substance that could affect the ball but simply a uniform or equipment issue, easily addressed with a pair of scissors.

However, when I told Frank about the laces, he said, "Did that son of a bitch ask you?"

"Mike did ask us," I told Frank.

Robinson, looking right at Scioscia in the Angels' dugout, screamed, "You're a fucking cunt."

Ouch!

The next day in the *LA Times* sports section, above the fold, I saw a photo of me and Tschida trying to get between both managers. In this photo—and frankly the angle wasn't doing either of us any favors—I looked like a walrus. I had so much fucking fat underneath my chin—or should I say, chins—that they seemed to be multiplying like guppies. Looking at that picture, I thought, *Good God, what the hell happened to me?* while the only thing I could hear in my mind was the Beatles' "I Am the Walrus." Without seeing my body but only my face, you would've thought I was six hundred pounds.

It was literally that day, because of that photo, that I said to myself, *We all get a playoff bonus in November. I'm going to see a doctor and see what I can do about this.*

I did exactly that. One of my off days later that summer, I saw a plastic surgeon in Portland at OHSU (Oregon Health and Science University). He said it would be "no problem" and explained the procedure. First, liposuction, sucking out all the fat from my walrus jowls. Second, a face-lift, tightening my now (after the lipo) droopy and extra skin by pulling it up and attaching it behind my ears. Somehow, that didn't *sound* like a "no problem" procedure. But I was game, so I scheduled it.

Mike and I had a trip to Europe planned right after the season. I knew I wouldn't have the World Series, because I'd had it the year before. So along with a couple of friends, we planned a departure for two days after a potential seven-game League Championship Series would be over. Scheduled to get back from our Europe trip on Halloween, I scheduled my face-lift for

November 7. I actually called it, and still do, my *radical facial reconstruction*. Sounds way cooler than face-lift.

Mike was great about the whole thing, saying, "I like you just the way you are. If you'd feel better and want to do this, absolutely. Go for it. But if not, don't worry about it."

Let the radical reconstruction begin!

It's outpatient surgery, so I was home that afternoon, all bandaged up and looking like a cheap horror movie. I wasn't in too much pain and fell asleep right after I got home. Of course, there was a reason I wasn't in much pain: the massive dose of hospital painkillers was going strong. When I woke up a few hours later, my face was barking like a mofo!

"MIKE!!"

The Oxy prescription for pain, which said one or two pills every four hours, wasn't going to last long if I kept taking two every *two* hours. The pain was excruciating.

My radical facial reconstruction was on a Monday. Wednesday, I checked under the bandages . . . Ugh. I looked like I'd been run through a meat grinder. Just awful. Of course, the doctor had said it wasn't going to look pretty at first. But looking in the mirror, I thought, *My God, what did I do to my face? I actually asked for this?*

I was already in pain, and I started wondering if I'd ever look remotely normal again. Thursday, I went to see the doctor. After taking the bandages off, looking right at me, he said, "Aw, that's beautiful."

What, seriously? This is a hell of a situation, Doc.

It was another month before I looked like a human being again.

The next spring, only a couple of guys said anything. I'd been with Tschida, Iassogna, and Kulpa when the walrus picture ran in the *LA Times*, and they were the only umpires I told about the surgery. The first time I saw them was two months later, at our retreat.

Before I had radical facial reconstruction, I know many thought I had gained weight, because of my many chins and my "I Am the Walrus" look, even though I hadn't.

Afterward, very few noticed or commented on my facial reconstruction, but many commented about my (negligible) weight loss. In the before and after pictures, you can really see the difference.

I also have very obvious before and after pics from 2014, when I got the Bosley hair transplant. Of course, since I was wearing a hat on the field, it's tough to pick that up.

So now, with a face-lift and hair transplant, I can check off the "You're So Vain" *and* "stereotypical gay man" boxes.

26

Postseason from Hell

In 2009 I was assigned the AL Championship Series, Yankees versus Angels, and there was no way around it—we had an ugly series. Especially the fourth game.

But even before that, umpires had been on *SportsCenter* way too much. In the very first game of an American League Division Series, C. B. Bucknor—and it's worth mentioning, this was before we had video review—made a couple of questionable calls at first base. In the second game of the *other* AL Division Series, Phil Cuzzi missed a fair-foul call in the tenth inning that might well have kept the Twins from beating the Yankees. And over in the National League, the Phillies beat the Dodgers in a Division Series game when Jerry Meals didn't see a batted ball strike Chase Utley after he checked his swing; Utley wound up with a single that helped keep the game-winning rally alive.

So by the time our series began, people were already talking about umpires.

The first three games were, from our perspective anyway, uneventful.

The fourth game was a shithouse.

In the fourth inning, the Angels thought they had Nick Swisher picked off at second base. I had him safe. I knew it was close, but I didn't think I missed it. Looking at replay, he was out. Angels shortstop Manny Aybar didn't argue at all, but I know well enough that doesn't mean you're right, just as a player arguing doesn't mean you're wrong.

But just a few minutes later, Swisher got wiped off the bases when Tim

McClelland, working third base, ruled on appeal that Swisher had left too early when tagging up on a fly ball; again, replay suggested that Tim was wrong.

Both of those calls were, however arguable, at least nothing extraordinary without the benefit of slow motion and instant replay.

What happened in the fifth inning was different. On a fielder's choice and throw home, Angels catcher Mike Napoli got Jorge Posada in a rundown all the way up the line back to third base and then tagged both Robinson Canó arriving at third and Posada while both were off the base. It should have been a double play, which was obvious to everyone watching on TV . . . but Tim didn't realize Canó was off the base when tagged and left him safe at third.

I didn't see Canó off the base when he was tagged, either, although I wasn't looking for it. I was behind second base looking down the baseline toward third while keeping an eye on the batter-runner Swisher and if he was continuing on to second; everything happened fast with a lot of moving parts. The only one of us who had any clue was Laz Díaz, working left field in his first LCS. However, he didn't react or come in signaling he might have something different, and the call stood.

After the game, Tim felt horrible, saying, "How did I miss it? How did I not see that?" I too was disturbed after seeing my miss on the pick-off attempt.

The Yankees wound up winning, 10-1, but all anyone wanted to talk about was us.

Working the fifth game, at first base, I had a wacker, calling Johnny Damon out to end the Yankees' third. I was confident I'd gotten it right. Looking at the replay, obviously I hadn't.

If that had been my (or our) only miss, I don't think it would have resonated. But after what happened the night before, not to mention the entire post-season to that point, we made it easy for Joe Buck to say on Fox's broadcast, "Well, just add this one to the pile of blown calls this October."

I'm not sure that anyone who has never umpired or officiated knows how low you feel when you miss a call, even more so when it's in a postseason or extremely important regular-season game. It haunts you, follows you, and can (unfairly) brand you not only for the rest of your career but well after you've left the field.

Ten nutcutter correct calls in big games, like my Game Three foul ball in the 2001 World Series, are wiped out, forgotten with just one big miss. Fair? Not really. Inevitable? Unfortunately, yes. Even though you should be judged on your entire body of work, fans, media, even casual observers will always remember a mistake that's talked about and shown repeatedly for hours, days, sometimes decades. I'm not complaining, just pointing it out. All of us know it's part of the package when we sign up for this.

So with an umpire postseason from hell and me kicking calls in back-to-back games, now I had to strap it on for the sixth game, in Yankee Stadium. You do everything you can to block out all of that and focus on the present. Move on; do the job in front of you.

I had a good, solid game. In the fourth inning, the Yankees had the bases loaded, and a 3-1 pitch on Alex Rodriguez was a nutcutter, just missing the inside corner. I had it off for ball four, forcing in a run. Angels manager Mike Scioscia gave me a couple of shots from the dugout.

Watching it after the game with the strike zone box on the screen, the pitch is inside and doesn't touch any part of the line, meaning it was a ball according to their own graphic. Yet after the pitch, our buddies Buck and Tim McCarver weighed in.

"Well, I thought it was a strike."

"So did I."

Hold on. According to your almighty on-screen graphic that you swear by, I got the call right, but you're *still* going to say I was wrong? That's just not fair. On that same pitch, without the issues of the past couple of games, they might have said, "Close pitch, but good call by Dale Scott." Oh, who am I kidding?

The Yankees wound up winning that game and clinching the series, then beating the Phillies in a World Series that, thankfully, was relatively free of controversy.

But the damage had been done. The following January, we got the shocking news that supervisors Marty Springstead, Rich Garcia, and Jim McKean had all been fired by Major League Baseball.

We were not happy about this at all.

Jimmie Lee Solomon—whose title was executive vice president of baseball operations—was the one who purged those guys. From my discussions with

Marty, Jim, and Richie, as well as others within our ranks, I don't think he even liked his job; he always had wanted to be a Hollywood movie producer. That's fine; nothing wrong with that. But he just didn't seem like someone who really enjoyed what he was doing.

Jimmie Lee came off as someone whom you could not talk to because he knew everything. Marty and Richie, and to a lesser extent McKean, were a threat to him, because he felt his decisions concerning umpires—crew composition, postseason assignments, crew chiefs, or whatever—weren't necessarily respected, or were second-guessed, by Richie and Marty.

I think the perception was that he got rid of those guys because they were a threat to his leadership. Also, he and other high-ranking people in MLB wanted younger blood in supervisor positions. I understood that part. But the thing about Richie and Marty was that, even though they were longtime umpires getting older, they were *not* living in the seventies or eighties. They understood changes in the game, changes in umpiring. They recognized that the game evolves, and they weren't stuck in some past era they couldn't get out of.

I swear to God, if right now you talk to the staff that was around Marty, either when they were in the American League or after the league staff consolidated in 2000, you'd get nothing but praise for him.

Marty was a guy who could chew you out for screwing up and also get you in the mindset to correct whatever it was and move forward, and all in such a beautiful way that you'd be open to it, without getting discouraged or defensive. You took it all in and felt better about yourself afterward. He had that ability, which is rare.

Meanwhile, Richie was (and is) one of *the* best instructors for young umpires. I spent five years on his crew, trying to dig out of the hole I had dug, and then fell into, during the '87 season. He brought me a long way, helped me build a lot of confidence, and also taught me so much of the nuts and bolts of umpiring, just because he's that good of an instructor, as well as an outstanding umpire.

I understood Jimmie Lee wanting to get some younger blood in there, because the game certainly was evolving. Maybe he didn't think those two fit that mold, that they were stuck in the past, just a couple of old men.

But like I said, there was also a real perception that he was in a job he didn't like and that he was a guy who, if you challenged his leadership or his decisions, wasn't open to a lot of discussion. It was his way or the highway.

We didn't see it coming, and we were not happy. There hadn't been any rumors, so it caught all of them by surprise. This all happened suddenly in January, like Nixon's infamous Saturday Night Massacre. It just happened— *boom*, they were gone.

With Marty especially, because of all the years he devoted to this game, both on and off the field, and because of all the good he did for umpires—and Richie, too, as far as that goes—we really felt that the move was made out of spite. We felt that Jimmie Lee could have said to Marty and the others, "Listen guys, we're going in a different direction next year, so this will be your last season," and given them a sort of farewell tour.

Marty knew people in every fricking town—not only people involved with baseball but also the bellmen, bartenders, and restaurant workers. At the ballpark, Marty knew *everybody*. I remember in 2003 we had Boston at Philadelphia in a weekend series, with Marty there supervising. The crew and Marty went to dinner Saturday night. Sunday was a day game, and afterward the other guys left town. But Marty and I stayed. We went to dinner and then hit a couple of other places for a drink. Marty knew *all these people* . . . bartenders at Ruth's Chris, the maître d' at Morton's, this guy, and then this guy too.

"Christ, Marty," I said, "you were in the American League for twenty years. Philadelphia, you've been to very few times. How do you know everybody?"

"Scotty," he said, "that's what I do. I know people."

That's just the way he was. He was such a great ambassador for the game, as well as an excellent mentor for young umpires.

So when Jimmie Lee let them go, it seemed cheap, and spiteful, that they didn't allow those guys a graceful way out. That caused some real bitterness among us, as a group.

Quite frankly, Jimmie Lee was not well respected by umpires, mostly because he didn't seem to care about anything we said. When etiquette demanded, he would listen to you, and when you were done, he'd say, "Okay, thanks," and then go do whatever the hell he wanted to do. Wouldn't even consider it.

In the immediate wake of the firings, MLB's Rob Manfred—later the commissioner, of course, but at the time vice president of labor relations and human resources—told ESPN, "When things go less than perfectly, as they did in the postseason, you're going to think about making changes. And part of it is just the natural turnover in an organization. It's no more complicated than that."

I think that's a very convenient thing to put out there to justify what they did. Obviously, I had been right in the middle of that postseason, so I understand that everything didn't go perfectly. But I think—and this is my personal opinion—that was just an excuse, with a lot of other things involved.

If Jimmie Lee was truly concerned that supervisors were getting too old, that's a legitimate point. When I went to umpire school, Al Barlick was supervisor of the National League, and Johnny Stevens was for the American. I thought at the time, *These guys are fossils*. There were times when they would tell us something, and then, off to the side, we would be corrected by an instructor, because those two had been talking about how *they* had umpired back in the 1950s and 1960s.

Well, the game had changed. It wasn't that Barlick and Stevens weren't great umpires. But it was hard for me to relate to them, as a young guy, and it certainly wasn't what we were being taught. So that's a legitimate thing. It's just that Marty and Richie were not in that category. With Jimmie Lee, we had a real sense that he had his own issues and agenda.

27

Get the Hell Out of the Way

Usually, baseball "fights" aren't fights at all. What they always *are*, though? A pain in the ass, since we have to write a report if we have one.

Team protocol (and something I hate) is that if a player from one team starts screaming at or approaching a player from the other team, then here we go: both dugouts have to empty, and all the pitchers and catchers and coaches in both bullpens have to sprint all the way to the infield, although I'm being nice by saying they sprint. Hey, why not just square off in center field and save everybody some time?

And then what usually happens? Everybody yells at each other, grabs somebody, and hugs. Whichever player was pissed and started the whole thing gets *really* aggressive only after he's being held back by teammates, which looks really badass but pretty much guarantees he won't actually have to risk getting his ass kicked or suffer an injury that could cost him and potentially his teammates a great deal of money.

In my career, I did have a couple of interesting bench clearings, instigated not by players but by their managers.

I already told the story about Angels manager Mike Scioscia and Nationals manager Frank Robinson getting into a screaming match. Because there was never much chance of someone actually getting hurt, we all sort of enjoyed that one. And I write about Tony La Russa elsewhere in the book too. But La Russa's in the Hall of Fame, and after I retired, he *unretired* at seventy-six—having been voted into Cooperstown seven years earlier—to manage the White Sox to the AL Central title in 2021. So he deserves at least one more story in this book.

In a Cardinals-Pirates game in June 2004—which coincidentally was Yadier Molina's MLB debut—La Russa and Pittsburgh manager Lloyd McClendon both got ejected. This was the last game of a four-game series, and two days earlier, the Cardinals' Scott Rolen had suffered a concussion after being hit in the head by a first-inning pitch. When La Russa suspects his guys are being thrown at, he'll retaliate in a heartbeat and maybe more than once. Anytime I had La Russa, whether with Oakland or St. Louis, if any of his players was hit by a pitch (or close), the crew was automatically on alert for the rest of that game and, for that matter, the rest of the series.

In this instance, I don't think Rolen was intentionally thrown at. But he did get smoked, so when, with two outs in the ninth inning of the getaway game, the Cards' Tony Womack had to hit the dirt on an up-and-in ball four, La Russa started yelling from the first-base dugout at Pittsburgh pitcher Mike González.

Of course, that pissed off McClendon. He stormed out of his dugout, making a beeline toward the Cardinals' dugout, so now La Russa pops out too. I had first base, and Brian Gorman was working the plate. So we were the two closest umpires to what was now two managers charging at each other.

Brian and I tried to get between them as they wound up face-to-face, screaming at each other. Naturally, both dugouts and bullpens emptied. But unlike most bench clearings, the players weren't after each other and, instead, just watched as their managers unloaded on each other. We ejected both of them, Brian got to write everything up, and the whole crew had a good laugh over the unusual baseball fight we'd witnessed.

The worst actual brawl I ever saw was during the second game of a doubleheader on August 24, 1993, Oakland at Milwaukee, with me working the plate. This included a few things that I, like most umpires, hated:

1. A doubleheader. Hated them. At least this was a straight doubleheader, and not the dreaded split, where you have two distinct start times, like one o'clock in the afternoon and seven o'clock in the evening. That way *they* get two gates, and *we* get a really long day.

2. An additional game added to our schedule. If you are making up a game that originally was on your schedule, that's fine. If you lose a game and another crew picks it up, that's even better! But the worst is picking up a game from another crew's postponement. Hated that. Every time you see a postponement on the board, especially early in the season when there are more weather issues, you immediately figure out if you have those same two teams later in the year. If so, there's a good chance you just got assigned an extra game, either as a straight doubleheader, a split doubleheader, or (worst of all) a lost off day.

3. Working the second game of a doubleheader on the plate. Hated that too. If your rotation had you on the plate in one of the two games, I always preferred the first. And what happened in *this* doubleheader illustrates why.

The first game started at 5:08 and went smoothly enough, with Milwaukee coming from behind with four runs in both the seventh and eighth innings to win going away, 9–2. We started the second game at 8:44, and again everything was routine enough as Oakland entered the bottom of the ninth with a 6–4 lead and with future Hall of Famer Dennis Eckersley back on the mound after getting two outs in the eighth.

Eck was usually damn near automatic (especially when pitching just one inning, which he wasn't this time). I was pretty confident that with Eck and a two-run lead, extra innings weren't in my future. At least I hoped not, as we were now past midnight.

But Eck struggled, missed his spots, and they hit him. He still could have finished it off, but with runners at second and third and with two outs, he walked Dickie Thon to load the bases and then gave up a game-tying hit to Pat Listach. Eck wasn't happy with how I'd called a couple of pitches before the hit, and as he walked to the A's dugout after finally getting the third out, he let me know it. I told him to keep walking, and he did. But as we were just getting ready to start the tenth, Eckersley yelled at me from the dugout, "You fucking cunt!"

I ejected him, and that's when the fun began.

Eckersley charged out of the dugout repeating his first statement a few times as well as issuing a ton of F-yous and go-fuck-yourselfs and saying how I was a piece of shit. After saying again, "You're a fucking cunt," I came back with, "Well it takes one to know one, Eck!" By this time, Davey Phillips had joined the "discussion" and was standing next to both of us when something happened that, frankly, I did not see coming.

Eck, about six inches away from me, puckered his lips and attempted to spit in my face. I heard the sound one makes when spitting, and I felt the *poof* of air hitting my cheek.

I was repulsed! I brought my hand up to my face, fully expecting to feel a sizable wad of spit . . . but felt nothing. It was dry, as somehow he did everything *except* actually spit on me. I don't know if he was too dehydrated to muster up enough moisture or if he intended this.

I looked at Davey, who had this part-horrified, part-surprised look, as he, too, fully expected to see Eck's DNA dripping down my cheek. Don't get me wrong—I was thrilled there wasn't any, but I was also incensed by what he *had* done. I screamed that this was going in the report, to which Eck responded on his way back to the dugout, "I don't give a fuck! You think I can't afford it?"

Meanwhile, La Russa had now joined the festivities and picked up where Eckersley left off, yelling about my horseshit strike zone and how I was fucking them. Then Tony said what I consider the worst thing you can say to an umpire. He accused me of cheating. Specifically, he claimed I'd been purposely calling balls on pitches in the strike zone.

There are many ways you can get ejected: say the magic word, throw your hat or equipment, show me up, or, of course, make physical contact. But one that will quickly get you tossed as well—and really set me off as most of those other things wouldn't—is to accuse me of cheating. It strikes at the heart of your integrity, an umpire's single most important quality. It's as low as you can go without, you know, actually spitting on me.

I almost threw out my shoulder ejecting La Russa, while letting him know how *bullshit* and *bush league* his comment was. We kept going at it, and by now it had been a while since the ninth inning ended. Milwaukee's Jesse Orosco had already warmed up when Eckersley started all of this with his cheap shot from the dugout.

Suddenly, Brewers manager Phil Garner appears, yelling to anyone who would listen about how long this was taking. This further aggravated La Russa, who started yelling and gesturing at Garner. So now I was old news (which I didn't mind) while the two managers were marching toward each other, screaming and cussing.

Davey and I, now joined by crewmates Mike Reilly and Rocky Roe, were trying to separate Tony and Phil as both dugouts and (of course, per their stupid protocol) both bullpens emptied onto the field. Next came another unexpected, never-seen-before turn of events.

Although both teams had come onto the field, they were still on their respective sides, probably enjoying the spectacle of their managers screaming at each other. Suddenly, without warning or provocation, A's outfielder Troy Neel, a former Texas A&M linebacker, charged the Brewers' line and took down Dickie Thon and Dave Nilsson with one tackle. I mean he seriously ran full steam for fifteen yards and just buried them.

Then, as I stated in my official report, "A major brawl erupted."

Let me stop here to explain the procedure umpires follow when benches and bullpens empty.

It's pretty simple, really: GET THE HELL OUT OF THE WAY. It's one thing when it's just a couple of players (or managers) going at each other. In that case, you at least try to get in the middle and keep them from doing much damage. But once the teams join in, all bets are off. I'm not a math major, but there are about fifty of them and four of us. If the multimillionaire ballplayers want to beat the shit out of each other, have at it! Our job now is to observe and take numbers.

But this wasn't your typical grab someone and do a little do-si-do. There were clusters of real fighting going on. Thon was fighting with A's coach Tommie Reynolds, and then Brewers coach Tim Foli joined in. (Later, while viewing the video, I realized Foli was actually trying to be a peacemaker, which was reflected in my report and was, considering Foli, a minor miracle.) You had two players on the field who were actually on the disabled list, Oakland's Mark McGwire and Milwaukee's Graeme Lloyd. Players on the DL can suit up and sit on the bench, but they're prohibited from participating in any activity, including harassing umpires or opposing players and, of course, joining any altercations on the field. Those two would be hit with automatic fines and suspensions.

But the most dangerous situation involved Oakland's Edwin Núñez, who had pitched for the Brewers the year before, and Milwaukee's B. J. Surhoff (or as umpires sometimes called him, B. J. Surlyhoff). Often in the confusion among all those bodies during a brawl, we might miss the more aggressive instigator or the first punch. So before finishing our report after the game, we would always check the video to make sure we saw everything from beginning to end.

We didn't need video for this, though, as both Rocky and I saw it clearly.

Núñez, who had pitched in the first game of the doubleheader, was in the clubhouse when the brawl broke out and ran back onto the field. Surhoff had shoved A's outfielder Scott Lydy and then was restrained by La Russa, Garner, and Oakland's Mike Aldrete. Núñez took offense to Surhoff's shove and—later claiming he didn't realize B.J. was being held back—decked him with a massive, blindside blow to the face. Surhoff never saw it coming and toppled to the ground, eyes rolled back in his head. There was blood everywhere, and he wound up needing stitches.

Rocky and I glanced at each other: *Wow, did you see that??* It was a crushing blow, the worst shot I had ever seen on a baseball field (only matched years later in Texas by Rougned Odor).

Finally, order was restored, and the crew got together to compare notes. As we decided who would be ejected, I wrote the names on the back of my lineup card. Davey and I then went to each manager to let them know who was staying for the rest of the game and which lucky bastards got to go home.

Remember, this all happened before the start of the tenth inning. We still had a game to finish, with no idea how long it would last. Personally, I needed to refocus and get back to calling pitches. We came close to ending the game in the Brewers' eleventh when they loaded the bases with no outs . . . but somehow didn't score.

Mercifully, in the thirteenth inning at 1:55 in the morning, Dave Nilsson hit a walk-off single. So five hours and eleven minutes after the first pitch, the second game was in the books. Our doubleheader, including a game that wasn't originally ours (again, hate that), from the first pitch of the first game to the winning run of the second, lasted eight hours and thirty-six minutes.

But my night wasn't done. Not yet. Not by a long shot.

Any time you have ejections, warnings, equipment violations, anything else out of the ordinary (including brawls, of course), you have to write an umpire report. Depending on the incident, the report needs to be filed in the league office immediately or, in some cases, within twenty-four hours. With the "Tuesday Night at the Fights" we'd just experienced at County Stadium, this report needed to be done and faxed—yes, faxed, since email wouldn't come to our world until 2000—tonight. Or rather, this morning.

I went with Davey to his hotel suite so that we could start our rather long report. We didn't arrive until around three in the morning, twelve hours after leaving the hotel for the stadium. To help with our writing—okay, actually to soothe our tired and aching bodies—we raided Davey's minibar. It took us about two hours (and several minibottles of gin) to write, edit, and fax everything.

We wound up with eleven ejections: two for arguing balls and strikes (Eckersley and La Russa) and nine for fighting or participating in team activities while on the disabled list (Oakland's Neel, Reynolds, McGwire, Núñez, and pitching coach Dave Duncan and Milwaukee's Garner, Foli, Lloyd, and Thon).

A few days later American League president Dr. Bobby Brown issued the following fines and suspensions:

Edwin Núñez	$7,500	10 games
Tony La Russa	$2,500	5 games
Phil Garner	$2,500	5 games
Troy Neel	$1,500	4 games
Tommie Reynolds	$1,000	5 games
Mark McGwire	$1,000	3 games
Graeme Lloyd	$1,000	3 games
Dennis Eckersley	$500	—
Dickie Thon	$150	—
Dave Duncan	$100	—
Tim Foli	$0	—

That makes the grand total $17,750 and thirty-five games.

Fines and suspensions are supposed to serve as a deterrent. You know, so you'll think twice before repeating such behavior. As you can see, participating while on the DL will get you $1,000 and three days, but attempting to spit in an umpire's face and calling him a cunt (more than once!) gets you just $500, which is otherwise known to these guys as a clubhouse tip.

Nice deterrent.

28

From Frank's Friendly
to Jimmy Fallon

The first time any of my colleagues said anything to me about being gay was during spring training in '98 or '99. There was this little bar, Frank's Friendly Tavern, just on the edge of the Arizona State campus in Tempe. It's gone now. But Greg Bonin started going there in the early eighties, and it became an umpires' hangout. Especially Minor League umpires.

In spring training, MLB guys like myself, who'd been going there forever, would stop by a few times and meet up with umpires who were working Minor League camps. A lot of them, I didn't know well or was meeting for the first time. On any given night, the MLB umpires on hand would pick up the tab for the Minor League guys.

One of those nights, Derryl Cousins and I were sitting at a table off to the side. Out of the blue, Derryl said, "Scotty, I know you have a different lifestyle than most of us. I just want you to know I think you're a great guy, and I would walk on the field with you any day. So it's not an issue."

Now my full defense mechanisms fired up immediately. For one thing, I've got no idea why this came up. So I just said, "I appreciate that, Derryl." But I didn't really admit to anything; I just took the compliment and moved on to something else. Later that spring, Rick Reed did the same thing, and I responded the same way, not really responding.

But if those guys knew? It seemed likely that just about everyone else did too.

In my first full season as a chief, in 2002, my crew was Jimmy Joyce, Jeff Nelson, and Ron Kulpa. But we all had single weeks off during the first month of the season. So our first game on the field together, as a complete crew, wasn't until May 7. And our first opportunity for a crew dinner was May 18 in San Francisco. After our Saturday afternoon game, we went to Morton's, one of our favorite hangouts.

After we'd ordered and the wine had been poured, Kulpa pipes up, "Okay, chief. Let's talk about the elephant in the room. Dale, we know you're gay. We don't care. We want to be able to joke and bust balls this season without walking on eggshells."

At that, Jimmy grabbed the wine bottle and tipped it up, making it look like he was guzzling it, while I'm pretty sure Jeff did a spit take across the table. I froze for a second and then smiled, not too surprised Ron would make a statement like that, since he basically has no filter.

I was actually happy about Ron putting it out there. Jimmy then shared a conversation he'd had with his wife, Kay. *She* had figured it out and tried to explain it to Jimmy. But guys like Jimmy and Davey Phillips, they were mostly oblivious. For one thing, they had a stereotypical idea in their mind of what a gay person is like. And when you're not that, when you're not checking those boxes, I think a lot of them just sort of say, even when there are other signs, "Nah, there's no way."

The same thing goes for my father. There were a hundred things saying, *Dale's gay.* But hey, he went to the prom with a girl, so I'm sure that can't be true. Unless Dale actually tells me, I'm not going to believe it.

A decade or so later, it became sort of official when I got Mike, who's now my husband but wasn't then, listed as my domestic partner on my MLB insurance benefit. All my colleagues were aware by then, and now my employer was too. When Cathy Davis, umpire senior administrator, was making arrangements for the opening series trip to Australia in early 2014, she gave the names of the umpires and their guest to MLB International, who were booking the flights and hotels. When Cathy gave Mike's name as my guest, the person at International responded with, "So Dale wants a room with two beds?"

"No, he wants a room with one king-size bed."

"Are you sure?"

"Yes, I'm sure!" Cathy was one of the first to know about Mike and I, and she was a huge ally.

But that was about as far as it went until later that year, when *Referee* magazine was putting together a story about me for their October issue and asked for some nonbaseball photos from before I got to the big leagues.

The story's about me growing up in Eugene, working at KBDF, the beginning of my umpiring career, first in high school and then professionally. The writer, Peter Jackel, did a great job interviewing friends from high school, my radio program director, and the local umpire association commissioner who got me started in 1975, with everything accompanied by corresponding images.

Just after the season in 2013, Mike and I had been legally married in the backyard of our winter home in Palm Springs, with the ceremony officiated by then mayor Steve Pougnet. That felt like another huge victory for equal rights and a victory I no longer wanted to hide. Meanwhile, this *Referee* article would be coming out, and the most important person in my life wasn't even mentioned?

That's why I submitted the photo of us with a telling caption: *He and his longtime companion, Michael Rausch, traveled to Australia for the 2014 season opener between the Diamondbacks and Dodgers.*

I understood this would potentially (and finally) out me, quite publicly. While it might have seemed somewhat accidental, I wanted that and was ready for it. With all the sacrifices and hardships the LGBTQ community and individuals had made and continue enduring, it had become hypocritical for me *not* to come out, to *not* be proud of who I am and our (at the time) twenty-eight-year relationship.

The magazine was delivered to subscribers in late September . . . and nobody really seemed to notice. Maybe because the article wasn't published online. But one D-1 college football official picked up on it and emailed the editors of a website called *Outsports*, who contacted me about doing a story. I wasn't interested at that moment, with the postseason about to begin, but I agreed to do something after the World Series. The *Outsports* story, written by Jim Buzinski, came out on the second of December, and that opened the floodgates publicly.

About a week later, I was in Palm Springs, half asleep with *The Tonight Show* on. As Jimmy Fallon was doing his monologue, he started out, "Some pretty big sports news here," and I perked up a little. "Dale Scott recently became the first Major League umpire to come out as gay. Well, he says he's out, but the other umps said he's safe. So now they gotta look at replay."

I jumped out of bed, not believing what I just heard. It was so surreal.

In February, just as spring training was starting, I was contacted by *USA Today*, HBO's *Real Sports*, and CNN. I told all three the same thing: I'm still gay. So there's really nothing to talk about. Right now, the focus should be on the thirty teams that think they can win the World Series. If you want to talk *after* the season, about how everything went, I'll be happy to. But right now there's no story.

That spring I was in Arizona. My first game was in Goodyear: Reds versus Indians. First two innings, I was at first base; then I switched to third base. Between the third and fourth, Marlon Byrd, running from the outfield to his dugout, stopped and gave me a big bear hug, saying, "Buddy, I'm so proud of you. You're free. You're free!"

Same game, Joey Votto shook my hand and also said he was proud of me. Honestly, the only comments I got all spring were positive. And that continued into the regular season. Business as usual, never heard anything from the stands about being gay. Not a thing. Also, I received hundreds of email messages, most of them from people I didn't know and all of them positive.

So why didn't I come out earlier? Part of me wishes I had.

It's an enormously personal thing. No one can make that decision except the person who's contemplating it. In a perfect world, everyone gay would come out and blow away the stereotypes and preconceived notions of who, what, and how many we are. I encourage our community to live and be their true selves, to unchain themselves from hiding, lying, having to play the game.

But I also live in reality, and although many like myself have come out and found acceptance and love from family and friends, many others have received the opposite.

Outing someone is also wrong. With one exception. I do believe outing is warranted when closeted elected officials at any level, or someone who leads or controls an organization, actively promote or implement policies or laws that attack, oppress, or demoralize our community or infringe upon rights due every American citizen. That hypocrisy actively hurts our community.

Are there gay umpires working in Major League Baseball right now? None that I know about. Are there gay players? Of course. But I have no idea who, and if I did, I certainly wouldn't say. I do hope a player comes out and breaks the silent barrier that has gripped the sport. Once that happens, it should help others to take that step.

Following the *Outsports* story, I received hundreds of emails from around the world, along with comments on various websites. Many were personal and touching, some were funny, a few were juvenile, and, yes, a couple were insulting.

I was contacted by officials, coaches, and participants in multiple sports: baseball, softball, football, basketball, hockey, soccer, cricket, even professional wrestling. I heard from police officers, firemen, members of the military, mothers, fathers, from those who were straight, gay, bi, out, closeted. Of the hundreds of messages and comments, literally two were hateful or homophobic.

Parents expressed hope that my coming out would make it easier for their kids. Closeted gay coaches, police and fire personnel, teachers, and many others said this took them another step closer to walking through that closet door. The response was overwhelming and humbling, but not all were as serious.

A woman from New York wrote how proud she was of me, happy that I could finally be myself. She wished Mike and I nothing but love and a long life together. Then, in her second paragraph, she said, "However, as a longtime season ticket holder with the Yankees, for the life of me, I do not understand how you made some of those calls against them! What were you looking at?" I loved that! Because I want to be known not as "that gay umpire" but, instead, just as an umpire who happens to be gay.

In the *Outsports* story, I mentioned my love for the Ducks, which was repeated on several websites. An (anonymous) comment had me laughing: "I am shocked, SHOCKED Dale Scott has come out as an Oregon Duck fan. Then again, with all their uniform changes, it's not too surprising."

Then there was the email I received from Sal Fernandez, a seventeen-year-old high school senior from the LA area. It caught my attention immediately, because his email address was dalescott5@. I was, he wrote, his all-time favorite umpire since he'd started working games four years earlier. Now, I'll admit, after seeing his email address, I wasn't sure, at first, if I should be flattered or inform MLB security that I had a stalker. But as I began to read his message, I quickly realized how my coming out could change a person's life.

Sal was in the closet and afraid that if anyone found out, it would sabotage his dream to work in the Major Leagues. But now, he wrote to me, "I know I may not have the skill to be a Major League umpire, but it won't be because of who I am."

Wow. I was blown away. I'd never second-guessed my decision to come out, but hearing from Sal confirmed that I'd made the right call.

Sal asked if we could meet for lunch when I was in the LA area. In early June I had a series with the Dodgers, staying in Pasadena. We had a great lunch, chatting as if we had known each other for much longer than a few emails. He was graduating the next week and looking forward to starting college that fall.

A couple of months later, just weeks before Sal departed for Northern Arizona University, I was back in LA, and we had lunch again. I asked how graduation went.

"Well, I came out to everybody that night. My family, friends at school, all because of you!"

"Really?" I said. "So how did that go?"

"It went well, but I wouldn't have had the confidence to say anything if we hadn't met the week before."

I was so proud of Sal and, must admit, a little proud of myself too. He did something at seventeen that I didn't fully do until my midfifties.

I wondered how things would have been different if I'd had an umpire to look up to, a role model doing what I was striving to do and who, oh by the way, happened to be gay? Would I have lost the fear of being outed, ostracized, and blacklisted with no chance of getting out of umpire school or of being skipped over, if I had been hired initially, because of my sexuality?

I was lucky. I was able to handle those fears and anxieties relatively well. Now I hope my coming out has made it easier for a current or future closeted umpire in the Minor or Major Leagues to simply be his or her true self. A player or umpire—for that matter, anyone—should be judged on their work and how they treat others, not on their sexuality or the person they love.

29

Flip

In 2014, just a few months before my official coming out, I'd been named crew chief for my eleventh Division Series: Cardinals and Dodgers. I had the plate in the third game, and Los Angeles's Matt Kemp was *not* happy with my strike zone. Kemp got in my face after striking out in the ninth, but I didn't eject him. After the game, Kemp said some truly choice things about my plate work. There were reports that he'd be fined, but MLB fines aren't large enough for a guy with a $21 million salary to notice. The Cardinals finished off the Dodgers in the fourth game. I didn't get assigned the World Series, and the third-game controversy probably hadn't helped.

A year later, I had another Division Series, this time an American League affair between the Texas Rangers and the Toronto Blue Jays.

Texas won the first two games, in Toronto. Toronto won the next two games, in Texas. So we all headed back to Canada for the decisive fifth game. And the seventh inning that night in Toronto might be the single most memorable moment of my career.

Right before walking out of the locker room to work the plate, if somebody had said to me, *Oh by the way, tonight you're going to have a play you've never seen before, a protest, several bench clearings, a couple of ejections, a few delays for fans throwing stuff on the field, and a seventh inning that takes an hour. Okay, now go get 'em!* I might have said, "You know what? I'm good," and just retired, right then.

For the first six innings, though, everything—I mean everything, except for this being a winner-take-all playoff game with nearly fifty thousand people in Rogers Centre and much of Canada, Texas, and the rest of the United States watching on TV—was relatively routine. Until the seventh inning, which was anything but.

In the bottom of the sixth, Toronto's Edwin Encarnación had tied the game, 2–2, with a line drive homer. In the top of the seventh, the Rangers' Rougned Odor led off with a single and then advanced to third on a couple of infield outs.

Shin-Soo Choo, a lefty-hitting outfielder who'd homered in the third inning, came up. Choo took a 1-2 pitch for a ball and then took a step back, starting his normal postpitch routine, with his bat held upright and no part of it in the space above home plate. In other words, he wasn't in Russell Martin's way at all. But when the Toronto catcher casually threw the ball back to the pitcher, the ball hit Choo's bat and rolled toward third base.

This was a situation I have never seen, and how many times have I watched a catcher throw the ball back to the pitcher in almost four thousand Major League games?

With the deflected ball rolling on the turf, I confused what was actually happening with a rule interpretation I had a year earlier in Milwaukee. With a runner at first and less than two outs, Jonathan Lucroy swung at a pitch in the dirt for strike three. Blocked by the catcher, the ball ended up in front of the plate as Lucroy started walking toward his dugout. Inadvertently, his foot made contact with the ball, causing it to dribble away from Colorado catcher Wilin Rosario. Seeing this, the runner at first advanced to second. The controlling rule there was, if contact by the retired hitter was inadvertent, the ball is dead, and all runners return to their original bases (if the kick had been intentional, whole different story).

Now, in the heat of the moment, I confused the Choo deflection while still at bat with the play in Milwaukee. So I threw up my hands and called time, while Odor was sprinting home from third. In the span of a couple of seconds, rapidly replaying the situation in my head, an unsettling wave hit me like a ton of bricks . . . that horrible realization that I'd just screwed up. *Wait! That ball's live. Why do I have my hands in the air?*

Almost immediately after recognizing my mistake, I went into full damage control—what could I do, *if anything*, to correct this?

The ball had glanced off the bat, rolling softly toward third. With two outs, the Blue Jays' infield was playing back and also shifted for the lefty pull hitter Choo. Third baseman Josh Donaldson was nowhere near the ball, while Odor, with no hesitation, broke for the plate the moment he saw the ball come off Choo's bat. When I erroneously called time, that sent Odor back to third.

Rangers manager Jeff Banister, a former catcher, came out and said, "Dale, I've had this happen before. That ball is alive." We had a brief conversation, but I already knew what I had to do.

I signaled for the crew to come together. Once all five were around me, I covered my mouth, just in case anyone wanted to lip-read (the mic I was wearing for television had already been turned off).

"I think I just screwed up here," I said.

I told them exactly what happened and what I'd done, and they all agreed: "Yeah, the ball's live."

"Okay," I said. "The ball was nowhere *near* a fielder, right? My calling time did not stop someone from making a play on Odor?" I knew the answer but wanted it confirmed so that we'd all be on the same page. Again, they agreed—no Blue Jay was in position to make a play on Odor if I had kept the ball live.

"Okay, this is what we're going to do. I'm going to score the run, and then I'll take care of John," meaning Blue Jays manager John Gibbons, knowing he would go crazy. And after I pointed to the plate to indicate Odor's run counted, he did.

Busting out of his dugout, John was livid, first arguing that Choo interfered with Martin's throw. I told him Choo was perfectly legal, so he continued on, trying to convince me that even if it wasn't interference, the ball was dead. I told him by rule the ball was still alive.

"John, we got the play right. I didn't look good doing it, but we got it right. And that's what counts." I explained that although I shouldn't have, me killing the ball had no bearing on the outcome of the play. Odor would have scored regardless, because none of John's players were in a position to make a play and he never hesitated when the ball was deflected.

Gibbons said he wanted to protest. So not only do I have a play I've never seen, but now I get the first protested game in my career . . . all in a series-deciding fifth game.

"John, I have to know what you're protesting."

"All of it," he said, "the whole damn thing. I'm protesting all of it."

"You can't have a blanket protest, John. So what *exactly* are you protesting?"

"Well, you guys screwed it up," he said. "I protest the rule. I say the ball is dead; he doesn't score."

Once a protest is lodged, we have a protocol we're required to follow. I got on the headphones with MLB Replay Operations Center (ROC) in New York and explained what had happened and why I'd made my final call. One of the reasons we're required to communicate with ROC is to confirm that the rule in question was enforced correctly. If not, you correct it then, so you don't lose a protest later and have to replay the game starting from that point. ROC confirmed that when I scored the run, I had correctly applied the applicable rule. If I had returned Odor to third, Banister could have protested and most likely won, because the rule would have been misapplied if I'd killed the ball.

As umpires, one of our mantras—and maybe the most important of them—is, "Common sense and fair play," which means what it says. In this case, common sense tells me the run would have scored, regardless of me calling time. And fair play tells me I'm not going to deny the Rangers a run because of my mistake, not to mention the one made by the Toronto catcher.

Let me be clear. If any Blue Jay had been in position to make a play on the runner and, by me calling time, I'd prevented that, then I would have to live with my time-out call, keep Odor at third, and live with the consequences. But nobody had been.

Around the country (and Canada, I'm sure) I was criticized by umpires on social media, for killing the ball and *then* allowing Odor to score. They said once I called time, I didn't have the right, by rule, to change my mind and advance the runner. Technically? Maybe. But does *common sense* say the runner would have scored? Yes. Would it have been *fair* to deny that run? No.

Finally, after signaling to the press box the game was under protest, I said to Gibbons, "John, the run scores, your protest is lodged, and now it's time to get this thing going." He continued to argue, so I had to ask him, "Do you want to get run? It's time to move on."

During the entire argument, John never cussed me or got personal, nothing to get ejected. But there are times when there's nothing left to argue, you've explained what you're going to do, and the game needs to continue. Now it's either get run or get back in your dugout. Because we're done here.

"No! I don't wanna get run, I don't wanna get run!"

"Fine. Then let's go."

The moment I scored the run, fans began throwing whatever they could heave onto the field. At one point, a Toronto police officer standing next to me, with garbage flying by us both, offered his advice: "My suggestion to you and your buddies, when this game is over, you need to get off this field as fast as you can." This perfectly matched what I'd already planned on doing.

By the time I talked to Banister, my crew, Gibbons, and ROC *and* the field had been cleared of all the debris thrown by fans, there were eighteen minutes between pitches. That might be some sort of modern record, and it completely screwed my pace-of-game numbers.

When we finally started playing again, Shin-Soo Choo struck out. But Odor's run had given the Rangers a 3–2 lead.

Fortunately, and somewhat magically, in the bottom of the inning, nearly everyone forgot about Dale Scott.

After three Texas errors and one unearned run to tie the game, José Bautista blasted a three-run homer. Bautista's posthomer bat flip is forever famous, at least in Toronto, as *the flip*.

Working the plate, there are times when the ball is hit and you think it will clear the fence and doesn't or you think there's no way it's going out and yet somehow it does. Then there are times when you know. When Bautista hit it, I knew. *That ball was smoked!*

What is so vivid, and I've heard plenty of loud crowds, was how deafening Rogers Centre became at the crack of Bautista's bat. The place detonated, and I can't remember another moment like it. Watching the ball as it was sailing out of the park, I saw *the flip* out of the corner of my eye and thought, *This could be interesting.* Given how everything had been building to that point, his emotional flip seemed understandable. But in the "don't show me up" world of baseball, I knew better.

In addition to the crowd erupting, they once again decided to delay the game and throw debris onto the field, but this time in ecstasy rather than outrage. The Rangers took exception to *the flip*, the celebration, the flying garbage, pretty much everything at this point. Twice the benches emptied, but no fights broke out. I did eject Toronto pitcher Mark Buehrle for entering the field while on the disabled list (and earlier, Vic Carapazza had ejected Buehrle's teammate Michael Saunders while I was arguing with Gibbons).

The Blue Jays won, 6–3, and advanced to the American League Championship Series. The fans, who'd wanted that evil plate umpire strung up not so long ago, forgot all about me. With the win, Gibbons's protest was never filed.

I still had to write a report, though. As an umpire, you're taught that your reports are essentially legal documents, so you need to be precise. I was up most of the night doing that, and I had an early flight home to Portland the next morning. So I never slept.

The next afternoon, I was at a grocery store back home in Portland when Joe Torre, chief baseball officer, called. He wanted to congratulate me and the crew for the way we handled ourselves during the chaos of the night before. He complimented me for keeping calm and steady, dealing with everything professionally.

The last game of the Division Series round was that evening, with World Series umpire assignments to be announced the next day. The seven World Series umpires would be drawn from the twenty-four who worked in the divisional round. But Torre never brought that up, a sign that I wouldn't be one of them.

I felt I had a solid season in 2015, and when assigned as crew chief and plate umpire in the fifth game of a Division Series, I thought I had a better-than-decent shot at working my fourth World Series and first since 2004. But even though my plate job in that fifth game was consistent and steady, I realized my error in that seventh inning, regardless of the outcome, would jeopardize any shot at a World Series assignment. I'd been praised for getting it right but looked horrible getting there. Much better than looking good and kicking a play, but perception matters.

This was the same disappointment I'd felt after the 2007, 2008, 2011, and 2014 seasons, with good evaluations and feedback the entire season, Division Series assignments . . . but no World Series call.

That unbelievable game in Toronto was my ninety-first in the postseason. I didn't know it, *couldn't* know it, but it was also my last. I didn't work the playoffs in 2016, probably because of 2015 (but I'll never know for sure). Five games into the 2017 season, my career was over.

Coincidentally, in Toronto.

30

"I Can't Believe This Is
Happening Again"

September 18, 2016, I'm in Philadelphia. So are the Miami Marlins. I've got the plate, and I'm having a horrible day.

I call Martín Prado out on strikes when he checks his swing on an outside pitch, and I suppose he's pissed off because I don't ask for help. This isn't my finest hour, and he might be right—like I said, not my best day.

He immediately fires his bat into the ground, and as I'm pointing toward the bat—that's an automatic fine, however small and ineffectual the amount—he sends his helmet after the bat. I eject him. Prado comes back for a little chat and is soon joined by his manager, Don Mattingly.

It's all routine stuff, really, but I mention it only because Prado is the last ejection of my career.

On April 14, 2017, my crew had opened our season with a week in the Replay Operations Center in Chelsea, Manhattan. Week two, we were on the field in Washington DC, with the Cardinals visiting the Nationals. As crew chief, I worked our first game on the plate, followed by games at third and second. Then off to Toronto for a four-game series with the Orioles; in the opener, I was on first base. That set me up for my second plate game of the season.

It would also be the last game of my thirty-two-year MLB career.

Just a quirk in the schedule, but I hadn't visited Toronto in 2016. So this was my first plate job there since the famous fifth game in 2015, which prompted me to joke with the crew, "Well, this should be interesting. It's my first time strapping it on here since they threw a bunch of shit at me."

Things went fine until the eighth. Mark Trumbo led off for the Orioles. Ryan Tepera had just entered to pitch for the Blue Jays. Tepera wasn't exactly a superstar, but like seemingly half the guys in the big leagues now, he routinely threw in the midnineties.

Tepera's first pitch was a ninety-five-mile-per-hour fastball for a called strike. His second, the same pitch, missed low and outside. Then another midnineties fastball, this one up and a little in. This time Trumbo took a rip—the same rip he used to hit forty-seven home runs in 2016, most in the Majors—but instead of zooming over the fence, the ball caromed off his bat straight to the lower jaw area of my mask.

It happens so quickly. You're getting lower to see a pitch, and the next thing you know, you're on the ground.

I never lost consciousness or a sense of my surroundings after any of my concussions. I just knew I'd gotten smoked. Things are cruising along, and then *BOOM!* Obviously, you feel the impact, but the loud thud, the clamorous explosion as the ball hits your mask, really sounds like something is blowing up in your face.

This time, I spun around and then dropped to one knee. Blue Jays catcher Russell Martin immediately bent down, telling me, "Just stay down, Dale. Stay down. You're okay." His sympathy didn't exactly surprise me, but I was somewhat touched, if only because we had a history over the years. Not one of my favorite catchers to work behind, Russell wasn't shy about reacting either verbally or with negative body language when he disagreed with a pitch.

Quickly the trainer appeared, while I was trying to process what just happened. Besides my head pounding, I told the trainer I felt a sharp pain in my neck, which triggered a whole series of events. Rightfully so. When it comes to the neck or spine, they're going to be as cautious as possible, and so here came the medical cart with the backboard and neck brace.

By now, Toronto team doctor Irv Feferman was on the field, too, talking to me the entire time about what they were going to do and telling me to remain still. The doctor, trainers, medical cart personnel, all were running around doing what they were trained to do, while I just felt helpless and defeated. I was thinking, *I can't fucking believe this happened again.*

Helpless, I laid motionless on the Rogers Centre turf. Defeated, knowing what was in front of me the next several weeks, if not longer, I'd already become way too familiar with concussion recovery.

After slipping the neck brace on, sliding me onto the backboard, and then lifting me onto the cart and strapping me in, off we went. Traveling from the plate area to an exit in the left-field corner, I could hear but (because of the neck brace) couldn't see the fans as they applauded. Of course, the last time I'd worked the plate in Toronto, fans pelted the field with debris. Now, applause. *Should I give 'em the thumbs-up as we drive off the field?* I didn't, but now really wish I had.

Once off the field, the cart drove back to the umpires' change room (as they say in Canada), where the ambulance was waiting. I'd worked the very first game at SkyDome, nearly thirty years earlier, and in every game since, I'd walked by a parked ambulance on my way to our locker room. I never imagined that one day I would be riding in it.

As I lay on the cart, parked in front of our locker room, my uniform shirt was slipped off and my chest protector was removed without disturbing the neck brace. They also slipped off my shin guards and (somehow) removed my cup.

Someone retrieved my phone and wallet and gave them to Dr. Feferman, who had been by my side since I went down. Traveling in the ambulance for the short drive to the hospital, I was coherent. I could still only look straight up. I heard the siren as we traveled and thought back to when I was young. *I always wondered what it would be like to ride in an ambulance. Well, here I am. So I guess that one comes off the bucket list.*

But then I kept thinking the same thing, over and over. *I can't believe this is happening again. Why did this happen again?* The last time I had to leave a game was the year before in Phoenix. First inning, second hitter of the game, Dodger Jean Segura fouled a Brandon McCarthy pitch off the bottom of my mask. Another in a string of injuries involving a fast-moving baseball hitting me and causing me to leave the game. Just in the previous few years? Concussions (foul off my mask) in 2012, '13, and '16; forearm injury (uncaught pitch) in 2015 spring training; and cup shot (foul ball) in 2016.

So now I've taken one on the mask for the second time in nine months, but really it's the second time in four working months. Segura's foul ball had knocked me out for the rest of July. I'd made it through last August and

September and through spring training this year, and now I was hurt again, in my second plate game of the regular season. It was deflating.

We arrived at a crowded Friday night emergency room. I don't think foul balls rate as highly as gunshot wounds and car accidents, so it took about forty minutes before I was wheeled into an exam area. While waiting on my gurney, immobilized, looking straight up at the ceiling and listening to the chaos around me, a jumble of thoughts ran through my head, including, *I don't want to do this anymore. I just don't wanna do this.*

Back home in Portland, a friend called Mike and said, "Oh my God, I just saw Dale was taken to the hospital. He got hit. It was on ESPN's ticker." But Mike already knew. Before I was put in the ambulance, my two man, Jim Reynolds, asked me, "What is Mike's number? I'll call him." Jim told Mike I was heading for the hospital and that I would call him when I could. Mike also got texts or calls from a few friends who saw me being carted off the field on ESPN.

My parents lived, at the time, in Fairfield, California, and got a call from friends in Alaska who happened to be watching the Mariners game when they showed my "highlight." With no information, they were freaked out. They knew I got hit; they knew I was in the hospital; but at that point, that was all they knew, even after speaking with Mike.

I finally was able to call Mike from the ER, about ninety minutes after I arrived.

"I'm okay," I said. "Another concussion, plus it looks like I have whiplash. I think I'm flying to Phoenix on Sunday, hopefully home Monday. I'll keep you informed."

The ER doctor talked to Dr. Feferman and myself, asking several questions. I'm sure they ran some tests, but all I really remember is being there, although I do recall a woman from admitting asking for my card. I handed her my MLB Blue Cross insurance card. Looking at it like it was written in Chinese, she replied, "Oh, you're not Canadian? You're American? That's a *whole* different thing." She left and then soon returned with a bill, putting my credit card on the hook for $600 (pretty cheap, really) for a CT scan and x-rays. I had a concussion and a headache, but I still kicked into political mode, thinking, *You know, we should have a health system where you just show them a card.*

After the game, my crew showed up. I wasn't nauseous, and my neck issues were muscular (not skeletal), so I was released. After a few instructions, the guys got me back to my room, and I gave Jim a key, just in case.

Eventually, I went to sleep. I don't remember any issues, except I was depressed and thinking again, *This isn't fun; I don't want to do this anymore.*

The next day, we had a 1:00 p.m. game. Dr. Feferman asked me to come to the stadium with the crew so that he could examine me. We arrived around 11:30, and Triple-A umpire Nic Lentz was already there. (Nic wound up working 109 MLB games that season and 149 in 2018, but he wasn't officially hired on staff until 2020. Yes, it's an odd system.)

Dr. Feferman asked me a few questions, examined me, and then cleared me to fly the next day to Phoenix, where I would see Dr. Steven Erickson, the longtime MLB umpire medical consultant who also runs a concussion center.

I went back to the hotel, relaxed all afternoon, and then had dinner with the crew: Jim Reynolds, Brian Knight, Lance Barrett, and Lentz. I always loved crew dinners. Going to awesome restaurants where we usually had great connections after a day game was one of my all-time favorite things. To me, this one felt solemn, like a goodbye dinner. *This might be the last time I do this with a crew, as an active umpire.*

When Sandy Alderson joined the Commissioner's Office, he hired Mark Letendre as the first director of umpire medical services. Essentially, he was the first dedicated trainer for umpires. At the Replay Operations Center in Chelsea, MLB tracks every pitch in real time, and immediately after an umpire takes a head blow from a foul ball, Letendre receives a text with the details and can access the video. Oftentimes, when someone on my crew got hurt and had to leave the game, by the time I walked into our locker room and called Letendre, he already knew everything. A Triple-A umpire was already notified and on his way; that's how quickly this shit goes. The logistics of bringing the guy up can be complicated, so they don't waste any time.

So when I spoke to Letendre about flying to Phoenix, everything was already set. "I'll pick you up when you get in," he said. "You're staying at the Courtyard Marriott. Monday morning you've got an appointment with Dr. Erickson; I'll take you."

Monday in Phoenix, Dr. Erickson asked a lot of questions and helped set up physical therapy for my neck in Portland.

I asked him, "What are the long-term effects, if any, of these concussions and head blows I keep getting?" Not to mention the ones before 2003, before anybody was paying much attention at all.

"We don't know," he said. "There's research going on, and we're certainly learning more every day. But we just don't have definitive data. We don't know what, if any, long-term effects you may have. One thing I *do* know is that the more head blows and concussions you get, the higher probability of long-term issues."

The other thing I remember him saying—and this was the first time I had heard this—was, "Another thing we know is that if you have Parkinson's or dementia in your family history, multiple concussions and head blows can cause that to occur earlier and more severely."

Whoa. My dad's father and my dad's brother both died of Parkinson's, and his sister had dementia, as did my mom's sister. So it's certainly in the bloodline. I filed away that information.

Dr. Erickson cleared me to fly to Portland that afternoon, so Mark gave me a ride to the airport. Sitting at the gate with a couple of hours to kill, I called Dan Purtell, our union attorney. I knew I'd remain off the field for at least two weeks and probably longer, as I wasn't sure how long before I would recover from whiplash. "I'm just throwing this out there," I asked Dan, "but what are my options for getting off the field, permanently?"

"Well," he said, "let me think about this."

"With concussions," he said, "we're not going to be able to get long-term disability. They don't have the data yet to prove that these concussions will affect you years down the road."

If I had blown out my knee and could never umpire again, sure, I could get long-term disability. If I had some other medical issue, maybe. But this? Not good enough for an insurance company.

"We certainly can try," he said, "but I can almost guarantee that it will be rejected." I did expect him to say this, but that's why you have attorneys.

"The other thing," Dan said, "is that once you're recovered from your concussion and whiplash, you can just retire. Then they can do a couple of things.

"We can try to negotiate some kind of a deal, because you have a very legitimate injury situation that has now happened four times. And you want to leave the field before you suffer another concussion that could result in significantly negative effects for you, not only now, but for the rest of your life. So maybe there's some room there to negotiate.

"But if you choose to do this, they could also say, 'Okay, you're retiring. As of today, you're off the staff, and you're not being paid anymore. You're now a retired umpire.'"

If I did that in April or early May, I would actually owe *them* money. Getting paid year-round means that every January through March you're paid for work you haven't done yet, while from October through December, you're paid for work done months ago.

Bottom line, they could simply accept my resignation and move on.

In 2017 I was fifty-seven years old and in my thirty-second year in the big leagues. I had planned to retire after the 2019 season, at sixty. So I would have had three seasons left—the current one and two more. If I'd suffered multiple concussions ten years earlier, knowing I wouldn't get long-term disability, it would have been tough to just walk away from the job.

Later, as Purtell and I were sorting through my options, I said, "We really need to come up with some sort of framework that allows us to negotiate with them. Because these concussions aren't going away, and I won't be the last umpire whose career is ended by them. Especially for the younger guys, who aren't near a natural retirement age, it would be nice if we had some sort of a safety net within the contract."

"It's funny you should say that," he said. "MLB and I have talked about that. Just in general terms—that in the next negotiation, we need to address this, see if we can figure something out."

When I finally got home, Mike said, "I was really worried about you. And I can't help thinking, maybe this is a sign."

"Mike, I thought the same thing. It definitely crossed my mind this time, where with the other concussions it didn't."

Over all those years, I'd never once thought, *Oh, this is too dangerous.*

After my first (diagnosed) concussion, back in 2012, one of my friends in Portland said, "So when you go back, do you think that first time behind the plate, when the pitcher starts to wind up, you're going to start thinking about it?"

"No. Not until you just said that." Because it really hadn't entered my mind. I just thought I'd recover and get back to work. I mean, things happen. You get hit.

And things did happen after that, yes. But this was the first time—flying from Toronto to Phoenix, flying from Phoenix to Portland—when I really thought, *What am I doing here? At this point, am I just doing it for the paycheck? I've got three World Series, a ton of postseason games, All-Star Games. I've been a crew chief. I've done basically everything you can do in this profession.*

How do I defend this to myself? And how do I defend this to other people, when they're carrying me off again? Odds are it's going to happen again, right? Because it keeps happening. When they carry me off again, how do I defend that? I'm not a young guy who's never had the playoffs, twenty years ahead of me, a family to support. I'm not that guy. I've actually got it all, literally just a couple of years away from retiring, according to my own plan.

And for the first time, after four concussions, this finally entered my mind: *If I go back on the field and strap it on, as the first pitch is coming in, will I think this is the one that's gonna get me?*

And if that's on your mind? Get off the field. You're done.

I also had several friends text me, saying, "Dude. This is real. Don't be a hero."

Mike never said, "I don't want you doing this, and I'm gonna put my foot down." Nobody close to me—not Mike, not my family—said, "Dale, you need to stop; you need to retire."

But after hearing Dr. Erickson talk about Parkinson's and dementia and after having all those other thoughts, I called Purtell and said, "Okay, let's try to negotiate something."

Now, depending on what MLB said, I might still have gone back to work. But I was pretty confident that we could come up with some sort of a settlement, where they didn't just cut me off.

In reality, I knew at the Phoenix airport when waiting for my flight to Portland that I was going to retire. After my evaluation from Dr. Erickson and learning about my elevated risk of Parkinson's and dementia, I knew I would walk away.

I would be retiring two years before planned. At twenty years of service, when I was forty-six, I became vested in our pension plan. And for every year I drew on my pension before sixty-two, I would get penalized. My original plan was to retire after the 2019 season, at age sixty, with my severance package serving as a two-year bridge to sixty-two and my full pension.

If I retired because of concussions now, just a few months short of fifty-eight, my two-year bridge would suddenly become four years. I could start my pension at sixty, but I didn't want to take the extra two-year hit.

Although Mike and my parents knew, I didn't announce my retirement decision to anyone else, since it would take at least a month, if not longer, for me to recover from my concussion, as well as my weekly physical therapy for whiplash. I wanted Purtell to exhaust whatever options I might have with the Commissioner's Office, while I sought another opinion from a doctor who wasn't associated with MLB.

I contacted Dr. James Chesnutt, associate professor at Oregon Health and Science University in Portland, whose expertise is sports medicine, with a special focus on concussion management. We talked for almost an hour at his clinic, and afterward I was even more certain that retirement was the prudent choice.

I was ready. I'd been ready for a while.

A couple of months before my Toronto concussion, while getting prepared for spring training, I told Mike I was having trouble getting excited. An MLB season is a marathon, with rain delays, extreme heat and humidity, umpire reports, running for flights, scores of hotels, restaurants, and countless trips and days on the road between now and October. I was fully prepared to work three more seasons, but that doesn't mean I was *eager* for them.

In 2016 Bob Davidson was on my crew. For various reasons, MLB wanted Bob off the field, so that August they proposed that any umpire who (a) turned sixty by the end of the calendar year *and* (b) had twenty-plus years of service could retire with a nice package. At the time, there were ten umpires who qualified for that package.

I was too young; otherwise, I would have jumped on it. Of the ten, Tim Welke and John Hirschbeck had already announced their retirements at the end of 2016. Besides Bob, there were probably four of the remaining eight whom MLB happily would have seen retire.

But the deal was designed specifically with Bob in mind; if he didn't accept it, the deal was off for everybody. That put a lot of pressure on Bob.

I love Bob, who would do anything for you. I called him No Filter Bob, as he, at any time, would say or do damn near anything. However, MLB was always on him, saying his ejections weren't "warranted" or that his actions were violations of our *Umpire Manual*.

Bob loved the job—loved being on the road, loved the camaraderie. Bob loved all of it, but he was old-school. He wanted to do, and sometimes actually did, things that umpires could get away with when he broke into the big leagues, which they continued getting away with until 2000, when everything changed.

When Bob was first informed of MLB's retirement offer, his initial response was, "*Fuck 'em*. I'm not doing that, and they can kiss my ass."

A few days later, after going home and talking to his wife, Denise, on an off day, Bob showed up in the locker room with a different tone. "I think my thoughts are changing on this," he told me.

"Really, Bob? Why is that?"

"Because Denise told me our thoughts are changing on this."

Denise had lived the often-lonely life of an umpire's wife for more than thirty-five years. They weren't getting any younger; not to mention this nice retirement had just fallen into their lap . . . take it!

Hirschbeck and Welke, already on their way out, also had this fall into their laps. I talked to Jimmy Joyce, who wasn't planning to retire, and told him, "Jimmy, you do what you need to do. In my opinion, you would be insane not to take this. I would take it in a heartbeat. I just don't qualify." He took it. In the end, those were the only four who took the enhanced retirement package.

Now it was just a few months later, and I asked Dan Purtell, "So why not the same package for me?"

Well, here's why: We worked under a *collective* bargaining agreement. MLB can't make an offer to just one member without that offer being valid for others who are, legally speaking, your cohorts. For example, the CBA prevents baseball from paying two umpires with the same service time different salaries or paying four umpires more than the other two on a playoff crew. Bob was sixty-four, so any union member that age or older would have to be included. MLB, by crafting the offer to those who were sixty-plus, included a few others on staff they weren't reluctant to lose.

MLB's answer, which Purtell and I were expecting, was, "But if we do it for you, Dale, we would have to make the same offer to everyone else in your age cohort. We're not going to do that."

I proposed to Dan a different deal, but he got the same answer from MLB.

Whoever replaced me, as a first-year umpire, would make approximately $300,000 less per year than what I was currently making. Therefore, I proposed that MLB could then pay me an annual payment of $150,000 (half of what MLB would be saving) for the next two years, since I would be retiring early for a legitimate reason (i.e., concussions) that doesn't happen to be covered by long-term disability. That would get me to sixty, when I planned to leave anyway.

"It's worth a shot," Dan said. "But I doubt they'll go for it. Again, MLB doesn't want to set a precedent."

And that, of course, is exactly what they said.

Okay. I understood, but I was still disappointed.

When we first approached MLB about me getting off the field because of multiple concussions, their reaction was, "Man, we don't want to see him go. We love his work and his leadership."

"Dale, here's the ironic thing about this," Dan told me. "If they wanted you off the field, they would work something out with you. But because you're a good employee, because you've done what you *should* do for the last thirty-plus years, you actually lose out. They are not going to give you anything that might *encourage* you to retire."

MLB said they wanted me back on the field but understood where I was coming from, so they offered to keep me on staff the rest of 2017, with full pay plus the postseason bonus that everyone receives, even if I didn't work another game all season.

Now, none of this was done from the goodness of their hearts. They'd already budgeted for my salary, and my games would be worked by Triple-A fill-ins. They also wouldn't have to name a crew chief, officially. All those decisions would be on hold until January. So there were good reasons for them to make that deal.

By the end of May I'd recovered from my concussion, and physical therapy had resolved my whiplash, so it was time to either get back on the field or . . . walk away.

Of course, I'd already made up my mind. Now I just had to make it official.

On June 1 I signed an agreement that kept me on staff for the remainder of the 2017 season, with full pay, benefits, and bonuses. What's more, this left me eligible for any (beneficial) changes to the CBA during the calendar year (about which there had been some talks, but ultimately nothing changed).

So upon signing, I was free from professional baseball for the first time since 1981. I could now enjoy my first free summer in thirty-seven years, and boy did I!

For decades, I'd been jealous of Mike and our friends enjoying Oregon's beaches and mountains, lakes and rivers all summer long, while I was sweating my balls off in Baltimore and Kansas City. Now I got to enjoy all those things, too, and more.

Shortly after making my retirement official, I drove to Fairfield, California, to visit my parents and my brother and his family. Next, it was Palm Springs, to check on our winter home before driving back to Portland. Mike and I enjoyed barbecuing several days a week, walking to a movie, or going for a nightcap downtown on a beautiful summer evening. In August we witnessed a total eclipse of the sun that passed right over Oregon, and we went to concerts under the stars at the Oregon Zoo. I did things that summer that I rarely could during the previous thirty-seven summers, and I loved it!

In June I went to an Oakland A's game with my dad, Jess; my brother, Tim; and my nephew, Shilo, arriving early to say hello to Gerry Davis's crew in the umpire room. I also drove to Seattle for a Labor Day game when *my* crew was there: Jim Reynolds, Lance Barrett, Mark Wegner, and Ben May. Only Jim and Lance had been with me in Toronto three and a half months earlier, with Brian Knight and myself both on the disabled list now.

Going to those games was very strange. When I sat in the stands in Oakland, it was my first time watching an MLB game as a spectator since 1983, when my Texas League partner Terry Mann and I saw an Astros game in the Astrodome. That June in Oakland, I was just two months removed from being carted off the field, but already it seemed like years.

Sure, I knew I'd always be part of the umpiring brotherhood, but never again among the working few. It was a sad feeling but one that all of us will experience. Even so, I never regretted my decision to walk away, and instead, I looked forward to the next chapter in my life.

31

No Complaints, No Regrets

My career spanned a ton of changes in the game of baseball. I worked in forty-nine different Major League ballparks (including nineteen new ones). I umpired in the Dominican Republic and opened the 2014 MLB season in Sydney, Australia. My first fourteen seasons were in the American League; the last eighteen, working both leagues. When I was hired in 1986, we didn't have an annual retreat for going over rules, positioning, or any new regulations or interpretations. In fact, in my first several years, we didn't meet at all, and later, just twice before the transition to the Commissioner's Office in 2000.

When I came up in the mideighties, umpires were still working like it was the Wild West, where supervision was lax and inmates ran the place. Today, every game is televised somewhere; back then, not so much. If you had a two-week West Coast swing, your crew might end up on a milk carton—*MISSING!*—with the Tuesday night game in Seattle showing up in the Thursday morning newspaper in the East. Ejection reports were mailed to the league office. In an envelope, with a stamp. Later we would fax them to the office, which, at the time, seemed like a miracle.

The late nineties did bring the internet, computers, and email. And then in 2000 everything changed. New management, new union, more supervisors, more money, *and* more rules and responsibilities: from the Wild West to just short of military discipline. QuesTec tracking and evaluating every pitch you call, electronic ejection forms with immediate notification to multiple department heads, videos of odd plays sent to every umpire, rare rulings or pitchers with questionable moves to study (and you damn well better be prepared when he used it).

The strike zone was tweaked, pace of game became a thing, crew consultations went from rare to mandated, and the days of giving as good as you were getting in an argument were over. Fining umpires before 2000 was rare; now, not so much. Mechanics became more streamlined and generic, with an umpire's added flair or personality becoming less and less acceptable, let alone encouraged. Baseball, including its umpires, went corporate.

Of course, that trend flowed into replay—limited at first and then expanded. As we knew it would be.

Personally, I like replay. You cannot outrun technology. So instead of fighting it, better to embrace it, with a seat at the table, and help shape its use in an umpire-friendly way. I always thought it was ridiculous that the four people deciding on a possible home run, spectator interference, or ground rule two hundred feet away, with shadows, reflections, bright video boards, and seats full of fans in white shirts . . . that those four could basically become, within thirty seconds, the only four who don't know for sure what actually happened.

Both teams could watch the replay in their tunnels, most fans in the stadium have a monitor they can view, and obviously the millions watching at home, in a bar, or a Vegas sportsbook will get multiple looks. And here we are on the field: one guy has a homer, another thought a fan interfered, one was blocked out, and another just couldn't tell. So as a crew chief, I'd take all that in and come up with . . . *something*, while, like I said, everybody else already knows. That makes no sense.

No umpire wants to miss a call. When you do, it tears you up. If it can be corrected, that's a good thing. It's no fun when every twenty minutes on *SportsCenter* for the next twenty-four hours (if not longer), they show your missed call that ended up scoring the winning run. But when a big call is overturned, it's nearly always just a footnote and everyone moves on. Why? Because eventually the play *was called correctly*. You didn't look good getting there, and you're still not happy, because you failed. But at least you're not the story.

Does it take an extra minute or two? Sure. But that extra time often used to be spent arguing, so the game was going to stop regardless. At least now when play resumes, almost always the correct call will have been made. Replay will never completely eliminate controversial calls, because, like the umpires themselves, perfect is impossible. The technology is great, and it's always getting better. But there are still plays where you just can't get the perfect angle you need.

I still have close relationships with current active umpires, and they'll reach out when things didn't go well in a particular game or when a call blows up in the media. If nothing else, I'm happy to offer a sympathetic ear. I've been there, weathered the storm, taken the hits.

That brings me to the automated, *robotic* strike zone.

Be careful what you ask for. I've always said there is both a science *and* an art to umpiring. The science is the rules, the basics of what the game is all about. The art is applying those rules to how the game is actually played, especially in the Major Leagues. An automated umpire has the science but completely misses the art. Although fans of the game may not realize it yet, to make a game run smoothly, to prevent issues and maintain the standards of the highest level in the world, you need both.

As much as baseball can be a whirlwind, I always tried to remember who I was and where I came from. That can so easily get lost after a few years in the Show.

You are a rock star with amateur umpires, a novelty when meeting fans, and someone to brag about with relatives. You meet owners, managers, bartenders, and servers in some of the nicest restaurants and bars across the country, where, with a phone call or a text, you have the best table, without a reservation, on a Saturday night, not to mention reduced checks when leaving (if you get one at all). You're often upgraded to a hotel suite when checking in and have connections to half-price clothes, shoes, luggage, even jewelry.

While struggling financially in the Minor Leagues, making next to nothing, you're paying for everything. When you've made it and can afford anything, things are just given to you.

Because of people I knew or was introduced to, I was a guest at the White House to watch *Marine One* leave for Camp David with President George W. Bush and the First Lady and had private tours of Arlington National Cemetery and the Johnson Space Center in Houston, where I sat in the same chair in which so many flight directors made life-and-death decisions.

I've been to *Saturday Night Live* five times, David Letterman twice, and once each to *The Tonight Show with Jimmy Fallon* and *Late Night with Seth Meyers*. For ten years, while in New York, I would spend time in Pine Valley (i.e., the set of *All My Children*), visiting friends Dominick Maldari and Carole Shure, who worked there. Tim Tschida got me started on AMC when we were together in the Cal League. He convinced me it was a terrific way to kill an hour while sitting in our (barely) air-conditioned Bakersfield hotel room—and then I watched year-round until they were unceremoniously canceled by Disney-owned ABC.

I've attended NBA and NHL playoff games and met the Oregon Ducks' ticket manager, who, when I told him I planned to buy football season tickets, set me up with two seats on the 40-yard line, which I've now had since 1989.

The opportunities I've had and the connections I've made, all because I was an MLB umpire, have left me forever grateful. I've also tried to pay things forward, going back to Eugene and the Lane County Umpires Association, where it all started, with talks and clinics; giving uniforms and equipment to the Portland Umpires Association; and speaking and working at camps, clinics, and other engagements all around the country.

As fulfilling and enjoyable as teaching and helping umpires and associations have been, my coming out publicly is one of the best calls I ever made.

What's ahead for me? As I've said, even though concussions caused me to retire a couple of years earlier than planned, I was ready to retire.

I mean *really* ready.

Well into my MLB career, during my off-seasons, I officiated Portland-area football and basketball games. Even with a full regular baseball season through September, I would get back to Portland around week five of the football season and then work through the high school playoffs. So I'd work maybe four varsity games, might work a JV game, too, and then the playoffs. And then I could work pretty much the entire basketball season before leaving for spring training.

In basketball, what I enjoyed was the exercise. I am *not* an exercise guy. But when you're up and down the court, you don't feel like you're exercising; you're *doing* something. But as for what I enjoyed more, it was football by far. I officiated basketball for twenty years. The first ten, I enjoyed. The last ten, it became worse every year. The attitudes of the players and coaches had changed; a lot of these high school coaches were imitating college coaches, or at least the theatrical ones. And I felt like a babysitter in stripes. But I enjoyed the exercise, and I actually did enjoy the officiating. I could have kept doing basketball, because it didn't conflict with the baseball season, but I chose to stop.

I kept wishing I could work part of the football season, because I really did enjoy that. I liked the responsibilities on the field. I liked being outside. Compared to umpiring baseball, when I would do a football game, I was officiating, I was getting exercise, there was the camaraderie with the other officials, and there was just so much less pressure. That doesn't mean I didn't take it seriously. And Lord knows I made mistakes, like anybody else. But compared to walking on a big league field and working with professionals, it was . . . almost quaint. There wasn't as much scrutiny, with the cameras and the media and all the stuff you'd see all year umpiring baseball.

During the winter of 1983–84, while I was still living in Eugene, besides officiating, I worked at Grocery Cart, a locally owned chain of convenience stores. Just a temporary job to get me to March and spring training, the job could be frustrating at times because of how rude some customers treated people making minimum wage or just barely more.

One Sunday afternoon, a woman maybe in her early fifties drove up in her Mercedes, wearing a fur coat and some rather expensive jewelry. She went to the dairy cooler and brought to the checkout stand a gallon of milk. Plopping it down with a bit of attitude, she said with an annoyed tone, "I see your milk went up again."

First of all, I'm not the person who prices the inventory, and second, I don't care. But I tried to be nice and quipped, "I think the cows went on strike."

"You know, I can get this at Safeway for twenty cents cheaper," she said snottily.

"Lady, I don't care where you buy your milk. Why don't you and your fur coat jump in your Mercedes and save twenty cents at Safeway."

With that, she left the milk and whipped toward the door, letting me know that this would be my last day working at Grocery Cart. It wasn't, but I knew I was wrong (and the next day, my manager did have a little talk with me).

I also got back into radio briefly, working some off-season shifts in Portland early in my umpiring career. Then, starting in 1987, I taught at weekend umpiring clinics up and down the West Coast, with other Major and Minor League umpires. Every winter, we would produce three camps in places like San Diego, Long Beach, Las Vegas, Sacramento, the Bay Area, Portland, and rural Centralia, Washington.

The West Coast Umpire Camp went strong for ten years, with Gary Darling, Mike Winters, Larry Poncino, Ron Barnes, and Dan Wickham as the core group that got it started, joined by Bill Miller, Ted Barrett, and others at different times. We worked more than thirty camps with over one thousand umpires attending, before we stopped after the 1998 off-season.

I stopped officiating football and basketball in 1996 and, afterward, spent my off-seasons traveling with Mike and enjoying the time off at home. We've gone to Australia twice, as well as Amsterdam, Paris, London, Prague, Madrid, Barcelona, and Puerto Vallarta, and taken a Caribbean cruise. We also have enjoyed traveling around the country, with several trips to New York, San Francisco, San Diego, Chicago, Washington DC, New Orleans, Key West, Dallas, Las Vegas, Reno, Seattle, Palm Springs, and many trips to the Oregon coast (including our favorite spot, Yachats).

Palm Springs is a beautiful oasis located in the vast Sonoran Desert, up against the San Jacinto Mountains that rise almost eleven thousand feet to the west. Located 115 miles east of Hollywood, Palm Springs became a mecca for movie stars and moguls starting in the 1930s and accelerated after the war. It also became a favorite gay destination that hosts numerous circuit parties and festivals throughout the year. Dan Zilka, a close friend of ours, bought a home there in 1994. Mike and I would visit during my off-season, and we ultimately fell in love with Palm Springs and the entire Coachella Valley.

In fact, Mike and I enjoyed Palm Springs so much that we bought a house there in 2007.

Since my last concussion took me off the field, we've spent more time in the desert. Now, instead of leaving in February each year to prepare for another baseball season, Mike and I won't migrate north to Portland until May, with Wylie, our yellow Lab, in tow.

We love the beauty and of course the weather but also the large, active gay scene. With more than ten gay resorts, many shops and boutiques, and an abundance of bars and restaurants, Palm Springs is a community where, as a gay man, you don't feel any need to "play the game."

Thirty-seven years of traveling, of being away from home, of the continued pressure and stress of umpiring baseball at the highest level in the world—it all takes a toll. I realized that even more once I was away from the game.

Some journey, though, and unimaginable that day in March 1975, when I first walked onto the field to work the bases at Madison Junior High in Eugene, Oregon.

No complaints. No regrets.

ACKNOWLEDGMENTS

I have been blessed, and am beyond grateful, for the opportunities I've been given:

From my parents, who always backed me, even when I told them I was going to umpire school to try to make a career as the guy everybody yelled at.

From Ken Larson, who took a chance on a fifteen-year-old kid and let him put the uniform on for the first time.

From Dick Nelson, who took the time and interest to help me develop and blossom while in the Minor Leagues.

From Minor League partners who shared part of my journey: Matt Fairchild, Mike Felt, J. B. Hance, Phil Janssen, Terry Mann, Keith Meastas, Tim Tschida, Jim Uremovich, and Larry Young.

From Dick Butler, who took a shot and hired a twenty-six-year-old guy who had worked a total of one game in the American League.

From Marty Springstead, who watched in real time a young, deflated umpire devoid of confidence and saw a ton of potential, enough to put time and energy into bringing it out of him, when he could have let him drown and sent him on his way. To put it bluntly, he saved my career.

From the many veteran MLB umpires in my early years, as I struggled and learned: Larry Barnett, Nick Bremigan, Joe Brinkman, Al Clark, Derryl Cousins, Don Denkinger, Jim Evans, Rich Garcia, Ted Hendry, John Hirschbeck, Tim McClelland, Larry McCoy, Jim McKean, Durwood Merrill, Dan Morrison, Steve Palermo, Dave Phillips, Rick Reed, Mike Reilly, Rocky Roe, Tim Welke, and Larry Young.

From the many other umpires I had the pleasure to work with or have on my crew: Lance Barrett, Ted Barrett, Cory Blaser, C. B. Bucknor, Mark Carlson, Gary Cederstrom, Eric Cooper, Fieldin Culbreth, Bob Davidson, Dana DeMuth, Laz Diaz, Doug Eddings, Paul Emmel, Mike "Shooter" Everitt, Tripp Gibson, Brian "Rooms" Gorman, Chris Guccione, Adam Hamari, Marvin Hudson, Dan Iassogna, Jim Joyce, Brian Knight, Ron Kulpa, Alfonso Marquez, Jerry Meals, Chuck Meriwether, Bill Miller, Mike Muclinski, Jeff Nelson, Brian O'Nora, D. J. Reyburn, Jim Reynolds, Todd Tichenor, Tim Timmons, Tim Tschida, John Tumpane, Mark Wegner, Quinn Wolcott, Jim Wolf, and so many more (during my thirty-two years in Major League Baseball, I worked with 134 partners at least once).

And of course, from my husband, Mike—my rock who's been with me on this journey since 1986; who listened, advised, comforted, cheered, and always had my back; who spent countless nights home alone but never once complained; who has, in so many ways, made me a better person. Oh, and also made innumerable airport runs, including way too many of those ridiculous predawn jaunts.

We're a team. The best.

Dale Scott

I'll keep this shorter than usual, because this is Dale's book.

I do want to thank Rob Taylor, our editor at the University of Nebraska Press, for his enthusiasm for this project from the get-go. I've long admired Rob's work with the press, and it's both a thrill and an honor to actually work *with* him.

I also need to thank my parents for their continuing support and my wife, Angela, and daughter, Olive, for hardly complaining at all about all the times I needed to work instead of play board games or watch a movie with them. We'll get caught up someday, I promise.

Special thanks to my dear, longtime friend Rich Burk for reconnecting me with Dale Scott *after* Dale changed his mind about writing a book.

And finally, I need to thank Dale. I have long wanted to help an interesting baseball person write a book, but it always had to be the *right* person. Well, in countless ways Dale's been the right person, and I'm honored to share my little space on the cover of *his* book.

Rob Neyer

APPENDIX

DALE SCOTT CAREER EJECTIONS
MLB 1986–2017

Date	Team	Ejected	Reason
5-29-1986	California Angels	Doug DeCinces	Called third strike
6-15-1986	Detroit Tigers	Sparky Anderson	Balls and strikes
6-15-1986	Detroit Tigers	Lance Parrish	Balls and strikes
6-22-1986	Oakland Athletics	Tony Phillips	Play at the plate
6-28-1986	Baltimore Orioles	Jim Dwyer	Postgame
8-2-1986	Oakland Athletics	Tony Phillips	Called third strike
5-22-1987	Toronto Blue Jays	George Bell	Balls and strikes
6-20-1987	Texas Rangers	Pete Incaviglia	Called third strike
7-9-1987	Kansas City Royals	Danny Tartabull	Called third strike
8-16-1987	Seattle Mariners	Bill Connors	Balls and strikes
8-19-1987	California Angels	Ruppert Jones	Play at first
5-30-1988	New York Yankees	Billy Martin	Catch/trap call (threw dirt on umpire)
8-5-1988(2)	Boston Red Sox	Joe Morgan	Called third strike
8-5-1988(2)	Boston Red Sox	Spike Owen	Called third strike
6-17-1989	New York Yankees	Dallas Green	Fair/foul call
5-8-1990	Toronto Blue Jays	Cito Gaston	Balls and strikes
8-3-1990	Toronto Blue Jays	Cito Gaston	Balls and strikes
4-15-1991	New York Yankees	Álvaro Espinoza	Check swing
6-6-1991	Kansas City Royals	Hal McRae	Play at third (bumped umpire)
9-21-1991	Detroit Tigers	Pete Incaviglia	Balls and strikes

7-8-1992	Chicago White Sox	George Bell	Called third strike (threw helmet)
5-25-1993	Detroit Tigers	Tony Phillips	Balls and strikes
7-5-1993	Kansas City Royals	Hubie Brooks	Play at third
7-27-1993	Minnesota Twins	Kent Hrbek	Play at first
8-6-1993	Oakland Athletics	Tony La Russa	Balls and strikes
8-24-1993(2)	Oakland Athletics	Dave Duncan	Balls and strikes
8-24-1993(2)	Oakland Athletics	Dennis Eckersley	Balls and strikes
8-24-1993(2)	Oakland Athletics	Tony La Russa	Balls and strikes
9-18-1993	Minnesota Twins	Chuck Knoblauch	Play at first
5-17-1994	Seattle Mariners	Lou Piniella	Balls and strikes
7-27-1994	Toronto Blue Jays	Roberto Alomar	Balls and strikes
6-7-1995	Oakland Athletics	Tony La Russa	Balls and strikes
6-7-1995	Oakland Athletics	Terry Steinbach	Balls and strikes
6-12-1995	Toronto Blue Jays	Cito Gaston	Balls and strikes
4-6-1996	Boston Red Sox	Stan Belinda	Intentional HBP
4-6-1997	Cleveland Indians	Mike Hargrove	Balls and strikes
6-4-1997	Chicago White Sox	Bill Simas	Throwing at batter
4-27-1998	New York Yankees	Willie Randolph	Called third strike
5-6-1998	Tampa Bay Rays	Jerome Walton	Called third strike
9-6-1998	Toronto Blue Jays	Tim Johnson	Play at first
9-6-1998	Toronto Blue Jays	Paul Quantrill	Play at first
9-6-1998	Boston Red Sox	Jimy Williams	Balls and strikes
9-15-1998	Minnesota Twins	Eddie Guardado	Balls and strikes
9-15-1998	Minnesota Twins	Tom Kelly	Balls and strikes
10-17-1999	Boston Red Sox	Jimy Williams	Play at first
7-29-2000	Chicago White Sox	Paul Konerko	Balls and strikes
9-2-2000	Texas Rangers	Bill Haselman	Balls and strikes
9-11-2000	Seattle Mariners	Kevin Hodges	Throwing at batter
4-25-2001	Detroit Tigers	Phil Garner	HBP noncall
6-19-2001	Minnesota Twins	LaTroy Hawkins	Balls and strikes
7-12-2001	Colorado Rockies	Buddy Bell	Balls and strikes
8-14-2001	Arizona Diamondbacks	Mike DiFelice	Fighting
8-14-2001	Pittsburgh Pirates	Kevin Young	Fighting
9-11-2002	San Francisco Giants	Bruce Bochy	Postgame
4-23-2003	Milwaukee Brewers	Dave Nelson	Fair/foul call
6-9-2004	Seattle Mariners	Bob Melvin	Fair/foul call (reversed)

4-4-2005	Chicago Cubs	Carlos Zambrano	Balls and strikes
4-30-2005	St. Louis Cardinals	Tony La Russa	Balls and strikes
4-30-2005	St. Louis Cardinals	Alberto Reyes	Balls and strikes
4-30-2005	St. Louis Cardinals	Jim Edmonds	Postgame
6-14-2005	Anaheim Angels	Brendan Donnelly	Doctored ball (pine tar)
6-18-2005	Seattle Mariners	Mike Hargrove	Called third strike
6-18-2005	Seattle Mariners	Richie Sexson	Called third strike
5-2-2006	Oakland Athletics	Jason Kendall	Fighting
5-2-2006	Anaheim Angels	John Lackey	Fighting
5-2-2006	Anaheim Angels	Mike Scioscia	Arguing for intentional HBP ejection
5-13-2006	Chicago White Sox	Ozzie Guillén	HBP call
5-14-2006	Minnesota Twins	Ron Gardenhire	Called third strike
7-18-2006	Florida Marlins	Gary Tuck	Balls and strikes
5-11-2007	Houston Astros	Phil Garner	Check swing
5-23-2008	Cleveland Indians	Eric Wedge	Home run noncall
9-3-2008	St. Louis Cardinals	Dave Duncan	Balls and strikes
7-25-2009	Cleveland Indians	Winston Abreu	Intentional HBP
7-25-2009	Cleveland Indians	Eric Wedge	Intentional HBP
4-21-2010	Detroit Tigers	Johnny Damon	Called third strike
4-23-2010	Arizona Diamondbacks	A. J. Hinch	Catch / no catch
5-12-2010	Boston Red Sox	Terry Francona	Called third strike
9-10-2010	Texas Rangers	Ian Kinsler	Called third strike
6-10-2011	Cleveland Indians	Orlando Cabrera	Called third strike
9-7-2011	Atlanta Braves	Fredi González	Catch/no catch (reversed)
4-15-2012	San Diego Padres	Bud Black	Fair/foul call
6-17-2012	Houston Astros	Doug Brocail	Balls and strikes
7-14-2012	New York Mets	Terry Collins	Catch/trap call (reversed)
6-3-2013	Chicago White Sox	Mark Parent	Balls and strikes
9-13-2014	Milwaukee Brewers	Johnny Narron	Called third strike
4-25-2015	Milwaukee Brewers	Ron Roenicke	Balls and strikes
10-14-2015	Toronto Blue Jays	Mark Buehrle	Coming onto the field (not on roster)
5-15-2016	Texas Rangers	Steve Buechele	Fighting

5-15-2016	Toronto Blue Jays	José Bautista	Fighting
5-15-2016	Toronto Blue Jays	Josh Donaldson	Fighting
5-15-2016	Toronto Blue Jays	Tim Leiper	Balk noncall
5-15-2016	Texas Rangers	Rougned Odor	Fighting
5-21-2016	Anaheim Angels	Yunel Escobar	Called third strike (threw helmet)
9-9-2016	Arizona Diamondbacks	Welington Castillo	Called third strike
9-18-2016	Miami Marlins	Martín Prado	Called third strike (threw bat and helmet)

Minor Leagues*
1981 Northwest League (Short-A)

6-27-1981	Eugene	Danny LaMar	Play at the plate
7-3-1981	Salem	Rick Ingalls	Balk
7-7-1981	Bend	Kent Keiser	Called third strike
7-7-1981	Bend	P. J. Carey	Balls and strikes
7-7-1981	Bend	Luis Gómez	Postgame
7-24-1981	Bend	P. J. Carey	Play at the plate
8-14-1981	Medford	Brad Fischer	Play at the plate

1982 California League (Long-A)

6-11-1982	Modesto	Gary Dawson	Charging the mound
6-13-1982 (1)	Visalia	Phil Roof	Play at the plate
6-13-1982 (1)	Modesto	Tim Conroy	Balls and strikes
7-25-1982	Fresno	Jim Maloney	Non–home run
7-31-1982	Visalia	Steve Lombardozzi	Pickoff at first
8-3-1982	Redwood	Goldie Wright	Balls and strikes
8-12-1982	Stockton	Mike Felder	Balls and strikes
8-15-1982	Bakersfield	John Burden	Postgame
8-23-1982	Stockton	Bill Max	Check swing
8-25-1982	Stockton	Rick Bass	Balls and strikes

1983–84 Texas League (Double-A)

4-21-1983	Arkansas	Nick Leyva	Play at second
4-29-1983	Jackson	Sam Perlozzo	Catch / no catch
5-17-1983	San Antonio	Rick Ollar	Non–home run
6-25-1983 (2)	Shreveport	Duane Espy	Home run
7-11-1983	Tulsa	Steve Buechele	Play at second
7-16-1983	Shreveport	Bob Cummings	Balls and strikes
7-16-1983	El Paso	Ernie Riles	Play at the plate
7-18-1983	El Paso	Jack Lazorko	Balls and strikes
7-23-1983	Midland	Tom Harmon	Balls and strikes
7-27-1983	Midland	Tom Lombarski	Balls and strikes
8-20-1983 (2)	Jackson	Bob Schaefer	Play at first
8-20-1983 (2)	Jackson	Sergio Beltre	Postgame

1984–85 American Association (Triple-A)

7-19-1984	Evansville	Gordy McKenzie	Catch / no catch
8-4-1984	Iowa	John Perlman	Play at first
5-14-1985	Iowa	Bill Hayes	Balls and strikes
5-24-1985	Indianapolis	Gene Glenn	Pickoff at first
5-26-1985	Indianapolis	Razor Shines	Postgame
5-28-1985 (2)	Denver	Dann Bilardello	Play at the plate
6-4-1985	Louisville	Bill Lyons	Balls and strikes
6-20-1985	Oklahoma City	Jeff Kunkel	Balls and strikes
6-24-1985	Iowa	Larry Cox	Play at the plate
7-9-1985	Louisville	Curt Ford	Catch / no catch
7-15-1985	Nashville	Louie Pasado	Fighting
7-30-1985	Buffalo	Marv Foley	Play at the plate
8-11-1985	Indianapolis	Mike O'Berry	Balls and strikes
8-11-1985	Indianapolis	Felipe Alou	Balls and strikes
8-12-1985	Indianapolis	Fred Manrique	Play at second
8-17-1985	Buffalo	Cliff Wherry	Check swing
8-17-1985	Buffalo	John Boles	Check swing

* Some Minor League ejections are missing.

MOST GAMES ALL TIME PARTNERS

Derryl Cousins	Joe Brinkman	2,123
Beans Reardon	Larry Goetz	1,910
Al Barlick	Lee Ballanfant	1,631
Larry Barnett	Greg Kosc	1,491
Bob Engel	Paul Runge	1,491
Johnny Stevens	Larry Napp	1,455
Lee Weyer	Ed Montague	1,435
Ted Hendry	Jim Evans	1,399
John Rice	Larry Napp	1,398
Doug Harvey	Shag Crawford	1,326
Babe Pinelli	Dusty Boggess	1,274
Frank Secory	Frank Dascoli	1,268
Bill Williams	Tom Gorman	1,228
Stan Landes	Al Barlick	1,227
Doug Harvey	Jerry Crawford	1,201
Mike Reilly	Rich Garcia	1,200
Mel Steiner	Augie Donatelli	1,129
Frank Umont	Jim Honochick	1,124
Harry Wendelstedt	Randy Marsh	1,123
Frank Pulli	Doug Harvey	1,113
Augie Donatelli	Al Barlick	1,104
Dale Scott	Dan Iassogna	1,097
Bill Stewart	George Magerkurth	1,077
Lee Weyer	Dutch Rennert	1,071
Dana DeMuth	Nestor Chylak	1,069
Bill McKinley	Doug Eddings	1,069
Hank Soar	Bill McKinley	1,061
Tim Welke	Gary Cederstrom	1,046
Larry Goetz	Frank Dascoli	1,029
Dutch Rennert	Ed Montague	1,024
Mike Winters	Bruce Froemming	1,022
Augie Donatelli	Jocko Conlan	1,020
Ed Sudol	Tom Gorman	1,012
Terry Cooney	Joe Brinkman	1,010
Ed Vargo	Al Barlick	1,009
Dick Nallin	Bill Dinneen	1,000

UMPIRE PARTNERS OF DALE SCOTT

Dan Iassogna	1,097
Ron Kulpa	789
Rocky Roe	601
Dave Phillips	556
C. B. Bucknor	537
Tim Welke	390
Jerry Meals	367
Rich Garcia	355
Bill Miller	352
Jim Joyce	350
Durwood Merrill	330
Mike Reilly	308
Dan Morrison	276
Gary Cederstrom	201
Lance Barrett	190
Jim Evans	184
Bob Davidson	155
Larry McCoy	154
Marvin Hudson	136
Tim Tschida	136
Laz Diaz	135
Derryl Cousins	133
Todd Tichenor	130
Joe Brinkman	126
Brian Gorman	126
Mike DiMuro	124
Fieldin Culbreth	122
Jeff Nelson	120
Jim Reynolds	120
Mark Wegner	116
Rick Reed	114
Larry Young	114
Paul Emmel	112
Brian O'Nora	111
Tim McClelland	107
Don Denkinger	105

John Hirschbeck	101
Vic Voltaggio	101
Andy Fletcher	99
John Shulock	98
Jim McKean	90
Al Clark	87
Bill Hohn	84
Drew Coble	74
Ted Barrett	72
Steve Palermo	69
Lance Barksdale	68
Tripp Gibson	68
Rob Drake	62
Chuck Meriwether	62
James Hoye	55
Chris Guccione	49
Ted Hendry	49
Nick Bremigan	47
Quinn Wolcott	46
Ken Kaiser	43
Terry Craft	41
Jim Wolf	36
John Tumpane	33
D. J. Reyburn	31
Terry Cooney	30
Adam Dowdy	30
Mike Estabrook	30
Mark Johnson	29
Tim Timmons	29
Ed Hickox	28
Angel Campos	27
Brian Knight	26
Gabe Morales	25
Scott Barry	23
Adam Hamari	21
Larry Barnett	20

Damien Beal	19
Toby Basner	17
Eric Cooper	17
Dale Ford	17
Mike Fichter	17
Mike Muchlinski	17
Chad Fairchild	14
Greg Kosc	13
Ramon De Jesus	12
Ray DiMuro	12
Mike Everitt	12
David Rackley	12
Vic Carapazza	10
Doug Eddings	10
Ian Lamplugh	10
Alfonso Marquez	10
Jordan Baker	9
Delfin Colon	9
Ben May	9
Scott Packard	9
Cory Blaser	8
Justin Klemm	8
Ramon Armendariz	7
Sean Barber	7
Phil Cuzzi	7
Kerwin Danley	7
Tom Hallion	7
Mike Vanvleet	7
Clint Fagan	6
Casey Moser	6
Mark Ripperger	6
Pat Spieler	6
Mark Carlson	5
Marty Foster	5
Adrian Johnson	4
Matt Hollowell	4

Larry Vanover	4
Bill Welke	4
Chris Conroy	3
Bruce Froemming	3
Pat Hoberg	3
Travis Katzenmeier	3
Kevin Kelley	3
Randy Marsh	3
Paul Nauert	3
Alan Porter	3
Brian Runge	3
Jack Samuels	3
Chris Tiller	3
Hunter Wendelstedt	3
Dusty Dellinger	2
Dana DeMuth	2
Angel Hernandez	2
Travis Reininger	2
Steve Rippley	2
Bruce Dreckman	1
Jerry Layne	1
Tom Lepperd	1
Marcus Pattillo	1
Chris Segal	1
Darren Spagnardi	1
Joe West	1

INDEX